Inclusive Growth Through Social Capital Formation

About the Author

Christabell, P.J. is Assistant Professor in the Department of Futures Studies, University of Kerala. She got her Ph.D. in Economics from the Department of Economics at University of Kerala in 2004. She was a Faculty Member in ICFAI National College (2004-2005). She served as Assistant Professor in University of Gondar, Ethiopia (2005-2006), Government College Nedumangad and Government College for Women, Thiruvananthapuram (2006-2013). She is the author of the book "*Women Empowerment through Capacity Building: The Role of Micro-Finance*" and had published research papers in various reputed and peer reviewed international and national journals. She was the resource person of various international as well as national seminars and conferences. She is an active commentator on social and economic issues in popular media.

Inclusive Growth Through Social Capital Formation

Is Micro-finance an Effective Tool for Targeting Women?

Christabell, P.J.

CONCEPT PUBLISHING COMPANY PVT. LTD.
NEW DELHI-110059

ISBN-13: 978-93-5125-222-1

First Published 2016

Published and Printed by

Concept Since 1974

Concept Publishing Company Pvt. Ltd.
Regd. Office:
A/15-16, Commercial Block, Mohan Garden,
New Delhi-110059 (INDIA)
Phones : 25351460, 25351794,
Fax : 091-11-25357109
E-mail : publishing@conceptpub.com
Website: www.conceptpub.com

Editorial Office: H-13, Bali Nagar, New Delhi-110 015, India.

Cataloging in Publication Data—DK Courtesy: D.K. Agencies (P) Ltd. <docinfo@dkagencies.com>

Christabell, P. J., author.
Inclusive growth through social capital formation : is micro-finance an effective tool for targeting women? / Christabell, P.J.
pages cm
Includes bibliographical references and index.
ISBN 9789351252221

1. Microfinance—India—Kerala. 2. Social capital (Sociology)—India—Kerala. 3. Poor women—Government policy—India—Kerala. I. Title.

HG178.33.I4C47 2016 DDC 332.095483 23

Foreword

After some euphoria over reduction in poverty rates and the arrival of a 'virtuous cycle of growth' in Kerala, social scientific discourse on this society now increasingly acknowledges that the remarkable social development achieved in the twentieth century through strong 'public action' in a context of the lack of economic development (referred to often as the 'Kerala Model'), is under serious threat. Most of these studies find inequalities to be growing in both urban and non-urban sectors, but the groups worst-off largely continue to be those who have already been identified as heavily disadvantaged in Kerala's history of social development. For example there is work now that criticizes claims regarding Kerala's entry into a 'virtuous growth regime' citing studies of income and head-count ratios, noting that the worrying trends in inequality and poverty reduction apply to both rural and urban contexts. It is also noted that the Dalits and Adivasis in the state are the worst sufferers in both, and that in urban context, the Other Backward communities too have seen a fall in real consumption.

Nevertheless, even in this bleak scenario, certain experiments in Kerala in poverty-alleviation and self-help now attract the attention of development researchers as new beacons of hope. One such is the Kudumbashree, the vast all-Kerala network of women's self-help groups created under the aegis of the Kerala government's Poverty Alleviation Mission. At present, the Kudumbashree includes the vast majority of poor families in Kerala, covers the length and breadth of the State, and consists of nearly forty-two lakh women members. After 2008, the three-tier Kudumbashree federated structure in each panchayat plays a key role in local governance in the panchayats, and projects itself as not really a sub-system of the panchayat, but as an equal partner in local development. Research on Kudumbashree's economic success is, however, mixed. Nevertheless, it has been argued that even when the intended or stated consequences (poverty alleviation and socio-economic upward mobility) of such programmes have not fructified, their unintended consequences and effects may be democratizing. Thus, when women use the Kudumbashree as a gateway to enter politics and public and not for self-help in livelihoods alone, that must not be seen as a perversion of goals but as a desirable if unintended consequence that remedies one of the acknowledged failings of Kerala's social and political history, the segregation of women from public life. However, there is also indication now that Kudumbashree groups do engage in successful economic activities. Scholars like Ananya Mukherjee-Reed now argue that Kudumbashree women's groups have successfully revived a culture of group farming in the State; there is also evidence that women turning their domestic skills, especially culinary skills, into marketable purposes, as in the well-known experiment of Café Kudumbashree, are increasing their incomes considerably.

It is perhaps also vital to remember that Kudumbashree has not been a static programme since its origin in the late 1990s; it is equally important to also take into account the fact that it has had a history in the state that goes back directly to the early 1990s, when women began to be identified as agents of community development and well-being and were invited to engage in public life on those terms. Since the 1990s when the programme was heavily geared towards micro-finance, it has sought to pay greater attention to micro enterprise and group ventures on the one hand, and in seeking equal partnership in local development with local self-governments, on the other hand. Its institutional structure, too, has been remoulded considerably to these ends. In short, at present, the Kudumbashree is well-recognized to play a key role in the widely-improved distribution of welfare resources in the panchayats, especially, and is equal in importance to the panchayat itself in the space of the local body. But this does not indicate a smooth and tranquil scenario by any means. Indeed, one may only describe the present scene as one of struggle, in which the Kudumbashree seeks to assert itself and play a noteworthy role in development decisions in the panchayat. Nor does it mean that a revolution of sorts has swept local governments – far from it, the initial conditions prevailing in the very diverse regions that it covers seem to play a vital role in realizing the potential of the enabling changes in Kudumbashree's institutional structure, and in many areas, they work against the democratizing potential of these changes.

However, it is necessary to keep a close watch on whether the programme is delivering its intended benefits – such watchfulness cannot be avoided in assessing public welfare programmes even though watchfulness must mean much more than that if a holistic and fair understanding of programme impacts is sought. Christabell P J's present work draws our attention towards a core concern about Kudumbashree, which, however, has been addressed insufficiently in available critical research on the programme. She examines, broadly, the impact of the programme on the extremely poor communities in Kerala. Given that Kudumbashree was envisaged as a poverty alleviation programme, it is surely all-important to assess whether the extremely poor in the state have benefited from it or not. Her observations seem to confirm worrying signals that are emerging from other studies as well: the extremely poor seem to benefit less. As she remarks, much of the poorest do not seem to be reasonably aware even of its modalities even and their ability to save and their confidence to acquire loans is abysmally low. Grievously, some sections of the poorest, for example, plantation workers, are not even recognized as Below-Poverty-Line groups despite their participation in the Kudumbashree – such participation has, apparently, not empowered them to claim this status till date.The very form of self-help groups, and its practices, such as regular meetings, do not seem to serve them well, given that most of the extremely poor also suffer from high time-poverty. They also lack the wherewithal to avail of the trainings and other opportunities for new skill-acquisition provided by the programme. Not surprisingly, loans for enterprise end up being used for purposes of 'consumption-smoothening' (though this is not exclusive to the extremely poor). Christabell also notes that nearly ninety-seven per cent of the groups surveyed maintained a common fund for emergencies: again, not surprising, given the skyrocketing prices of health care and education in Kerala.

In general, her work indicates that the micro-enterprise-centred self-help group and savings-and-credit model is perhaps not only inadequate, but actually inappropriate for the extremely poor who have no assets and have to rely entirely on selling their labour power to make a livelihood – if the aim of such an intervention is to enable upward mobility of these groups. On the flip side, it seems to indicate that it does allow for survivalist strategies and poverty management – through 'consumption-smoothening', mainly. This implies the need for much stronger efforts to improve the condition of the extreme poor by not only enabling adequate consumption, but also encouraging the acquisition of marketable and culturally-respectable skills that would secure high-paid and better-status employment to the poorest. This calls for a focus on developing the access of the young people among the poorest to education and employment that enhances their incomes and social status, and especially, their socio-economic and spatial mobility. This, in turn, would call for greater and more effective investments by the government in the social development of extremely poor communities. Nevertheless Christabell concludes on an optimistic note, arguing that the resource base of once-resourceless women has been considerably enriched now, and "As Kudumbashree is a government sponsored programme, it could significantly change the lives and outlook of the poor women in the local settings of the State." (p.260). They have also now gained much greater confidence in dealing with local governance and handling micro-finance and micro-enterprise.

While the manuscript is in need of much tightening and strong editing as well as a thorough copyediting, I congratulate the author for choosing an area that is not only important but also challenging because of the diversity of contexts. It contributes to a growing area of research that is vital to our understanding of the successes, failures, and the many effects of poverty alleviation pivoted on the empowerment of women in the era of 'responsibilising' neoliberal welfare in Kerala.

J Devika

Acknowledgements

I am thankful for the financial support given by the University Grants Commission, New Delhi for conducting the present study.

I am deeply indebted to the Principal, Government College for Women, Thiruvananthapuram for facilitating and providing all kinds of support for carrying out the research work in the college.

I do convey my gratitude to all my colleagues in the Department of Economics, Government College for Women, Thiruvananthapuram for their kind support and cooperation.

I do express my hearty thanks to Mr Vimal Raj, A., Project Fellow whose services are unparalleled and without his sustained support this work would not have been completed.

I do thankfully remember the co-ordinators and group leaders and I express my deep gratitude to members of Kudumbashree for their patience and helpful approach during the course of my conducting the field-work.

My family members supported me through prayers, unended love and assistance.

Christabell, P.J.

Contents

List of Tables

List of Figures

Abbreviations

ADS	Area Development Society
AIDIS	All Indian Debt Investment Survey
APPBO	Average Population Per Branch Office
ARDRS	Agricultural and Rural Debt Relief Scheme
APL	Above Poverty Line
ASA	Association for Social Advancement
ATM	Automated Teller Machine
BC	Banking Correspondent
BFs	Bank Facilitators
BIDS	Bangladesh Institute of Development Studies
BMI	Body Mass Index
BPL	Below Poverty Line
BRAC	Bangladesh Rural Advancement Committee
BSS	Bharat Sevak Samaj
CBNP	Community Based Nutrition Programme
CBO	Community Based Organization
CBs	Cooperative Banks
CDS	Community Development Society
CGAP	Consultative Group to Assist the Poor
CRR	Cash Reserve Ratio
DWCRA	Development of Women and Children in Rural Areas
DWCUA	Development of Women and Children in Urban Areas
EBT	Electronic Benefits Transfer
ECS	Electronic Clearing Service
FUNDELAM	Fundacion' de la Mujer Campesina
GB	Grameen Bank
GDP	Gross Domestic Product
GDI	Gender Development Index
GEM	Gender Empowerment Index
GoAP	Government of Andhra Pradesh
GoI	Government of India

GoK	Government of Kerala
HADP	Hill Area Development Programme
HDI	Human Development Index
IFAD	International Fund for Agricultural Development
IGA	Income Generation Activities
IGVGD	Income Generation for Vulnerable Group Development
IHSDP	Integrated Housing and Slum Development Programme
IMR	Infant Mortality Rate
IRDP	Integrated Rural Development Programme
JLLIs	Joint Liability Lending Institutions
JNNURM	Jawaharlal Nehru National Urban Renewal Mission
JRY	Jawahar Rozgar Yojana
KCCs	Kisan Credit Cards
LPS	Lower Primary School
MC^2	Mutuelle Communautaire de Croissance
MFIs/Ps	Micro-finance Institutions/Programmes
MFO	Micro-finance Organisation
MPCE	Monthly Per Capita Consumption Expenditure
MSMEs	Micro, Small and Medium Enterprises
NABARD	National Bank for Agriculture and Rural Development
NBFC	Non-Banking Finance Companies
NEFT	National Electronic Fund Transfer
NGO	Non-Governmental Organization
NHGs	Neighbourhood Groups
NSS	Nair Service Society
NSSO	National Sample Survey Organization
OBC	Other Backward Class
OEC	Other Economically Backward Caste
PAIS	Personal Accident Insurance Scheme
PAP	Poverty Alleviation Project
PASS	Pazhakulam Social Service Society
PPC	Peoples' Plan Campaign
PRI	Panchayati Raj Institutions
PSBs	Public Sector Banks
PTA	Parent Teacher Association
RASTA	Rural Agency for Social and Technological Advancement
RBI	Reserve Bank of India
RCF	Report on Currency and Finance
RD 12	Rural Development-12
RDP	Rural Development Project
RFIs	Rural Financial Institutions
RKBY	Rashtriya Krishi Bima Yojana

RLEGP	Rural Landless Employment Guarantee Programme
RMK	Rashtriya Mahila Kosh
ROSCAs	Rotating Savings and Credit Associations
RRBs	Regional Rural Banks
RTGS	Real Time Gross Settlement
SC	Scheduled Caste
SEWA	Self-Employed Women's Association
SGSY	Swarnajayanthi Grama Swarozgar Yojana
SHGs	Self-Help Groups
SHPI	Self-Help Promoting Institutions
SIDBI	Small Industries Development Bank of India
SJSRY	Swarna Jayanti Shahari Rozgar Yojana
SLDBs	State Land Development Banks
SLR	Statutory Liquidity Ratio
SME	Small and Medium Enterprise
SNDP	Sree Narayana Dharma Paripalana Sangham
ST	Scheduled Tribe
TRDEP	Thana Resource Development and Employment Programme
TRYSEM	Training Rural Youth for Self-Employment
UBS	Urban Based Services
UBSP	Urban Basic Services for the Poor
ULB	Urban Local Bodies
UPS	Upper Primary School
USEP	Urban Self-Employment Programme
WB	World Bank
WCP	Women Component Plan
ZP	Zila Parishad

1

Introduction

The 'inclusive growth' as a strategy of economic development received attention owing to a rising concern that the benefits of economic growth have not been equitably shared. Growth is inclusive when it creates economic opportunities along with ensuring equal access to them. A vast majority of the population remained outside the ambit of basic health and education facilities during this high growth phase. The approach of forming social capital for inclusive growth is widely used nowadays. Social capital is the quality and quantity of relationships, networks, and norms among people and organizations that facilitate collective action. The resurgence of interest in "social capital" as a remedy for the cause of today's social problems draws directly on the assumption that these problems lie in the weakening of civil society.

From an annual average growth rate of 3.5 per cent during 1950 to 1980, the growth rate of the Indian economy accelerated to around 6.0 per cent in the 1980s and 1990s. In the years 2003-04 to 2006-07, the Indian economy grew by 8.8 per cent. In 2005-06 and 2006-07, the Indian economy grew at a higher rate of 9.4 and 9.6 per cent, respectively. Reflecting the high economic growth and a moderation in population growth rate, the per capita income of the country also increased substantially during this period. An important characteristic of the high growth phase is its resilience to shocks. The Indian economy successfully avoided any adverse contagion impact of the East Asian crisis, post-Pokhran sanction era, and border conflict with a neighbouring country during May-June, 1999.

Despite the impressive numbers, growth has failed to be sufficiently inclusive. Agricultural sector which provides employment to around 60 per cent of the population lost its growth momentum from that point, though there has been a reversal of this trend since 2005-06. The percentage of India's population below the poverty line has declined from

36 per cent in 1993-94 to 26 per cent in 1999-2000. The approach paper to the Eleventh Plan indicated that the absolute number of the poor is estimated to be approximately 300 million in 2004-05. The seventh quinquennial survey by the National Sample Survey Organisation (NSSO) (61st Round) reveals that growth rate of employment increased from an annual 0.98 per cent in the period 1993-94 to 1999-2000 to 2.89 per cent from the period 1999-2000 to 2004-05, while the acceleration in the rate of growth of labour force from 1.03 per cent to 2.93 per cent during same period had negative impact on employment rate. Similarly, poverty ratio has been declining during the recent period, but it continues to remain at a very high level of 27.5 per cent (Uniform Recall Period) in 2004-05 from 36.0 per cent in 1993-94. The most disturbing fact is that the income inequality as commonly measured by consumption expenditure (Gini coefficient) has increased in India from 32.9 in 1993 to 36.2 in 2004 (Ali and Zhuang, 2007).

In short, though the Indian economy achieved a high growth momentum during the last two decades, it could not bring down unemployment and poverty to tolerable levels. A vast majority of the population remained outside the ambit of basic health and education facilities during this high growth phase. In these decades, economic and social inequalities have widened alongside high growth rates which have exacerbated regional inequalities (Chakrabarthy, 2009). The average monthly per capita consumption expenditure (MPCE) in urban areas in India is almost double than that of rural areas. In some States, the disparities are more glaring.

Economic growth is inclusive when it creates opportunities along with ensuring equal access to them. Inclusive growth by its very definition implies an equitable allocation of resources with benefits accruing to each section of the society. The concept "inclusion" is a process of including the excluded as agents whose participation is essential in the very design of the development process, and not simply as welfare targets of development programmes (GoI, 2007). The 'inclusive growth' as a strategy of economic development received attention owing to a rising concern that the benefits of economic growth have not been equitably shared. The inclusive growth by encompassing the hitherto excluded population can bring in several other benefits as well to the economy. It would translate economic growth into growth in poverty reduction, a process of growth to which the poor can contribute and from which the poor can also benefit. The employment opportunities and improvement in productivity across all sectors of the economy are also envisaged.

Apart from addressing the issue of inequality, the inclusive growth also make the poverty reduction efforts more effective by explicitly creating productive economic opportunities for the poor and vulnerable sections of the society. While it is quite evident that inclusive growth is imperative for achieving the equity objective it is now considered essential even to sustain the growth momentum. First, in India, the major chunk of population is based in rural areas. Significant increase in demand for manufacturing and services sectors has to come from the rural population. Therefore, it is important to ensure that growth takes place in agriculture, allied sectors as also in secondary and services sectors in rural areas, and amongst urban poor to provide a growing market for the goods and services produced by the expanding corporate sector. Second, from supply-side management, growth in agriculture is necessary in order to keep manufacturing prices under check, to provide food security and to keep inflation under control. Price stability is not merely important as an anti-poverty measure, but also as an instrument to ensure stable and sustained growth. Third, higher growth in agriculture and rural areas coupled with demographic dividend (i.e. growing proportion of population in the working age group of 15-65) will lead to a rise in the savings level for financing the increasing level of investments necessary to sustain the overall growth momentum.

Fourth, the limitations on increasing production and productivity in agriculture are driving migration to urban areas leading to population pressure in urban areas and increase in urban poor. Infrastructure in urban areas needs considerable investment to handle the migration—this requires significant investment in housing, water, sanitation, lighting and power, waste management, education, health facilities, and public transport. Hence, urban development policies have to focus on inclusive investment to deal with the huge armies of low-income population likely to move into these areas. Fifth, since in many countries such as India, the growth process is knowledge-based and services-led, the requirement of skilled labour is quite substantial in comparison to the present availability. In order to ensure adequate supply of skilled labour force, huge social sector investment is required covering the vast majority of people who may not be able to afford such education and skill development. Sixth, it is the unorganised non-farm sector that is increasingly absorbing most of the labour force. This sector has huge potential for growth once there is sufficient investment in infrastructure ensuring linkage to markets and easier access to assets and skills. Infusion of appropriate technology, skills, and easier access to credit, especially start-up capital, apart from facilitating market development, can make this segment an expanding base for self-sustaining employment and wealth generation.

Entrepreneurial development has to be encouraged by creating competitive environment and easy availability of finance for newer projects and enterprises. There are several factors to be considered for inclusive growth. Uppermost among these, is the need for raising the allocative efficiency of investment and resource use across different sectors of the economy—this can be met by addressing two basic supply-side issues *viz.* (i) effective credit delivery system to facilitate productive investment in employment impacting sectors especially, agriculture, micro, small and medium enterprises; and (ii) large scale investment in infrastructural facilities like irrigation, roads, railways, communication, ports, power, rural/urban reconstruction and in social infrastructure such as health care, education and sanitation (GoI, 2007).

Even if India succeeded in achieving broad-based and inclusive growth, there are many groups that still remain marginalised. These include primitive tribal groups, adolescent girls, the elderly and the disabled who lack family support, children below the age of three and others who do not have strong lobbies to ensure that their rights are guaranteed. A key element of the strategy for inclusive growth is an all out effort to provide the mass of people the access to basic facilities such as health, education, clean drinking water, etc. that they need. In the short run, these essential public services impact directly on welfare. In the longer run, they determine economic opportunities for the future. It is important to recognise that access to these basic services is not necessarily assured simply by a rise in per capita income. The governments at different levels have to ensure the provision of these services and this must be an essential part of the country's strategy for inclusive growth. It is also important to recognise that better levels of health and education are in fact the pre-conditions for sustained long-term growth. The private sector, including farming, micro, small and medium enterprises (MSMEs) and the corporate sector, have a critical role to play in achieving the objective of faster and more inclusive growth.

Thus, the Eleventh Plan Document tried to restructure the policies in order to make the growth faster, broad-based and inclusive by reducing the fragmentation of the society. It clearly stated that "The development of rural India is an imperative for inclusive and equitable growth and to unlock huge potential of the population that is presently trapped in poverty with its associated deprivations" (GoI, 2006). Huge investments in education and health, and rural infrastructure were the key elements of the inclusive growth strategy as envisaged. Broadly, the policies aim at increasing the income and employment opportunities on the one hand try to finance programmes which are capable of making the growth more inclusive on the other.

Social Capital Formation

The concept of social capital has taken a central role in the modern development discussions, especially in the case of local level development. The concept was developed by Robert Putnam in his study of Italy (1993) and was then employed in the United States situation (1995). It is also argued that its importance was stressed much earlier by a number of theorists of politics like Tocqueville. He had stressed the association between group bonding and political development. In general, the term of social capital can be explained as the quality and quantity of relationships, networks, and norms among people and organizations that facilitate collective action. Putnam (1993) has defined social capital as "features of social organisation such as networks, norms, and trust that facilitate coordination and cooperation for mutual benefit". According to Putnam, social capital "refers to the collective value of all 'social networks' and the inclinations that arise from these networks to do things for each other". Further, he explained that it "refers to connections among individuals—social networks and the norms of reciprocity and trustworthiness that arise from them." Another pioneer in the field Coleman (1998), had defined social capital functionally as "a variety of entities with two elements in common: they all consist of some aspect of social structure, and they facilitate certain actions of actors... within the structure"—that is, social capital is anything that facilitates individual or collective action, generated by networks of relationships, reciprocity, trust, and social norms. In Coleman's conception, social capital is a neutral resource that facilitates any manner of action, but whether society is better off as a result depends entirely on the individual uses to which it is put.

Social capital is about the value of social networks, bonding similar people and bridging between diverse people, with norms of reciprocity (Dekker and Uslaner, 2001). Sander (2002) stated that "the folk wisdom that more people get their jobs from whom they know, rather than what they know, turns out to be true". Adler and Kwon (2002) identified that "the core intuition guiding social capital research is that the goodwill that others have toward us is a valuable resource." As such they define social capital as "the goodwill available to individuals or groups". Its source lies in the structure and content of the actor's social relations. Its effects flow from the information, influence, and solidarity it makes available to the actor". Dekker and Uslaner (2001) posited that social capital is fundamentally about how people interact with each other.

Belliveau, *et al.* (1996) describes the social capital as "an individual's personal network and elite institutional affiliations". Bourdieu (1986) stated that it is "the aggregate of the actual or potential resources which are linked to possession of a durable network of more or less institutionalized relationships of mutual acquaintance or recognition". Social capital is "made up of social obligations ('connections'), which is convertible, in certain conditions, into economic capital and may be institutionalized in the form of a title of nobility". It is explained that it is "the sum of the resources, actual or virtual, that accrue to an individual or a group by virtue of possessing a durable network of more or less institutionalized relationships of mutual acquaintance and recognition" (Bourdieu, 1986). Boxman *et al.* (1991) stated that it is "the number of people who can be expected to provide support and the resources those people have at their disposal".

Burt (1992) explained that it is formed among "friends, colleagues, and more general contacts through whom you receive opportunities to use your financial and human capital". It can also be considered as "the brokerage opportunities in a network". Knoke (1999) "the process by which social actors create and mobilize their network connections within and between organizations to gain access to other social actors' resources". It can also be defined as "the ability of actors to secure benefits by virtue of membership in social networks or other social structures." (Portes, 1998). Brehm and Rahn (1997) describe it as "the web of cooperative relationships between citizens that facilitate resolution of collective action problems". According to Coleman (1998), "social capital is defined by its function. It is not a single entity, but a variety of different entities having two characteristics in common: They all consist of some aspect of social structure, and they facilitate certain actions of individuals who are within the structure". Fukuyama (1995) described it as "the ability of people to work together for common purposes in groups and organizations". "Social capital can be defined simply as the existence of a certain set of informal values or norms shared among members of a group that permit cooperation among them". Inglehart (1997) tells that it is "a culture of trust and tolerance, in which extensive networks of voluntary associations emerge". Portes (1998) explains that "those expectations for action within a collectivity that affect the economic goals and goal" seeking behaviour of its members, even if these expectations are not oriented toward the economic sphere. Putnam refers it as the "features of social organization such as networks, norms, and social trust that facilitate coordination and cooperation for mutual benefit" (Putnam, 1995). It is also described as "those voluntary means and processes developed within civil society which promote development for the collective whole".

Bourdieu (1972) distinguishes between three forms of capital: economic capital, cultural capital and social capital. He defines social capital as "the aggregate of the actual or potential resources which are linked to possession of a durable network of more or less institutionalised relationships of mutual acquaintance and recognition". His treatment of the concept is instrumental, focusing on the advantages to possessors of social capital and the "deliberate construction of sociability for the purpose of creating this resource". In other words "social capital enhances the benefits of investment in physical and human capital" (Putnam, 1993).

Loury (1992) thinks that it is the "naturally occurring social relationships among persons which promote or assist the acquisition of skills and traits valued in the marketplace... an asset which may be as significant as financial bequests in accounting for the maintenance of inequality in our society". Nahapiet and Ghoshal (1998) explains that it is "the sum of the actual and potential resources embedded within, available through, and derived from the network of relationships possessed by an individual or social unit". Social capital thus comprises of both the network and the assets that may be mobilized through that network. Pennar (1997) feels that it is "the web of social relationships that influences individual behaviour and thereby affects economic growth". Schiff (1992) has another view that it is "the set of elements of the social structure that affects relations among people and is inputs or arguments of the production and/or utility function". Woolcock (1998) explains in such a manner that it is "the information, trust, and norms of reciprocity inhering in one's social networks". As one might expect there have been a number of different definitions offered for social capital, but Robert Putnam's definition seems generally representative of the typical way of defining social capital. According to Putnam social capital is: "features of social life—networks, norms, and trust—that enable participants to act together more effectively to pursue shared objectives. Social capital, in short, refers to social connections and the attendant norms and trust". In essence then what basically constitutes social capital according to the commonly accepted definition are things like norms and relationships.

Social capital is the value of what individuals are willing to contribute, be it in terms of labour, materials, expertise, or financial support, for the social good and for which they are not expecting compensation. For now let it suffice to say that operationally social capital is defined herein as the provision of personal resources for social good in a way which is patently selfless. Individuals may usually derive some personal pleasure from their pro-social activity. However, it is clear that the predominant economic effect of this behaviour is frequently to benefit the social system at the expense of the providers.

The resurgence of interest in "social capital" as a remedy for today's social problems draws directly on the assumption that these problems lie in the weakening of civil society. However, this ignores the arguments of many theorists who believe that social capital leads to exclusion rather than to a stronger civil society. It can increase productivity (both individual and collective), so, social contacts affect the productivity of individuals and groups. Collective action is thus an indicator of increased social capital. Even though identical policies aimed at promoting democracy and development may be undertaken, the degree of success in realising these goals is determined by the fruitfulness of social capital that exists in individual situations. According to Putnam, social capital fosters reciprocity, facilitates information flows for mutual benefit and creates trust, and once these are in place, they tend to be self-generating as future generations are inducted into these norms through socialisation.

According to Putnam (2000), social capital is a key component to building and maintaining democracy. In other words, abundance of social capital is viewed as a necessary condition for modern liberal democracy. A low level of social capital leads to an excessively rigid and unresponsive political system and high levels of corruption, in the political system and in the region as a whole. Formal public institutions require social capital in order to function properly, and while it is possible to have too much social capital (resulting in rapid changes and excessive regulation), it is decidedly worse to have too little. High stocks of social capital, it is claimed, will lead to active civic engagement and the rise of an active civil society. Civil society highlights the role of interest groups, social movements, organised private, non-profit, self-governing and voluntary agencies, which occupy or create social space beyond the full control of the State apparatus.

Putnam speaks of two main components of social capital: bonding social capital and bridging social capital. A focus on external relations has also been called 'bridging' or 'communal' (Oh *et al.*, 1999) and a focus on internal relations 'bonding' or 'linking'. Similar categorization could be done according to other criteria such as strong or weak ties, horizontal or vertical, open or closed, structural or cognitive, geographically dispersed or circumscribed, and instrumental or principled. Baker explains it as "a resource that actors derive from specific social structures and then use to pursue their interests; it is created by changes in the relationship among actors" (Baker, 1990). Bonding refers to the value assigned to social networks between homogeneous groups of people and bridging refers to that of social networks between socially heterogeneous groups. Typical examples are that criminal gangs create bonding social capital, while choirs and bowling clubs create bridging social capital. It is argued that bridging social capital will generate a host of other benefits for societies, governments, individuals, and communities

Without 'bridging' social capital, 'bonding' groups may become isolated and disenfranchised from the rest of the society and, most importantly, from groups with which bridging must occur in order to denote an increase in social capital. Bonding social capital is a necessary antecedent for development of a more powerful form of bridging social capital. Bonding and bridging social capital can work together productively if in balance, or they may work against each other. As social capital bonds and stronger homogeneous groups form, the likelihood of bridging social capital is attenuated. Bonding social capital can also perpetuate sentiments of a certain group, allowing for the bonding of certain individuals together upon a common radical ideal. In mild cases, it just isolates certain communities such as suburbs of cities because of the bonding social capital and the fact that people in these communities spend so much time away from places that build bridging social capital.

There are two key issues in the study of social capital. First, social capital is not equally available to all, in much the same way that other forms of capital are differently available. Geographic and social isolation limit access to this resource. Second, not all social capital is created equally. The value of a specific source of social capital depends on the socio-economic position of the source with society. Portes (1998) identified four negative consequences of social capital: exclusion of outsiders; excess claims on group members; restrictions on individual freedom; and downward levelling norms. Putnam suggested that social capital would facilitate co-operation and mutually supportive relations in communities and nations and would therefore be a valuable means of combating many of the social disorders inherent in modern societies. In contrast to those focussing on the individual benefit derived from the web of social relationships and ties, individual actors find themselves in, attribute social capital to increased personal access to information and skill sets and enhanced power. According to this view, individuals could use social capital to further their own career prospects, rather than for the benefit of organisations.

Women and Micro-finance

As of today, more than a billion people live in poverty around the world, and a great majority of them are women. Poverty is a social phenomenon and can be defined in an inclusive sense as consisting of a number of elements: lack of access to, or availability of income-earning opportunities, basic health and education, food security; lack of adequate shelter, water or sanitation; lack of land or employment opportunities; and gender discrimination. The list is sometimes further enlarged to include: lack of participation in civil society, social exclusion, alienation, political instability and conflict. The more inclusive the definition is, the less specific it becomes.

Poverty is usually viewed as either a form of absolute deprivation or relative, but significant, deprivation. Absolute poverty is perceived as subsistence below the minimum requirements for physical well-being, generally based on a quantitative proxy indicator such as income or calories, but sometimes taking into account a broader package of goods and services. Alternatively, the relatively poor are those whose income or consumption level is below a particular fraction of the national average. As Sen (1999) notes, "relative deprivation in terms of incomes can yield absolute deprivation in terms of capabilities", depending on a person's ability to convert income into well-being; it is in turn based on, for example, health status, age, gender, and differences in social or ecological environment; poverty can be stated as a lack of capabilities, both intrinsic and instrumental (e.g. income, education, health, human rights, civil rights, etc.) that permit people to achieve functionings (the things they want to do) and beings (the States of existence they want to experience).

The defining feature of 'chronic poverty' is its extended duration. Poverty that is both severe and multi-dimensional but does not last a 'long' time, is by its nature not chronic. Thus, while those in severe income poverty at any given time are not necessarily chronically poor, the chronically poor are likely to be experiencing severe and multi-dimensional poverty. Commonly, the chronic poor experience several forms of disadvantage at the same time: these combinations keep them in poverty and block off opportunities to escape. An obvious example is lower caste widows living in remote areas in India: their poverty is sustained through the interaction of gender, caste and age discrimination and geographical location. In addition to people living in remote rural areas—often the homes of marginalized castes, tribes, ethnic groups, immigrants and pastoralists—vulnerable sub-groups identified in the literature include disabled people, older people, people living with HIV/AIDS, and women (particularly widows and female-headed households). It is likely that a significant proportion of the chronically poor are those who experience multiple and overlapping vulnerabilities.

Feminization of poverty has been noted by analysts since the late 1980s. It is a situation where women make up a majority of the poor. The number of women living in poverty has increased disproportionately to the number of men, particularly in the developing countries. Restrained access to physical assets, social assets and financial assets constitutes a large part of the problems. In addition to economic factors, the rigidity of socially ascribed gender roles and women's limited access to power, education, training and productive resources are responsible. Women bear the burden of attempting to manage household consumption and production under conditions of increasing scarcity.

According to general societal notions, women's work includes reproductive work (the childbearing and childrearing responsibilities, required to guarantee the maintenance and reproduction of the labour force), productive work (agricultural work and work in informal sector enterprises) and community managing work (provision of items of collective consumption). But even in these fields of activity, women are subordinated.

Gender planning and development has led to the conceptualization and improvement of micro-finance and other micro-level services, aimed exclusively at women. Micro-credit has been defined as "programmes that provide credit for self-employment and other financial and business services (including savings and technical assistance) to very poor persons" (Micro-Credit Summit, 1997). The basic idea of micro-finance is that poor people, especially women, are ready and are willing to pull themselves out of poverty if given access to economic inputs. Studies from all-over the world show that the Micro-Finance Institutions/Programmes (MFI/Ps) have significantly increased women's security, autonomy, self-confidence and status within the households by providing opportunities for self-employment. It has also helped in reduction of poverty through mutual help, solidarity and joint responsibility. Micro-finance programmes are currently being promoted as a key strategy for simultaneously addressing both poverty alleviation and women's empowerment.

Three main ways of making MFI services more poverty focused have been identified by various agencies in the world. They are: (i) identifying and reaching the poor; (ii) attracting the poor; and, (iii) discouraging or excluding the non-poor. In meeting the needs of the poor through micro-finance facilities, MFIs have to see to it that it provides flexible products and services that meet the need of every individual. Some may require flexible repayment schedules, others may require flexible loan sizes and many others may require a non-rigid deposit system and insurance facilities. MFIs have to see to it that the varying needs of its poor clients are met, in a cost effective and sustainable manner. If micro-credit is to reach the poorest, MFIs must focus on improving efficiency, bringing down high administrative costs in their operations, and, over time, passing on the benefits of efficiency to their clients through lower prices. MFIs must keep their costs at minimum levels through simple management structures and operational and delivery systems. Although scale is a factor that influences efficiency, delivery mechanisms and systems also play a key role. Therefore, it is necessary to continue to search for low-cost business models to serve not only the poor but also the poorest.

Statement of the Problem

The challenges of achieving more inclusive growth can only be met by policies that encourage easier and affordable access to financial services. Both theoretical and empirical researches highlight the role of financial development in facilitating economic development. At the cross-country level, evidence indicates that various measures of financial development are positively related to economic growth. The innovative credit delivery system—micro-finance—was a breakthrough in the world of finance. It changes the life of the poor, especially women, not only by providing financial services such as micro-savings and micro-insurance, but also by imparting training in entrepreneurial development. Over the past few decades, micro-finance institutions and programmes all-over the world have adopted numerous innovative ways of providing credit and savings services to the entrepreneurial poor. These include the provision of small loans to poor people, especially in rural areas, at full-cost interest rates, without collateral, repayable in easy instalments. Borrowers are organised into groups, which reduce the risk of default. There are also effective mechanisms to disseminate valuable information on ways to improve the health, legal rights, sanitation and other relevant concerns of the poor. In SHGs, credit is provided for agricultural activities and other livelihoods and could be several times the deposits made by the SHG. Most of the SHGs have been linked to public sector banks in view of the latter's dominant presence in the rural areas.

Many micro-finance institutions/programmes (MFI/Ps) have targeted women who live in households with very little or no assets. In addition to all the economic benefits attached to the micro-finance, it is a main strategy in the formation of social capital. The self-help groups show the bonding strategies that build trust and cooperation among individuals and within communities. It also promotes bridging strategies that break down barriers across groups and communities and enable collaborative action on shared objectives. Through connecting it to the higher levels, micro-financial activities help in scaling-up strategies that connect communities in collective action for social change and development at the policy and/or systems levels.

Kerala, a southern State of India, has gained international acclaim due to its development experience during the second half of the twentieth century. The basic characteristic of Kerala's experience is that it has gained high levels of social development despite low levels of per capita income. Kerala's development achievements have been considered by many as a model of viable development achieved through equitable distribution against the background of a relatively low economic growth. It has been attributed to the combination of public action and responsive governance. The achievement has been mainly due to the twin engines of education and health. In spite of these achievements in the social sector, women in Kerala face a variety of problems such as educational discrimination, gender discrimination in the labour market, wage discrimination, deprivation, lack of health care, violence and sexual atrocities and lack of public space. Many of the problems of women have gone unattended and neglected even by social reform movements and organisations in Kerala.

Kudumbashree: Social Capital Formation for Women in Kerala

In Kerala, the idea of micro-finance had germinated long before the advent of the modern MFI/Ps. Many church-based development institutions in Kerala had promoted credit unions early in the twentieth century. Micro-finance institutions/programmes of the modern type emerged in Kerala in the late 1980s and the early 1990s. In 1991, the centrally sponsored Urban Basic Services for the Poor (UBSP) and the Community Based Nutrition Programme (CBNP) of UNICEF converged to target the poor women of Alappuzha town. For that, a community-based administration system called Community Development Society (CDS) was set-up for enabling women from poor families to plan, implement and monitor schemes for their own benefit. The CDS has a three-tier federated structure. At the ward level, women from high-risk families form an Area Development Society (ADS) and all the ADSs of the town form a CDS. Both ADS and CDS have elected governing bodies.

Its basic unit is the neighbourhood group (NHG) comprising women from 25 to 40 families with high risk. A NHG has an elected five-member neighbourhood committee comprising: (i) a community health volunteer; (ii) a community infrastructure volunteer; (iii) a community income generation volunteer; (iv) a secretary; and (v) a president. The NHG conducts surveys of felt needs of each member family and of the NHG. The NHG committee also ascertains the sources of resources. Each NHG meets once in a week/fortnight. The members of the group are encouraged to cultivate the habit of thrift. Small savings of the members are collected on a regular basis and deposited in banks which could be further augmented by outside loan/grant/subsidy etc. The CDS, by working as a thrift society, is an informal banking system operating in the doorsteps, and carries one per cent interest per month. With the emergence of CDS, the influence of indigenous moneylenders has greatly decreased. Members get loans at any time in the year without undergoing vexing procedures (Suresh, 1998).

The CDS model of empowering women through self-management and economic activities was first extended to Malappuram district and then to other urban localities in Kerala. At present, CDS activities in the State are coordinated by a State Government Programme called 'Kudumbashree'. Kudumbashree is a woman-based participatory poverty eradication programme launched on 1st April, 1998 by the State Government with the financial support of National Bank for Agriculture and Rural Development (NABARD) and the Central Government. Thus, it is a partnership of four major agents—Central Government, State Government, local bodies and NABARD. The programme envisages a total investment of Rs. 858.80 crore. The main objective of the programme is to eradicate absolute poverty from the State within a decade by involving the poor actively in planning, managing and monitoring of programmes for their development. It is exclusively focused on women, women in family and women in community. It is an organisation of women from below the poverty line. The core activity of this is to empower women through micro-finance, micro-enterprise and convergent community action (Chathukulam, 2002b).

In Kerala, the State Poverty Eradication Mission implements the Kudumbashree Programme by organizing the poor by creating community based structures of women below poverty line with focus on self-help, demand-led convergence of available services and resources under the leadership of the Local Governments. The State Poverty Eradication Mission is the State Level Nodal Agency for the implementation of major centrally sponsored Urban Poverty Reduction Programmes *viz*. Swarna Jayanthi Shahari Rozgar Yojana (SJSRY), Integrated Housing and Slum Development Programme (IHSDP) and UBSP. Kudumbashree has organized Community Development Societies (CDSs) which act as a delivery system for the various Centrally Sponsored Urban Poverty Reduction Programmes. The physical and social developments and direct assistance to employment generation are the schemes taken up under these programmes.

The key components of the programmes are:

- Enabling certain minimum needs of infrastructure, setting up of micro-enterprises and capacity building of the poor.
- Providing high quality support services for the design and implementation of self-employment ventures.
- Setting up of a challenge fund to support pro-poor policies of the local governments, a technology fund to support transfer of technology relevant for poverty reduction, an innovation fund to support path breaking innovations in poverty reduction and a common revolving fund to provide seed capital for micro-enterprises.
- Generating jobs for educated youth.

Kudumbashree, from its very beginning, has promoted micro-enterprises as a means of livelihood for the poor women both in the rural and urban areas under various Government schemes. Kudumbashree regularly sets up monthly markets in each district on specified days and venues. The entrepreneurs are given opportunity to bring their products and efforts at standardization of product quality and presentation by them. Also, as part of its market development strategy, Kudumbashree exploits the opportunity of the Onam festival, by conducting State-wide Onam fairs. The project also envisages establishing 'Informal Bank of the Poor' at local body level under three-tier system, to act as the sub-system of the formal banking sector (GoK, 2012).

The unprecedented growth of micro-finance has taken place in Kerala due mainly to the initiatives and actions taken by the agencies in the field of micro-finance. This would certainly help to improve the overall status of women in Kerala because the self-help groups formed under micro-finance train women in income generation, sensitisation and democratic processes. The available evidence suggests that micro-finance has already made tremendous success in many parts of the State. It is in this context, the present study looked into the impact of the recent progress of micro-finance in Kerala on the capacity building of women in particular and development of the State in general. It further looked into how social capital formation among marginalized and vulnerable sections of the society through micro-finance helped the poor, especially in the context of inclusive growth.

Objectives

The specific objectives of the study are:

1. To analyse the factors that lead to the inequalities of women in rural/backward areas.
2. To study how micro-finance helps in the formation of social capital.
3. To examine whether micro-finance helps in the enhancement of democratic, economic and social capabilities of poor women.
4. To analyse the factors affecting bonding and bridging of social capital through micro-finance.
5. To examine how the actions taken by the authorities are effective in helping the women to have access to various financial and other services.
6. To find out the deficiencies of micro-finance in reaching the poor women effectively.
7. To understand the contribution of micro-finance to the poor women in accessing various financial products.

Hypothesis

It is hypothesized that micro-finance helps to enhance the resource base of women. Further, the micro-finance institutions effectively act as a tool of social capital formation for conferring inputs and services on the poor.

Data, Methodology, and Research Design

In Kerala, a large number of NGOs and other agencies are engaged in micro-financing. Most of them help in the promotion as well as financing SHGs. However, the study was conducted among the neighbourhood groups (NHGs) formed under Kudumbashree, a woman-based participatory poverty eradication programme launched by the State Government. The reason for the selection was that this programme has initiated NHGs among women both in urban and rural areas all-over the State. In order to understand the structure, functions and variations of NHGs under Kudumbashree, the researcher visited a few units in different localities of Kerala. Following that, a chart was prepared for choosing samples, with details such as names of the groups, year of their formation and number of members in each group. Discussions with facilitators were also held in order to select appropriate samples and cases.

Study Area

Of the fourteen districts in Kerala, for the present study, six districts are selected. They are Alappuzha, Idukki, Kozhikode, Malappuram, Thiruvananthapuram and Wayanad. The justification for the selection of the respective districts is that it is made on the basis of the concentration of six outlier communities in Kerala society—the tribals (Wayanad), marine fisherfolk (Kozhikode), slum dwellers (Thiruvananthapuram), agricultural labourers (Alappuzha), plantation workers (Idukki) and Muslims (Malappuram). For getting adequate representation of the poor women from all vulnerable sections of the society, approximately one hundred members of Kudumbashree were selected from each district.

Sources of Data

Besides the primary data collected through field investigations, secondary data are also used for the study, wherever found appropriate. The major sources of secondary data used are Decennial Censuses, NSSO, Directorate of Economics and Statistics (Government of Kerala), NABARD, Reserve Bank of India (RBI) and the print and electronic media.

Methodology

The adequate data were collected using two-stage sampling. In the first stage, NHGs of Kudumbashree were chosen and in the second stage, members were selected from the NHGs. Primary data were collected through an extensive field work. Two different schedules (Appendix I and II) were used in the primary data collection. Other qualitative methods such as case study and observation method were also used. In the analysis of data, both qualitative and quantitative methods were used.

Sampling Technique used for Selecting Neighbourhood Groups

At the first stage, details of 107 NHGs functioning under Kudumbashree from six districts of Kerala were collected. For that, two wards/panchayats from each district were selected, where the respective identified social group is concentrated. Special care was given to give appropriate representation of the vulnerable sections in the NHGs selected.

Sample Beneficiaries

At the second stage, five members from each neighbourhood group were selected for conducting a beneficiary survey using an interview schedule. Demographic particulars and information on standard of living, level of participation in other organisations and NHGs, personal savings and loan details and the micro-enterprises initiated by 590 members were collected from them.

Schedules

Two detailed schedules were prepared for collection of data: one for neighbourhood groups and the other for members of NHGs. The first was administered among leaders (secretary and president) of the neighbourhood groups (see Appendix I). Data were collected through interviewing them and holding focus-group discussions with all the members of the group. For supplementing the data relating to groups, reports and records of respective groups were checked. The details such as total savings, total loans of the group members etc. were collected beforehand. For collecting data from members of NHGs, a different schedule was used (see Appendix II). Both open-ended and close-ended questions were included in the schedule.

A pre-test had been conducted towards the end of May, 2010 before finalising the interview schedule. Data from ten neighbourhood groups and fifty members of NHGs were collected during this period. A preliminary analysis had also been done. On the basis of the field experience during the pre-test and the preliminary analysis, the schedules were modified and refined.

Interview Guide

Besides the field survey using pre-designed schedules, information was collected through interviews and focus group discussions with members. For this purpose, an interview guide was used which indicated the topics for further dialogue. Detailed information on members' views about the organisation, group activities and members' participation in them was collected. Relevant observations were systematically recorded and an informal approach was followed throughout the discussions.

Fieldwork

The information was collected during the weekly meetings of the SHGs and during the visits to the members' households. Other data related to the organisation were collected from reports and the newsletters published by the organisation and through discussions with the coordinators and leaders at various levels.

Data Processing and Analysis Plan

The statistical data were processed using the SPSS package. Simple tools like percentage, mean standard deviation and Chi-square were used to interpret the data and draw meaningful inferences. For evaluating the performance of SHGs, a performance rating technique (see Appendix III) was used. The indicators of the technique were drawn from NABARD and other sources.

Limitations of the Study

All the defects that could be raised against discussions based on data from a sample survey are applicable to this study too. In spite of the limitations, it is hoped that this study would bring out the nature and problems of micro-finance in general.

Chapter Scheme

Chapter two of the report attempts to give a brief review of theoretical and empirical literature by presenting the major debates in the field of micro-finance. After a discussion on financial inclusion in chapter three, the issues prevailing in the field of micro-finance in India is discussed. In chapter four, an exploration of micro-finance opportunities in Kerala is discussed, in which an evaluation of Kudumbashree is also done. The details of the study area are furnished in chapter five. The extent to which the tool of micro-finance helps in social capital formation has become the topic of discussion in chapter six. Chapter seven is devoted to an appraisal how the micro-finance helped in inclusive growth of poor women in the State. The summary and conclusions of the study are presented in the final chapter along with a few suggestions for improving the performance of the micro-finance system.

2

Major Debates in the Field of Micro-finance

Micro-finance has captured the imagination of many people working to reduce poverty, through its simple yet workable foundations. Apart from fulfilling its basic objective of poverty reduction, micro-finance institutions serve as "banks for the poor" by supporting the strong, but often untapped entrepreneurial spirit that exists in poor corners around the world through the building of an "inclusive financial system". As of today, micro-finance has been recognised as an effective poverty reduction strategy, which enables and empowers the poor through the provision of necessary financial services, and allows them to take advantage of income generation opportunities and reduces their vulnerability to livelihood shocks.

Micro-finance services are no longer considered a niche market activity with rigid delivery systems, confined largely to the development community and carried out solely by specialized micro-finance institutions. Conversely, it has gained importance as an innovative system, providing flexible financial opportunities for a vast clientele ranging from the poorest of the world to small and medium level entrepreneurs. The profitability and sustainability of the micro-finance industry is starting to make waves in the private commercial financial market as well.

Micro-finance—from its conceptualization to its present highly developed structure—has been marked by many issues and ideologies, brought forth by studies and researches from various viewpoints. Researchers have contributed immensely to the wide aspects of the core theory of micro-finance. The literature for micro-finance is burgeoned with many theoretical and empirical studies.

The various sections of the present chapter explain some of the major debates existing in the field of micro-finance *viz.*, sustainability of micro-finance institutions (MFIs), outreach to the poor, outreach to the extreme poor, impact on the poor, mistargeting and non-participation, drop-outs, delinquent clients, overlapping memberships, use of informal finance and commercialization of micro-finance.

Sustainability of MFIs

Sustainability is permanence (Navajas *et al.*, 2000). Sustainability of a micro-finance institution means its capability to operate as a development institution for the poor to maximize the expected net present social value comprising the net gain of users from loans and deposits, the profits or losses of the MFIs and the social opportunity cost of the resources used. Sustainability is a core value to micro-finance programmes. It simply reflects the financial and institutional ability of an MFI to continue providing its services to the target group. Financial sustainability means that the institution's income, in terms of interest and fees, can cover all its expenses including operating and financial costs, after adjusting for inflation and different sorts of subsidy (Christen, *et al.*, 1995; Johnson and Rogaly, 1997). Many MFIs have become increasingly self-sufficient and even highly profitable while reaching a target population of very small to medium borrowers, whom conventional formal lenders had traditionally considered not creditworthy (*The Microbanking Bulletin*, 2001). Hulme and Mosley (1996) have found that sustainable large-scale schemes are more able to pull down the real cost of lending to the borrowers and thereby attract more clients. At the same time, sustainability is the key to maintain the clients' loyalty to the institution, and thus their repayment discipline (Johnson and Rogaly, 1997).

Growth (reaching a large number of clients) is an essential condition for MFIs seeking long-term sustainability. MFIs are required to cover their costs with interest and fees generated from transactions of relatively small amounts, and, therefore, they need a large number of transactions in order to reduce their operations' unit cost (Johnson and Rogaly, 1997). An increase in the number of borrowers reduces average fixed handling costs of lending (Gonzalez-Vega, 1985). An analysis of 124 MFIs around the world in 2003 showed that those who have achieved financial self-sufficiency were more than two times larger (in terms of number of served clients) than the average, although operating from a similar number of branches. Christen, *et al.* (1995) propounds that the breadth (number of users) of outreach is essential to sustainably reach the poorest clientele. Financially, strong institutions with a large number of clients have the resources to innovate and develop new products that are suitable to poorer segments in the communities.

In pursuing financial sustainability, there is however a risk that some MFIs might lose their poverty focus. They find that their successful clients need to "graduate" to larger loans over time. Under the pressure of maintaining the interest income generated from their "best clients", MFIs might tend to increase the size of their loans, shifting away from their poorer clients (Johnson and Rogaly, 1997). Christen, *et al.* (1995) have observed that in order to reduce transaction costs and increase scale, it would be necessary for MFIs to expand its financial services and to strive to reach all possible persons within a geographical area. Thus, it might be necessary for an institution, in order to serve the poor in a specific geographic area, to extend its services to the non-poor as well.

Researchers have found that the poorest prefer individual loans; they do not wish to participate in group-based programmes, and do not like to attend regular meetings. Thus, to reach the poorest, different approaches are required. But there are no effective delivery mechanisms that can provide such flexible services on a large-scale to the poorest. For example, SafeSave in Bangladesh has been providing flexible services for the poorest for several years. However, it has so far not been able to achieve sustainability or reach a large number of clients. Reaching the poorest is obviously much more expensive than reaching the poor—those who are around the poverty line.

Rural Bangladeshi women who have little or no income opportunities, the Income Generation for Vulnerable Group Development (IGVGD) programme of Bangladesh Rural Advancement Committee (BRAC) has provided food grain assistance and savings and credit services to nearly a million participants targeted towards destitute over a ten year period. About 85 per cent of IGVGD members also received training and support in poultry and livestock raising, vegetable gardening, agriculture, fishery production, or grocery business. Two thirds of these women have 'graduated' from absolute poverty to becoming micro-finance clients, and have not slipped back into requiring government handouts (CGAP, 2009). BRAC keeps this programme on a sustainable level by providing smaller loans to IGVGD clients and cross-subsidizing these loans by its regular micro-credit programmes. Many micro-finance institutions (MFIs) offering only credit for micro-entrepreneurs face problems of inefficiency and instability in the long run. As recent studies have shown, the performance standards of outreach in quality and quantity, viability and sustainability of credit—only MFIs have not been widely met (Schmidt and Zeitinger, 1994). Few MFIs have reached financial self-sufficiency in terms of being fully financed by client savings and funds from formal financial institutions.

Outreach to the Poor

Outreach refers to the ability of micro-finance institutions to reach the poorest in society. Outreach in terms of financial services implies that MFIs should have to meet the goals of improved quality of life, and should provide short-term and long-term sources of liquidity and should serve the largest number of the targeted poor. The population of micro-finance borrowers has expanded quickly, as a growing number of public, non-governmental, and private micro-finance providers have entered to supply the market (Christen, *et al.*, 1995, Robinson, 1994, Poyo and Young, 1999). The Micro-credit Summit Campaign Report of 2007 reported a growth of 885 per cent in the number of clients from 1997 to 2006—an average annual growth rate of 29 per cent per year. In 2006, 3,316 institutions reported to the organization, and those institutions reached 133 million clients; a year later, the number had swelled to 154 million.

In Bangladesh, outreach had expanded at a rapid pace. At the end of December, 2000, the 585 largest MFIs in the country reported a total of over 11 million members with almost eight million holding outstanding loans in a total amount of about $440 million. In addition, the Grameen Bank reported over 2.3 million members with total loans outstanding of about $250 million making a total of some 13 million micro-finance clients out of a population of about 130 million people. Khandker, *et al.* (1995) that by 1994, Grameen Bank had more than two million members of which 94 per cent were women. In the same year, BRAC mobilised more than one million members, of whom 88 per cent were women. In 1994 alone, Grameen Bank disbursed US$385 million, while BRAC disbursed US$55 million. The loan recovery rate for both programmes has been consistently more than 90 per cent. Also in 1994, the savings mobilised by Grameen Bank were US$70 million compared with US$12 million of BRAC.

The Bangladesh Rural Development Board (BRDB) RD-12 programme is a successful replication of the group-based micro-credit programme. This programme started in December 1988 and by 1994 it had mobilised 4,52,000 members of whom 70 per cent were women, and disbursed US$17 million in the same year, and its loan recovery rate has also been consistently above 90 per cent. The savings mobilised by RD-12 from its members was US$5 million (Khandker, *et al.,* 1995). Land ownership, occupational criteria, and asset valuations are standard targeting tools used by micro-credit providers in Bangladesh in order to direct resources to the rural poor. In a sample of MFI members, it was found that 65 per cent of BRAC households had no agricultural land, compared to 55 per cent for Grameen members, and 58 per cent for a comparable government-run micro-credit programme. This supports evidence that a large proportion of extremely poor households join micro-credit programmes.

Studies have shown that in a limited period of five years, the CrediAmigo programme has provided micro-credit to over 3,00,000 of Brazil's working poor, and it is financially sustainable. Most of these families live on less than two dollars per day, and work in the cities and towns of the north-east region. More importantly, CrediAmigo has demonstrated to the development community that micro-credit can be delivered sustainably, on a large-scale, and with great impact on low income families. In 2000-01, micro-finance programmes assisted some ten million households (of a total of 30 million), with loans outstanding of about $1 billion. The organized NGO sector and Grameen Bank accounted for more than 86 per cent of micro-finance lending and commercial banks for just 14 per cent. But, some have reported concerns that the huge expansion of micro-finance has led to such intense competition for clients that it could undermine the industry (Wright, *et al.*, 2001).

Although the MFIs have reached close to 100 million clients (92 million clients by the end of2004 (Silverman, 2006) and 80 million clients in 2003, they actually only manage to meet around four per cent of the world-wide demand according to the World Bank. Despite the important contribution of micro-enterprises to output and employment in developing countries, and their sheer numbers, few of them are able to obtain loans or other services from banks, credit unions or finance companies. It is estimated that less than five per cent of micro-enterprises in Latin America have access to institutional sources of credit.

Outreach to the Extreme Poor

The World Bank (2001a) defines the extreme poor as those who have no land or house of their own, sell manual labour as their only means of income, have no savings, and who are unable to have three meals a day, cannot afford to purchase minimum clothing and have no ability to spend money on education. The other indicators include the following in the extreme poor category: households without any agricultural or homestead land, widows, husband-abandoned women, women-headed households,

households with disabled adult male members and households without any source of income or with very irregular income.

The extreme poor are trapped in chronic deprivation due to the combination of poor health, meagre education, and fractured families on one side and skewed resource distribution, inadequate infrastructure, varied forms of exclusion and scarce employment opportunities, on the other side. This sub-set of the poor lack the complementary resources that they can use to lift themselves out of the State of chronic deprivation. They are caught in a trap, below the threshold of a virtuous cycle of asset accumulation and sustainable livelihoods. It is commonly acknowledged that, despite the phenomenally rapid growth in outreach of NGOs particularly of micro-finance projects, NGOs have failed to reach the extreme poor. The second round Impact Assessment Study of BRAC's Rural Development Project (RDP), carried out by BRAC's Research and Evaluation, finds that 41 per cent of the eligible poor did not participate in any NGO programmes, micro-finance or otherwise (Hossain, 1988). Most micro-finance clients today fall in a band around the poverty line and the extremely poor are rarely reached by micro-finance (CGAP, 2009).

Rahman (2000) in a recent article find that almost three quarter of the hardcore poor did not participate even in non-financial NGO programmes. They argue that the hardcore poor's non-participation is due to micro-finance mechanisms and structures, through which most Bangladeshi NGOs deliver social development services like health care and education. The NOVIB Report on Bangladesh echoes very similar concerns: "The NGOs have not yet taken a pro extreme-poor approach to poverty alleviation". Micro-finance, the mainstay of most NGO projects in Bangladesh, is not suitable for all categories of the poor. For those trapped in chronic food insecurity with no asset base to protect themselves from the myriad of web of shocks, the micro-finance strategy may be ineffective and sometimes counter-productive. According to a World Bank report (2001a), about five per cent of the population in Bangladesh is destitutes, 31 per cent ultra-poor and 17 per cent moderate poor. An additional 20 per cent of the population, these studies suggest, though non-poor, are pretty vulnerable to pressures of downward mobility that could throw them into poverty. This distribution suggests that almost 70 per cent of those living below the poverty line would be either destitute or ultra-poor.

There are three camps of thought on the issue of financial services for the poorest.

- The first camp rejects the hypothesis that the poorest can be reached with financial services on a sustainable basis. According to them, credit is unlikely to help the poorest if they do not have the capacity to service the credit. As Robinson (1994) pointed out, "extremely poor households living in small, isolated communities in areas that lack basic infrastructure and markets may be unable to use credit in any way that would enable them to repay loan principal and interest."
- The second camp advocates that the poorest of the poor can be reached not only on a sustainable basis but also on a large-scale. They argue that there is a vast effective demand among the poorest for micro-finance services, particularly micro-credit. It is also argued that increasing numbers of micro-finance institutions (MFIs) with a focus on the poorest have achieved successful results and the required knowledge on delivery mechanisms is widely available. According to this group, if funding agencies and MFIs target the poorest and if funding agencies make more funds available to these MFIs, outreach to the poorest can be rapidly increased.
- The third camp recognizes that the potential for reaching the poorest on a sustainable and a large-scale basis is limited but the search for innovative approaches to expand the outreach to the poorest must be continued. Their view is that the search for sustainable models to deliver financial services for the poorest must continue; funding agencies have an important role to play in promoting innovations toward this end. This camp also recognizes that subsidies have an important role to play in developing sustainable mechanisms to reach the poorest.

The assumption that there is no effective demand for micro-finance services among the poorest does not seem to be realistic. Although the majority of clients in most sustainable MFIs—such as the Bangladesh Rural Advancement Committee (BRAC) and the Association for Social Advancement (ASA) in Bangladesh and the Share Microfin Ltd. in India—are not the poorest, these institutions serve some clients at the bottom 50 per cent below the poverty line. Also, the poorest households have an effective demand for safe deposit facilities (Rutherford, 2000). With flexible deposit and loan products, SafeSave in Bangladesh has been able to reach some of the poorest households in Dhaka slums. Similarly, about seven per cent of Mibanco clients in Peru belong to the poorest category.

Empirical evidence shows that appropriate products and services are effective ways of deepening the outreach to the poorest. MFIs must be provided with the right incentives and support to design appropriate products, particularly provide flexible deposit facilities, and extend their services to the poorest. ASA introduced a flexible product— business development services to improve capacity of the poorest to productively use credit—and a new service delivery system. Association for Social Advancement (ASA) established 1,200 outposts in remote locations to facilitate hard-core poor households' access to its products and services. The local staff responsible for the new flexible products operates from these outposts. Association for Social Advancement (ASA) reached one million hard-core poor households by the end of 2006 through this innovative programme.

Impact on the Poor

Micro-finance involves small-scale transactions in credit and savings designed to meet the needs of small- and medium-scale producers and businesses. Micro-finance programmes also offer skill-based training to augment productivity and organizational support and consciousness-raising training to empower the poor. The positive impact that these programmes have on the end customers determines its success.

A joint research project of the Bangladesh Institute of Development Studies (BIDS) and the World Bank find strong evidence that the micro-finance programmes help the poor through consumption smoothing and asset building (Khandker, 2000). The findings support the claim that micro-finance programmes promote investment in human capital (such as schooling) and raise awareness of reproductive health issues (such as use of contraceptives) among poor families. The studies also shed light on the role of gender-based targeting and its impact on household and individual welfare, finding that micro-finance helps women acquire assets of their own and exercise power in household decision-making. The research project estimates that the marginal impact of micro-finance on consumption was 18 per cent for women and 11 per cent for men (Pitt, 2000). The study finds that some five per cent of borrowers may lift themselves out of poverty each year by borrowing from a micro-finance programme, if the estimated impacts on consumption continue over time (Khandker, 2000). But even if this does happen, micro-finance could lift less than one per cent of the population out of poverty because it reaches only a quarter of the population.

The positive impact of micro-finance programmes has led to a decline in the proportion of the poor since the 1980s (Osmani, 1998). It has also been proved that these programmes are hugely sustainable (Khandker, *et al.*, 1995). The success of the Grammen Bank (GB) can be portrayed in the fact that one-third of Grameen's 2.1 million borrowers have pulled themselves out of poverty (Yunus and Jolis, 1998). Studies have termed Grameen as a model of hope for reducing poverty across the world; a significant contributor to poverty alleviation in a sustainable manner; provider of women empowerment and income; developer of family planning and a contributor to the increase in nutrition levels. While the micro-level impacts of programmes are largely evident, the impact over the national economy is still not very evident, but it is expected that macro-level impacts will become evident soon.

A study (Hossain, 1988) to assess the economic impact of the Grameen Bank on rural households found that the loans had generated new employment for one-third of the households of the GB participants. They had remained unemployed before joining GB. The average level of employment for members increased from about six working days to eighteen working days per month. Working capital for Grameen-supported enterprises increased nearly four-fold in 2.25 years. The study also reported increases in per capita food consumption in member households and in investments in housing, education and sanitation. Bangladesh Institute of Development Studies (BIDS) carried out an extensive study of the impact of PKSF PO's micro-credit programme using longitudinal data of 3,000 households between 1997 and 2000. One of the key findings was that "micro-credit has a positive and significant effect on poverty status of the programme household". The study also finds that members of micro-credit programmes are less vulnerable when faced with crises. Moreover, improvements in other social indicators (child immunization, use of sanitary latrines, and prevalence of contraception) are also more noticeable for micro-credit programme members compared to non-members. A study in 36 villages in Bangladesh showed that membership in micro-credit programmes positively affected a woman's decision-making role, her marital stability, her control over resources, and her mobility, but had less impact on her attitude regarding marriage and education of daughters. Navjas, *et al.* (2000) finds that the women participants in credit programmes felt their status had improved due to the fact that they were seen as income earners for the family because of their access to credit. If households served by the Grameen Bank are ordered by the amounts they have borrowed from the programme, it can be found that the top quarter enjoys 15 per cent higher consumption per capita than households in the bottom quarter. In addition, 62 per cent of the school age sons of Grameen Bank borrowers are enrolled in school versus 34 per cent of the sons of eligible households that do not borrow. For daughters, the Grameen advantage is 55 per cent versus 40 per cent.

Rahman (2002) summarised that the average food intake of a female Grameen Bank member is higher than that of a non-Grameen Bank poor female in the same area where the Bank is in operation. Although female borrowers of Grameen Bank have higher intake of food than their counterparts in the control group (non-Grameen Bank females), they never surpassed the males within the Grameen Bank category. Borrowing from a micro-credit programme such as the Grameen Bank increases per capita consumption, women's non-land assets, and women's labour supply to cash income earning activities, children's school enrolment, contraceptive use and fertility. Programme participation also increases profit for self-employed rural non-farm activities, as micro-credit programmes chiefly finance these activities in Bangladesh.

Khandker, *et al.* (1995a) observed that participants of micro-credit programmes are generally in a better position to meet their calorie requirements. However, the calorie intake depends on who participated (men or women) in the programme. Hashemi and Schuler (1997) observed that, although Grameen Bank does not provide family planning services directly, they influence the use of contraceptive by promoting family planning education, family planning norms and other relevant information. This general tendency has also been observed with organisations other than Grameen Bank. Grameen Bank put emphasises on installing proper sanitary latrines in order to control the diarrhoeal disease. The bank encourages its participants to install sanitary latrines in order to ensure better sanitation in the rural areas in Bangladesh. Grameen Bank beneficiaries are also encouraged to boil their drinking water or drink water from deep tube wells.

Khandker, *et al.* (1995b) has found "strong evidence that micro-finance programmes help the poor through consumption smoothing and asset building" and that "micro-finance helps women acquire assets of their own". They report that micro-finance "raises per capita household consumption for both participants and non-participants. A WB/BIDS study support the claim that micro-finance programmes promote investment in human capital (such as schooling) and raise awareness of reproductive health issues (such as the use of contraceptives) among poor families, and that micro-finance helps women exercise power in household decision-making. Credit services for the poor, and particularly poor women, reverse their systemic exclusion from access to public or private funds, thus altering systems of hierarchy and power (Todd, 1996).

Impact assessments show that micro-finance in general has positive economic impact on clients, in terms of income growth and reduced vulnerability, although the effects are often small (Mayoux, 1998), and all clients do not benefit equally. An early study of Grameen Bank noted its support for the poor, especially women, through employment and income generation and improvements in social indicators (Hossain, 1988). Some recent studies also find beneficial aspects of micro-finance operations in Bangladesh (Hashemi and Schuler, 1997).

Mistargeting and Non-participation

It is the primary goal of MFIs to provide flexible financial services to the poorest of the poor. In this sense, it is the mentally and physically challenged, the elderly, street children, destitute and refugees who are to be provided with micro-finance services. But, in recent years there has been considerable criticism from researchers about mistargeting. The researchers listed five sets of client-related barriers to participation: insufficient resources, ill health or vulnerability to crisis, being a female head of household, lack of education, and individual and household preferences.

According to Wright, *et al.* (2001), MFIs use the rhetoric of serving "the poorest of the poor", but it is generally understood that most do not reach the truly destitute groups composed of widows, orphans, the chronically sick, and the mobile landless. The reasons given for such non-participation vary from self-exclusion to the risk averse nature of the poor to participate and incur debt; as well as factors like the poor being busy eking out a living to participate in groups and attend meetings; exclusion of the poor by group lending programmes, out of fear that they will not repay on time; and exclusion by loan officers, who fear they will not repay, and thus, affect their loan recovery performance.

A survey conducted by the World Bank and the Bangladesh Institute of Development Studies, in Bangladesh revealed that in the year 1991-92, less than 45 per cent of all eligible households participated in the MFIs that operated in the 72 surveyed villages. The participation rates were 44 per cent in the Grameen villages, 52 per cent in the villages of the Bangladesh Rural Advancement Committee (BRAC), and 33 per cent in the villages of the RD-12 programme of the Bangladesh Rural Development Board (Khandker, *et al.*, 1995a).

A 1994 survey of areas served by the Rural Development Programme of BRAC revealed that 60 to 65 per cent of the eligible households did not participate in micro-finance programmes (Evans, *et al.*, 1999). Non-member households were found to have fewer assets, had lower income, were more reliant on wage labour, and were more likely to be landless compared to member households. In an access study conducted in four villages in which the Grameen Bank and Bangladesh Rural Advancement Committee (BRAC) were active, it was found that only 57 per cent of the target group households joined one of these MFIs (Hashemi, 1997). The major reason given for not joining was that people felt they would not have income to pay back loans and would be forced to sell what a little possessions they had in order to repay. Some women reported that leaving the home to attend required meetings would violate social norms. Thirteen per cent of the women wanted to join but were not accepted by group members who felt that they were too risky. In a 1997 study by the Association for Social Advancement (ASA), to determine why its programme did not reach many of the poor revealed that the most frequent responses included the lack of minimum clothing required to attend meetings, discouragement and threats from local elite, and age requirements (ages 18-50). By setting a relatively low maximum age requirement, ASA excluded old people who are often very poor. A study found that about 25 per cent of non-participants did not join MFI/Ps because they were unable to make weekly savings instalments, about 15 per cent could not make weekly loan instalments, seven per cent were not interested in getting a loan, and another seven per cent did not want to attend weekly meetings.

Several studies show that between 15 to 30 per cent of members of micro-credit programmes are from "non-target" households, as measured in terms of land. However, they typically are marginal farmers and can still be considered part of the vulnerable non-poor; prone to transient bouts of poverty. Rahman (2000) has found that almost three quarters of the hardcore poor in Bangladesh have never received social development services from NGOs. Focusing policy attention towards the extreme poor is important because their existing opportunities can be severely constrained due to mismatches between the structure of opportunities available and the complex structure of constraints they face. Market mediated opportunities may also bypass the extreme poor because they lack the human and social capital needed to participate and benefit from such opportunities, and/or because they live in areas or belong to ethnicities that are bypassed or excluded due to their lack of voice and representation in policy-making processes. It is by now accepted that mainstream development approaches, especially micro-finance, largely bypass the extreme poor. However, evidence also suggests that micro-finance has provided an important opportunity for moderate poor households to overcome poverty and reduce vulnerability (Morduch, 1999).

Drop-out

Drop-outs (persons who stop being clients) are a concern for an MFI because of the cost of recruiting and training new members or clients to replace drop-outs. Because of the cost of making the first small loan to new clients, lending usually does not become profitable in many programmes until the third or fourth loan to a client is given. Retention, therefore, is key to profitability and sustainability, although on the other hand, dropping out may be an advantage for a client if better services are obtained by switching to another MFI. Dropping out before overcoming poverty implies that the participant loses out on the possibility of economic graduation. Dropping out after overcoming poverty implies that the members would be deprived of other services provided by the programme. Also, even if they have moved out of poverty, they might face difficulty in maintaining that level without the help of MFI/Ps. For the organization, dropping out implies lesser credit disbursements and lesser profits. Also, marginal cost of new membership is high, and so, a high rate of drop-out is not feasible for the organization (Khandker, *et al.*, 1995).

Wright, *et al.* (2001) reported that in BRAC, drop-outs represented over 15 per cent of its membership in 1992 and almost 11 per cent the next year. Analysis of these drop-outs showed that Bangladesh Rural Advancement Committee (BRAC) was losing many of its older, experienced and more cost effective clients. The inflexibility of the BRAC model, especially the lack of access to savings in times of emergency, was identified as an important factor affecting drop-outs. Strict rules governing savings deposits and withdrawals suggest that members perceive that compulsory savings are an additional cost of borrowing (Montgomery, *et al.*, 1996). Zeller, *et al.* (2000) found that the average size of borrowing groups fell over time because drop-outs exceeded new members. For example, within the five-year period prior to 1994 survey, the average size of BRAC groups fell from 56 to 37, while the average size of ASA groups fell from 25 to 18 persons. Evans, *et al.* (1999) found that 11 per cent of the eligible non-member households in their survey were former members of BRAC's Rural Development Programme that had subsequently dropped out. Drop-out households tended to be smaller, with lower education, male, and more frequently participated in other non-governmental organizations (NGOs) than current member households.

Association for Social Advancement (ASA) grew by over 25,000 members during 2000, reaching more than 1.2 million. However, to achieve that increase, it had to recruit 3,22,000 new members to offset the loss of 2,96,000 members who dropped out during the year, a drop-out rate of almost 20 per cent. Annual drop-out rates during 1996 to 1999 varied between 15 and 18 per cent. A study conducted in 1995 by the ASA identified internal factors in the programme's design and operation as the major problem leading to drop-outs. The programme's low credit ceiling and the rule against multiple loans were the important factors, followed by frequent loan payments and joint liability. The Thana Resource Development and Employment Programme (TRDEP), a micro-finance programme started in the late 1980s by the Ministry of Youth and Sports in Bangladesh (Montgomery, *et al.*, 1996), also reported numerous drop-outs. To spread its benefits to more clients, the programme limits each client to a maximum of three one-year loans. Unpublished data from the project office show it had reached over 3,17,000 members with their first loan by the end of 2000. Over 30 per cent had graduated, meaning they had received three loans, but almost 28 per cent had dropped out before completing the three-loan cycle. Design and implementation factors contributed to the high drop-out rate. Some members switched to other MFIs that expanded into areas served by TRDEP, to escape the three loan constraints, even though the effective interest rate in The Thana Resource Development and Employment Programme TRDEP was roughly half of many MFIs. In addition, the temporary field staff hired to implement the TRDEP project were reportedly threatened with firing if they did not recover most loans, so, this may have induced them to seek clients who were somewhat better off than those served by other organizations. It is possible, therefore, that some TRDEP drop-outs qualified for commercial bank loans or were attractive candidates for other MFIs because of their above-average repayment capacity.

Another study surveyed members of the Shakti Foundation for Disadvantaged Women, found that the drop-out rate was 14 per cent in 1998 and nine per cent in 1999. A sample of drop-outs was asked to report their reasons for leaving, for which the largest number (33%) reported the loan amount was too small, followed by too many meetings (28%), long meetings (25%), not wanting to pay for a defaulting member (25%), and loans being too expensive (22%). Most MFIs in Bangladesh put their clients on a "treadmill of continuously increasing loan size", and it is alleged that loan officers have "pushed" larger loans to reach disbursement targets (Sinha and Matin, 1998). However, Wright, *et al.* (2001) reported that the MFI BURO Tangail experienced a drop-out rate of only three per cent in 1997 because it allowed members the possibility of borrowing when they wanted to and offered them attractive savings products. As a result, only about half the members actually had loans at any one time. This also suggests that not all members want loans all of the time.

Delinquent Clients

Delinquencies and defaults arise when borrowers are unable to repay, and also when borrowers do not value access to future services enough to maintain a relationship with the MFI. Matin (1997) studied borrowers in four villages where Grameen had been operating since 1980. Almost 56 per cent of the loans taken in 1994 were overdue as of the end of 1995. The repayment rates among the borrowing groups varied from 28 to 56 per cent. Many borrowers with overdue loans had stopped paying entirely while others were repaying intermittently. "Unzipping" of joint liability was occurring and the whole system was beginning to operate on the basis of individual liability. A follow-up survey conducted in the same villages in May 1997 revealed that 56 per cent of the loans were in default in 1995 and in 1997; the survey pointed that eventual loan losses would be high. Moreover, about 59 per cent of the loans that were not yet due in 1995 were delinquent in 1997. On-time loan recovery steadily deteriorated from 89 per cent in 1993 to 41 per cent in 1996 (Matin, 2000). Yet, none of the borrowers interviewed believed that poor repayment performance by the groups or centres affected their chances of getting future Grameen loans. Also, loan sizes increased rapidly during this period as loan officers were under pressure to meet disbursement targets. Since loan size was found to be positively correlated with delinquency and default, it was argued that this rapid expansion in lending contributed to the decline in recovery rates.

In a Grameen survey, it was found that some 60,000 borrowers with payments more than 25 weeks overdue had an unpaid amount of over

US$2 million. The huge expansion of micro-finance in Bangladesh has led to an intense competition for clients (Wright, *et al.*, 2001). Repayment discipline is declining, as clients are increasingly willing to default with one MFI confident in the belief that a competing MFI will make a follow-on loan. It is difficult to get a clear picture of loan delinquency and default rates by consulting MFI reports because many exaggerate their loan recovery performance to impress donors. Most of the 585 MFIs providing data to the Credit and Development Forum reported loan recovery rates of 90 per cent and above, so, the average recovery rate was over 95 per cent. However, these data may be misleading. Some MFIs use reporting definitions that are lax by international standards, such as not classifying loans as overdue until one year after the final installment falls due (Matin, 2000).

Matching repayment schedules with expected cash flow are an obvious way to reduce delinquencies and client fears that they will not have income when needed to repay loans. Even borrowers highly motivated to repay occasionally become delinquent because of emergencies, unexpected problems and shortfalls in income. Ex-post adjustments are needed in the members' repayment schedules, including extensions for those projected to quickly acquire sufficient liquidity to resume regular payments, and formal loan rescheduling for those expected to face major longer-term repayment problems. Those who experience major disasters need new contracts that roll over existing balances and provide new funds to restart businesses. The large MFIs in Bangladesh, and Grameen made these adjustments selectively for their clients most severely affected by the 1998 Bangladesh floods.

Overlapping Memberships

Most MFIs prohibit members from belonging to more than one organization at a time, yet multiple memberships or overlap exists. Since it is against the rules, it is difficult to get members to admit to it. Moreover, little is known about multiple memberships when all members of households are considered in contrast to just individual members. Wright, *et al.* (2001) reported that multiple memberships can be as high as 40 to 50 per cent in areas where many MFIs are operating. Part of the explanation is over borrowing by members who borrow from one source to repay another. But part of the explanation is that the rigidity of some MFIs forces clients to manage their finances by working with several organizations simultaneously. Moreover, if credit ceilings are low and all group members receive the same size loan, a dynamic borrower may need to borrow from several MFIs to obtain the total amount desired. Multiple memberships can also arise when members shop around prior to switching from one MFI to another to obtain more attractive services.

Chaudhury and Matin (2001) conducted a study of the dimensions and dynamic processes that prompt families to participate in multiple MFIs. The study was carried out in Tangail district of Bangladesh where 27 NGO-MFIs were found to be operating. Of the BRAC members that were interviewed, only 16 per cent of the 240 households surveyed had someone from the household who was a client solely of BRAC. In 30 per cent of the households, the BRAC member was also a client of another NGO. In 27 per cent of the households, the BRAC member was exclusively a BRAC client but other household members were clients of other NGOs. Finally, in 27 per cent of the households, the BRAC clients as well as other household members were members of other NGOs.

Informal Finance: The Moneylender Menace

One of the arguments given for expanding the micro-finance industry is to help poor people escape from the clutches of "evil moneylenders" who allegedly charge usurious rates of interest. Formal finance is expected to substitute for informal sources. Apart from giving handouts to poor households, micro-finance programmes offer small loans to foster small-scale entrepreneurial activities. Such credit would not otherwise be available, or would be only available at the very high interest rates charged by moneylenders (who often charge as much as ten per cent per month). Moneylenders used to operate with little competition, since potential entrants quickly find that costs and risks are high, and borrowers are usually unable to offer standard forms of collateral, if at all, any.

But, in spite of the entry of micro-finance institutions, there is widespread evidence that MFI clients widely use informal finance as part of their financial management strategy. Zaman (1998) reported that during the 1998 Bangladesh flood, the main source of cash for loan repayments by BRAC borrowers was interest-free loans from relatives. Even NGO clients involve in informal loans. They found that over ten per cent of NGO assets represented loans made to other persons. Todd (1996) describes how Gramen women cross-finance by borrowing from Grameen to pay moneylender and other informal loans, and borrow small sums informally to meet Grameen loan installments or to access large sums of money quickly in advance of their next Grameen loan. These practices are sensible ways for women to use financial services in response to demands for resources and cash flow constraints. Each source offers products with different attributes of size, repayment schedule, ease of access, and financial and transaction costs that make each attractive in given situations. For example, the higher interest costs of informal finance may be offset by lower transaction costs in securing loans. Individuals who have established repayment reputations with moneylenders can often count on them to make loans quickly in times of emergencies in ways that are nearly impossible for the typical MFI.

Sinha and Matin (1998) conducted a case study in northern Bangladesh in a region where several MFIs compete. Almost all households (87%) reported borrowing from informal sources and the proportion was higher for MFI clients than for non-clients. Household consumption and payment of other loans were the two most frequently reported uses of the informal loans. Surprisingly, these same purposes were among the most frequently reported uses of MFI loans as well. In an analysis of the Grameen Bank clients in the survey, it was found that due to the large increase in Grameen lending that was occurring, some internal cross-financing was taking place, in which the proceeds from one loan were being used to repay another. Moreover, clients reported borrowing from informal sources so they could maintain high repayment rates with Grameen and could be eligible for larger future loans. The study concluded that in the rural households they surveyed in 1994, NGO borrowers received 20 per cent of their total debt outstanding from friends and relatives and another 18 per cent from shopkeepers and other informal sources. Nine per cent of the funds borrowed from informal sources were reportedly used to pay the existing debt while eleven per cent of formal loans were supposedly used for that purpose. They reported on credit access and use in Bangladesh as part of a multi-country analysis. They found that the poor in Bangladesh, as in the other developing countries, borrow from a variety of sources. The poorer they are, the greater is the frequency of reported use of loans for consumption smoothing.

Commercialization of Micro-finance: A Business Opportunity

The total annual demand for micro-credit, the most developed sub-discipline of micro-finance, is estimated to $50 billion and it is currently growing with an annual growth rate of 15 to 30 per cent. Clearly, philanthropy and development aid is not capable of meeting this huge demand and the answer could be commercialization of micro-lending.

Only by letting profit oriented institutions enter a scene that still is largely dominated by donation-based ones, it is believed that one can raise the huge amounts of funds needed to meet the demand. In addition to the increased supply of funds, commercialization would also benefit MFIs and micro-borrowers by providing loans with longer maturities and by providing more diversified funding sources.

Today, it is believed that if micro-finance is to achieve its full potential, it must be fully integrated into a developing country's financial system with access to vast amounts of human, physical, and financial resources and management know-how. There are many reasons why micro-finance could give investors the chance to do well, by doing 'good':

- The sheer size of the micro-finance market is in itself an attractive feature. There are currently up to three billion people without access to proper financial services (CGAP, 2009). There are also an estimated 500 million micro-entrepreneurs worldwide. For international investment banks this means a largely untapped source of micro-credits that, for instance, can be pooled together, securitized and sold to investors all around the world. For local retail banks and the like, on the other hand, a focus on micro-credits to the poor could be a first step in building a brand name in a potentially huge future market for ordinary financial services.
- There is a good chance that the risk-adjusted returns from micro-lending are higher than returns from corresponding traditional lending. A poor farmer or entrepreneur in the developing world typically generates much higher returns on his or her assets than a corresponding business in the developed world. This means that many of these poor borrowers can afford to pay very much for capital. An example is the so called "5/6 loans" in the Philippines, where a moneylender lends you five pesos in the morning and you pay back six pesos in the evening. This is equal to a daily interest rate of 20 per cent, or much more than 5000 per cent a year. If one compares this to typical interest rates in the developed world and to well-documented micro-finance default rates in the range of one to five per cent, one can easily see the potential for commercial micro financing. Even if the cost of making micro-loans is high this is most likely not a market where all arbitrage possibilities have been exploited (CGAP, 2009).

- Commercially viable micro-lending could be an interesting alternative for private investors who (for altruistic motives or for commercially driven "marketing" purposes) want to contribute to the fight against poverty. By directly targeting the poor and therefore circumventing inefficient or perhaps even corrupt government structures, micro-lending could be an efficient means of doing well (financially) by doing good (socially).
- One can expect returns from micro-loans to be largely uncorrelated with returns from most other asset classes and a micro loan portfolio would therefore serve as a natural hedge for a typical investment bank, insurance company or pension fund in most of the developed world. Furthermore, since diversification is the only real free lunch in the financial world, the discovery of an asset class that is largely uncorrelated with the major economical and political events in the world should attract the interest of any rational investor, big or small.
- Financial markets in the developed world have recently faced a rapid development that could help speed up the commercialization of micro-credit. Recently introduced financial instruments and vehicles, such as credit derivatives and hedge funds, could make it possible for investors to tailor their risks and returns as they please and thereby transform the micro-finance landscape from a small subsidized market to a large efficient market with thousands of profit-maximizing investors with different appetites for risk.

A deal made by the Indian bank ICICI Bank in 2004 was one of the first (and the largest) direct micro-finance securitizations ever done. In this securitization, ICICI Bank bought a portfolio of 42,500 micro-loans from SHARE Microfin Ltd., a large Indian MFI, for $4.3 million (Meehan, 2004). The portfolio contained 25 per cent of SHARE's loans and the transaction was facilitated by a $3,25,000 guarantee provided by the Grameen Foundation USA. The purpose of the deal was purely commercial-SHARE could use the $4.3 million to scale up its lending (to the poor) and ICICI Bank could access a hard-to-reach market (the poor) through a well run MFI. Securitization—a process through which homogenous illiquid financial assets are pooled and repackaged into marketable securities—is the most recent innovation in the micro-finance market. Proponents of commercialization of micro-finance activities admit that there are hurdles to overcome, but argue that micro-finance securitization is in the same early stage of development, as credit card securitization was in the 1980s, and mortgages more than half a century ago. They contend that micro-finance will experience the same growing pains, but eventually become a well-established asset class.

The locus of micro-finance is just beginning to shift from the non-profit world to private investors, and the industry does appear to have growth potential. However, while micro-finance is allowing investors to tap a new emerging market within the emerging markets, its growth will ultimately depend on continued policy reform, standardization and transparency of information on lending institutions, and the industry's capacity to innovate and increase efficiency in order to serve the lowest end of the market.

3
Financial Inclusion
An Agenda of Inclusive Growth

In India, financial inclusion has been viewed as one of the major aspects of inclusive growth. The process of financial inclusion is an attempt to bring the weaker and vulnerable sections of society within the ambit of the organized financial system. Economic theory supports the view that access to affordable financial services enlarges livelihood opportunities and empowers the poor to change their lives. Such empowerment aids social growth as well as sustainable development of the economy. It is in this sense; the inclusive growth cannot be complete without financial inclusion.

Financial inclusion is not a concern only to India, but has become an issue of worldwide concern. It has been taken as a serious issue by all the economies of the under-developed, developing and developed nations of the world. One can cite innumerable examples of financial exclusion from around the world. In Cameroon, it takes more than $700 to open a bank account which is more than the country's Gross Domestic Product (GDP) per capita. In Sierra Leone, fees to maintain an account exceed 25 per cent of GDP per capita. In Bangladesh, more than four types of documents are required to open a deposit account. In Pakistan, it takes more than 20 days to process a consumer loan application. In the Dominican Republic, it costs $50 to transfer $250 internationally. All these show that in developed countries, most people take access to banking services for granted. The price and non-price barriers prevent large parts of the population in developing countries from accessing and using formal banking services (Beck, *et al.*, 2008).

The mainstream financial institutions have nowadays recognized that the poor too are bankable. They feel that the modern technology helps them make this possible. India has also introduced technology into different financial products and financial services. The country has allowed using its citizens the debit/credit cards and mobile banking. She also has allowed regional rural banks and cooperative banks to sell insurance and financial products. Different commercial banks have opened no-frills accounts with overdraft facility for their customers. The approach to financial inclusion in developing countries such as India is different from the developed countries. In the developed countries, the focus is on the relatively small share of population not having access to banks or the formal payments system. But in countries like India, majority who are excluded are focused and aimed to be financially included.

In the present chapter, a discussion on financial inclusion is presented along with the reasons for exclusion, present status of rural credit in India, reasons for low access to financial services, ways in which financial inclusion is possible and the present status of micro-finance in India.

Financial Inclusion—Definition

Financial inclusion can be defined as "the delivery of credit and other financial service at an affordable cost to the vast sections of the disadvantaged and low income groups" (GoI, 2008). It means access to the various financial services including savings, credit, insurance and payment and remittance facilities to all sections of society in an equitable manner. The objective of financial inclusion is to extend the scope of activities of the organized financial system to the people with low incomes. Through credit, it attempts to lift the poor out of poverty. It is not only providing accessibility of the entire range of financial products and services, it must also be appropriate, fair and transparent. In short, the essence of financial inclusion is in trying to ensure that a range of appropriate financial services is available to every individual and enabling them to understand and access those services.

Financial inclusion can be viewed from two sides. One is exclusion from the payments system i.e., not having access to a bank account. The second type of exclusion is from formal credit markets, requiring the excluded to approach informal and exploitative markets. The focus of financial inclusion is on establishing the basic right of every person to have access to affordable basic banking services (Thorat, 2008). Hence, financial inclusion has generally been defined in terms of exclusion from the financial system. The term financial exclusion is interpreted as "the inability to access necessary financial services in an appropriate form due to problems associated with access, conditions, prices, marketing or self-exclusion". In this context, financial inclusion can also be defined as "the process of ensuring access to appropriate financial products and services needed by vulnerable groups such as weaker sections and low income groups at an affordable cost in a fair and transparent manner by mainstream institutional players" (Chakrabarty, 2009).

Financial Inclusion for Inclusive Growth

The challenges of achieving more inclusive growth can be met by policies that encourage easier and affordable access to financial services. Finance is the lubricant, which oils the wheels of development. All economies rely upon the intermediary function of finance to transfer resources from savers to investors. Both theoretical and empirical researches highlight the role of financial development in facilitating economic development (Rajan and Zingales, 2003). At the cross-country level, evidence indicates that various measures of financial development are positively related to economic growth (King and Levine, 1993; Levine and Zervos, 1998). Even the recent endogenous growth literature, building on 'learning by doing' processes, assigns a special role to finance (Aghion and Hewitt, 1998 and 2005).

In market economies, this function is performed by commercial banks, financial institutions and capital markets. As a result, many people have to necessarily depend either on their own sources or informal sources of finance, which are generally available at high cost. Most of the population in developed countries (99 per cent in Denmark, 96 per cent in Germany, 91 per cent in the USA and 96 per cent in France) have bank accounts (Peachy and Roe, 2004). In many developing countries, capital markets are at a rudimentary stage, and commercial banks are reluctant to lend to the poor largely because of the lack of collateral and high transaction costs. The poor would borrow relatively small amounts, and the processing and supervision of lending to them would consume administrative costs disproportionate to the amount of lending. Several studies have confirmed that complicated loan procedures and paperwork, combined with a lack of accounting experience, limit poor people's access to formal sources of credit. Commercial lenders in rural areas prefer to deal mainly with large-scale farmers. The absence of commercial banks in certain areas has led to non-conventional forms of lending. However, formal financial sectors in most developing countries serve relatively a small segment, often no more than 20-30 per cent of the population, the vast majority of them are low income households in rural areas.

Table 3.1: Composite index of financial inclusion for selected developing countries

Country	*Composite Index of Financial Inclusion (% of population with access to financial services)*
India	48
Bangladesh	32
Brazil	43
China	42
Indonesia	40
Korean Republic	63
Malaysia	60
Philippines	26
Sri Lanka	59
Thailand	59

Source: World Bank (2006) and (2008).

The above mentioned fact can be clearly perceived (Table 3.1) with the help of the composite index of financial inclusion which explains the per cent of population with access to financial services. The general picture one can observe is that all the developing countries are lagging behind the developed economies in the case of financial inclusion. When Korean Republic and Malaysia have an index of 60 per cent or more, India is one among the lower rung along with Brazil and China.

The financial indicators of India *vis-à-vis* the international benchmark of OECD countries (Table 3.2) show a glaring divergence. The demographic branch penetration which is measured by the bank branches per 1,00,000 people is always around six and only shows a marginal increase over the last years. The demographic ATM penetration measured by ATMs per 1,00,000 people is only 3.28 in 2008 for India while for OECD nations it is between 47 and 167. Deposit accounts per 1000 people in India are around 400 and loan accounts per 1000 people are around 80, while the benchmark figure is incomparable. Geographic branch penetration is measured by branches per 1000 km^2 which is around 25 and geographic ATM penetration is measured by ATMs per 1000 km^2 as 13, where the OECD figures is not anywhere nearby.

Many studies on poverty indicate that, one of the reasons why poor households are unable to participate in the development process is their exclusion from the financial system. This is the fundamental flow of our conventional formal financial systems. As a result, these households find it extremely difficult to take advantage of economic opportunities, build assets, and finance their children's education, and protect themselves

Table 3.2: Financial indicators for India, 2001-08

Indicator	*2005*	*2006*	*2007*	*2008*	*Benchmark (OECD)*
Demographic branch penetration (branches per 100,000 people)	6.33	6.37	6.35	6.6	10-69
Demographic ATM penetration (ATMs per 1,00,000 people)	1.63	1.93	2.4	3.28	47-167
Deposit accounts per 1,000 people	432.11	442.87	459.52	467.35	976-1671
Loan accounts per 1000 people	71.42	78	83.59	89.03	248-513
Geographic branch penetration (branches per 1000 km^2)	22.99	23.46	24.13	25.49	1-159
Geographic ATM penetration (ATMs per 1000 km^2)	5.93	7.11	9.11	12.68	1-437

Source: Getting Finance in South Asia 2010, Kiatchai Sophastienphong, Anoma Kulathunga, The World Bank.

against external financial shocks. One can argue that financial exclusion not only pushes them but also tightly binds them into a vicious circle of poverty (Kochhar, 2010)

Table 3.3: Financial access of commercial banks in India

Deposits	
Accounts per 1,000 adults	747.29
Value (% of GDP)	55.03
Average account value (% of income per capita)	107.86
Loans	
Accounts per 1,000 adults	137.46
Value (% of GDP)	40.93
Average account value (% of income per capita)	436.09
Outreach (Branches per 100,000 adults)	
Total	10.11
Urban	3.82
Rural	6.29

Source: CGAP, 2010.

Financial Exclusion: A Harsh Reality in India

The responsibility of meeting the credit needs in the rural areas of India was entrusted primarily with the cooperative banking sector until about the mid-1960s. Nationalization of Indian commercial banks in two spurts in 1969 and 1980 indeed was intended for the improvement of the flow of formal institutional credit into rural households, especially to the poor. Although the banking system has experienced phenomenal growth in terms of geographical spread, deposit mobilisation and disbursal of credit in rural areas after nationalisation, bank credit remains by and large, inaccessible to the poor.

The poor both in rural and urban areas do not have the necessary capabilities to approach and negotiate with formal financial institutions. The drive of very poor people to help them through self-employment is ignored by the formal financial sector. Because the very poor have not traditionally been recognised as creditworthy or able to save, they are not perceived by the conventional agencies as profitable clientele for credit. As the poor have not been welcomed to the banking fold by the banks and financial institutions with a misconception that they are not bankable and there is no business opportunity in offering services to the underprivileged and poor people in the semi-urban rural and slum-dwellers in the metropolitan cities.

On the other hand, the rural credit system entrapped by the twin problems of high transaction cost and poor repayment performance, reduces the profitability of rural branches of nationalised banks. The incompetence of management of individual banks also increased the non-viability of the rural credit delivery system (Analyst, 1993). Several reasons such as complicated procedures, distant location, cultural gap between officials and the poor, short banking hours, political interference, unscientific lending policies, absence of provision for consumption credit made the poor customers away from the bank's doorsteps. Moreover, there is widespread belief that the poor are unbankable. There are also internal problems like absence of linkages of credit with marketing, investment credit having no provision for working capital. Inadequate staff and managerial deficiencies within the banking system have also been causing problems (Rajasekhar, 1994).

The financial sector reforms begun in 1992 were intended to liberalise the financial sector. But the proposed reforms have been systematically moving away from the social objective of the banking sector by abolishing concessional interest rates, insisting on collateral even for small borrowers and making large stipulated minimum balance compulsory for granting loans to small savers from the system (Mujumdar, 1995). In consequence, the number of small borrower accounts has declined and it has resulted in misallocation of funds, especially diversion to investment (in government securities and A class securities) from credit to the small borrower, expansion of foreign bank which only serves the elite in urban areas (Joshi, 1999).

In the last two decades, banking sector witnessed tremendous changes in terms of technological advancements, internet banking, online money transfers, etc. Reserve Bank of India has introduced the Electronic Clearing Service (ECS), Electronic Fund Transfer System, later extended as the National Electronic Fund Transfer (NEFT) and the Real Time Gross Settlement (RTGS). All these systems offered a secure and efficient platform for transfer of funds between bank accounts without the need for paper-based payment instruments (Chakrabarty, 2009). Despite the impressive growth in most financial segments over the past decades, there is still the under-penetration of most financial products/services. It is a reality that access to such technology is restricted only to certain segments of the society. Some trends, such as increasingly sophisticated customer segmentation technology have led to restricted access to financial services for some groups. There is a growing divide between the different sections of the population with an increased range of personal finance options for a segment of high and upper middle income population. On the other hand, a significantly large section of the population lacks access to even the most basic banking services. This is termed "financial exclusion". These people, particularly, those living on low incomes, cannot access mainstream financial products such as bank accounts, credit, remittances and payment services, financial advisory services, insurance facilities, etc. (RBI, 2008). Apart from the fact that exclusion itself is large, it also varies widely across regions, social groups and assets holdings. In short, the poorer the group, the greater is the exclusion.

An Enquiry into Financial Exclusion in India

Globally, over a billion poor people are still without access to formal financial services and some 200 million of them live in India. Based on the All Indian Debt Investment Survey (AIDIS) 2002, 111.5 million households in India had no access to formal credit. It also showed that 17 million households were indebted to moneylenders. The Arjun Sengupta Report on financing enterprises in the unorganized sector has pointed out that only 2.4 million out of 58 million units in this sector (with investment of less than Rs. 25,000) have got credit from commercial banks. The AIDIS 2002 also showed that lower the asset class or income, higher the degree of exclusion.

These findings are corroborated by Invest India Incomes and Savings Survey (2007). The survey showed that 32.8 per cent of households had borrowed from institutional sources and 67.2 per cent had borrowed from non-institutional sources. The survey also found that 70 per cent of earners in the annual income bracket of more than Rs. 4,00,000 borrowed from institutional sources as compared with only 27.5 per cent in the case of earners in the income bracket of less than Rs. 50,000. Geographically, only 5.2 per cent of the country's villages have a bank branch (Kochhar, 2009). Despite the vast network of rural branches, only 27 per cent of the total farm households are indebted to formal sources; of them, one-third also borrow from informal sources. There are parts of the country where more than 95 per cent of the farm households do not get any credit from institutional or non-institutional sources. There is evidence that farm debt is increasing much faster than farm incomes and the larger issue of the overhanging debt stock, as distinct from credit flow, has not even been on the agenda except of a few State Governments (Planning Commission, 2006). According to NSSO data in the situation assessment survey on "Indebtedness of Farmer households" (2003), 45.9 million farmer households in the country (51.4%), out of a total of 89.3 million households do not access credit, either from institutional or non-institutional sources. Further, only 27 per cent of total farm households are indebted to formal sources (RBI, 2009).

Extent of Banking Penetration

The penetration of banking services is uneven over various parts of the country as well as different categories of people. Various indicators clearly show that the backward rural areas and the marginalized sections of the population are lagging behind. The rural urban divide analyses of indicators of banking penetration of scheduled commercial banks in the country, including RRBs, testify to the rural urban divide existing in their operations/business.

Average Population per Branch Office

The average population served per branch office is an important indicator of banking penetration. The data on average population per branch office Average Population Per Branch Office (APPBO) is an eye-opener (Table 3.4). While the population Per branch has decreased for urban areas, the same has increased for rural areas indicating that branch expansion has not kept pace with the population increase in the rural areas. The trend in this indicator ever since the last decade shows a discerning picture of rural areas.

Table 3.4: Average Population Per Branch Office

	1991	2001	2005
Population per branch	13711	15209	15680
Population per Rural branch	13462	15667	16650
Population per Urban branch	14484	14137	13619

Source: Thorat, 2007.

Number of Accounts per 1000 Population

Another common measure of financial inclusion is the percentage of adult population having bank accounts. From the available data on the number of savings bank accounts and assuming that one person has only one account, it is found that on an all-India basis 59 per cent of adult population in the country have bank accounts—in other words 41 per cent of the population is unbanked. In rural areas, the coverage is 39 per cent against 60 per cent in urban areas. The unbanked population is higher in the North-Eastern and Eastern regions.

It is seen that the deposits (current plus savings) accounts per 1000 population in the rural areas as a whole, are about sixty per cent of the urban areas. North-Eastern States, Orissa Bihar and Chhattisgarh have particularly low ratio. Similar position is generally evident even in terms of credit accounts per 1000 population. However, Southern States are relatively better off in this regard (Table 3.5).

Number of Accounts per Branc

The number of deposit and credit accounts per branch in the rural areas is generally lower than the position in urban areas. In rural areas, the coverage is 9.5 per cent against 14 per cent in urban areas. Regional differences are significant with the credit coverage at 25 per cent for the Southern Region and as low as seven, eight and nine per cent respectively

Table 3.5: Deposit (current plus savings) and credit accounts per thousand population

Region/State	*Deposit (C+S) Accounts per 1000 population*		*Credit Accounts per 1000 Population*	
	Rural	*Urban*	*Rural*	*Urban*
Northern Region	338	652	55	71
North-Eastern Region	186	281	35	41
Eastern Region	185	413	45	47
Central Region	242	375	45	49
Western Region	263	526	46	121
Southern Region	393	486	136	185
All India	270	483	64	104

Source: BSR, 2005.

in North-Eastern, Eastern and Central Regions. The extent of exclusion from credit markets can be observed from a different viewpoint. Out of 203 million households in the country, 147 million are in rural areas. Of which 89 million are farmer households. 51.4 per cent of farm households have no access to formal or informal sources of credit while 73 per cent have no access to formal sources of credit. Similar data are not available for non-farm and urban households.

Looking at the different sources of credit, it is observed that the share of non-institutional sources decreased from 70.8 per cent in 1971 to 42.9 per cent in 2002. However after 1991, the share of non-institutional sources has increased; specifically, the share of moneylenders in the debt of rural households increased from 17.5 per cent in 1991 to 29.6 per cent in 2002. In urban areas the share of non-institutional sources has come down significantly from 40 per cent in 1981 to around 25 per cent in 2002.

Table 3.6: Number of deposit and credit accounts per branch

Region/State	*Deposit (C+S) Accounts per Branch*		*Credit Accounts per Branch*	
	Rural	*Urban*	*Rural*	*Urban*
Northern Region	4130	6677	675	771
North-Eastern Region	3716	5340	702	781
Eastern Region	3676	6087	887	693
Central Region	4586	6075	859	797
Western Region	3826	6630	663	1530
Southern Region	4549	5571	1577	2121
All India	4202	6155	1000	1321

Source: BSR, 2005.

Outstanding Balances per Branch

The deposits and credit outstanding per branch also reflect the rural urban divide. It is seen that deposits per branch in the rural areas is far lower than that in the urban areas, notably States in the North-East, Northern and Western region. In terms of credit per branch also, the difference is more pronounced in Northern and Western regions.

Table 3.7: Outstanding Balances per Branch

Region/State	Deposit (C+S) Accounts per Branch (Amt Rs. Crore)		Credit Accounts per Branch (Amt Rs. Crore)	
	Rural	Urban	Rural	Urban
Northern Region	6.43	25.22	7.19	46.99
North-Eastern Region	5.41	21.03	4.99	13.80
Eastern Region	4.99	18.80	3.99	23.62
Central Region	5.26	15.40	4.51	15.15
Western Region	4.67	26.51	7.72	63.77
Southern Region	4.01	14.41	8.73	32.68
All India	4.98	19.92	6.37	37.94

Source: BSR, 2005.

Outstanding Balances per Account

The outstanding balance per account, both deposit as well as credit, reveals the much larger values in urban areas. The average size of a deposit account in the rural areas is about one-third the size in urban areas and

Table 3.8: Outstanding Balances per Account

Region/State	Deposit (C+S) Balance per A/c (Rs.'000)		Credit Balance per A/c (Rs.'000)	
	Rural	Urban	Rural	Urban
Northern Region	15.56	37.78	106.46	609.72
North-Eastern Region	14.56	39.38	70.59	176.85
Eastern Region	13.57	30.88	44.58	341.00
Central Region	11.46	25.35	52.49	190.06
Western Region	12.19	39.99	116.42	416.71
Southern Region	8.82	25.87	55.39	154.08
All India	11.84	32.36	63.74	287.91

Source: Thorat, 2007.

ranged from about Rs. 7,000/- (in Andhra Pradesh) to about Rs. 17,000/- (in Punjab). The divide is as is to be expected sharper in terms of credit per account. The average credit account in rural areas ranged from Rs. 19,000/- (in Tripura) to Rs. 1.31 lakh (in Haryana).

Share of Different Credit Agencies in the total Cash Dues of Households

The share of different agencies in the total cash dues of rural and urban households reveals the extent of penetration of formal financial sources. Table 3.9 clearly shows that the coverage of banks in the rural areas has fallen from 64 per cent to 57 per cent while, significantly, the share of money lenders has increased from 17.5 per cent to 29.6 per cent in these areas (Table 3.9).

Table 3.9: Share of Different Credit Agencies in the total Cash Dues of Households

Credit Agencies	*Rural Households*			*Urban Households*		
	1981	*1991*	*2002*	*1981*	*1991*	*2002*
Institutional	**61.2**	**64.0**	**57.1**	**60.0**	**72.0**	**75.1**
of which						
Co-operative Soc./Bank	—	21.6	27.3	—	17.2	20.5
Commercial Banks	—	33.7	24.5	—	21.6	29.7
Government	—	6.1	2.3	—	11.1	7.6
Non-Institutional	**38.8**	**36.0**	**42.9**	**40.0**	**28.0**	**24.9**
of which						
Moneylenders*	—	17.5	29.6	—	10.2	14.1
Total	100.0	100.0	100.0	100.0	100.0	100.0

Source: Computed from the various decadal All India Debt and Investment Surveys.

Earners Having a Bank Account

One branch is catering to the banking needs of 16,000 population (June, 2007); only 17 credit accounts and 54 saving accounts are there per 100 persons with all the institutions (June 2007); only 13 per cent are availing loans from the banks in the income bracket of less than Rs. 50,000; and 53 per cent people are still taking loans from the institutional and non-institutional sources only for emergency purposes (Table 3.10).

Table 3.10: Earners Having a Bank Account—2007

Annual Income (Rs.)	*Urban*	*Rural*	*Total*
<50,000	43.1	26.8	28.3
50,000-100,000	75.5	71.2	73
100,000-200,000	91.8	87.4	89.9
200,000-400,000	95.5	93.6	94.9
>400,000	98.0	96.3	97.6
All	61.7	38.0	44.9

Source: Report on Currency and Finance 2006-08 (IIMS, 2007).

Access to Savings Accounts

A disaggregate data on the number of saving accounts with institutions in millions show that only 82 out of 100 adults hold an account in any of the formal financial institutions like commercial banks, Regional Rural Banks, Primary Agriculture Credit Societies, Urban Cooperative Banks and Post Offices (Table 3.11). Of the various institutions commercial banks get a lion share while PACS comes second.

Table 3.11: Access to Savings Accounts—Since 2002

No. of Saving Accounts with Institutions in Millions		
	2002	*2007*
Scheduled Commercial Banks	246.5	320.9
Regional Rural Banks	36.7	52.7
Sub-Total	**283.2**	**373.6**
Primary Agriculture Credit Societies	102.1	125.8
Urban Cooperative Banks	41.6	50.0
Post Offices	60.2	60.8
Total	**487.1**	**610.2**
No. of Accounts per 100 Adults (All Institutions)	72	82

Source: Report on Currency and Finance—2006-08.

Rural Credit in India: A Status Check

The National Sample Survey Organization's All-India Debt and Investment Survey (AIDIS), 2002 gives the subsequent result; 111.5 million Indian households had no access to formal credit. It also showed that 17 million households were indebted to moneylenders. Though the share of non-institutional sources of credit for the cultivator households had declined from 92.7 per cent in 1951 to 30.6 per cent in 1991, it had increased to 38.9 per cent in 2002 mainly due to increase in moneylenders' share. Simultaneously, the share of institutional sources such as commercial banks, co-operative societies, etc. increased from 7.3 per cent in 1951 to 66.3 per cent in 1991 and declined to 61.1 per cent in 2002.

As per the All India Debt and Investment Survey, 2003, nearly a fourth of the households were indebted in 2002. The per cent of indebtedness households in rural areas increased sharply from 23 in 1991 to 27 in 2003; the corresponding figures for urban areas during the same period were 19 and 18, respectively. As per the NSSO Survey (2003), out of 89.35 million farmer households, 43.42 million (48.6%) were reported to be indebted. Farmer's indebtedness was highest in Andhra Pradesh followed by Tamil Nadu and Punjab. The average outstanding loan per farmer household was highest in Punjab, followed by Kerala, Haryana, Andhra Pradesh and Tamil Nadu. According to NSSO data in the situation assessment survey on "Indebtedness of Farmer Households" (NSS 59th round-2003) estimated that 64.4 per cent farmer households are indebted in Kerala as against the national average of 48.6 per cent. The major reasons for arrears in repayment reported include high cost of cultivation, fall in prices of agricultural produce and crop failures. The data further shows that 45.9 million farmer households in the country (51.4%), out of a total of 89.3 million households do not access credit, either from institutional or non-institutional sources (RBI, 2008). The surveys underline the fact that lower the asset class or income, higher the degree of exclusion.

The Arjun Sengupta Report on financing enterprises in the unorganized sector has pointed out that only 2.4 million out of 58 million units in this sector (with investment of less than Rs. 25,000) have got credit from commercial banks. The Invest India Incomes and Savings Survey (2007) showed that 32.8 per cent of households had borrowed from institutional sources and 67.2 per cent had borrowed from non-institutional sources. The survey (Table 3.12) also found that 70 per cent of earners in the annual income bracket of more than Rs. 4,00,000 borrowed from institutional sources as compared with only 27.5 per cent in the case of earners in the income bracket of less than Rs. 50,000.

The underprivileged sections of the society such as farmers, small vendors, agriculture or industrial labourers, people engaged in unorganized sector, unemployed people, women, children, old people

Table 3.12: Sources of Loans (% of Indebted Earners)

Income	*Banks*	*Money-lenders*	*Other Institutional & Non-Institutional Sources*	*Total*
<50,000	13.0	34.0	52.1	100
50,000-100,000	34.5	19.6	45.9	100
100,000-200,000	49.3	12.0	38.7	100
200,000-400,000	51.6	11.8	36.6	100
>400,000	62.8	5.5	31.7	100

Source: Report on Currency and Finance 2006-08 (IIMS, 2007).

and the physically challenged are poorly banked. The extent of financial exclusion is alarming. Only 40 per cent of the people in India have a check in account, ten per cent have taken life insurance products, 0.6 per cent have taken non-life insurance products, only two per cent have access to credit cards. Geographically speaking, only 5.2 per cent of the country's villages have a bank branch (Table 3.13).

Table 3.13: Coverage of various indicators

Check in accounts	40 per cent
Life Insurance	10 per cent
Non-Life Insurance	0.6 per cent
Credit Card	2 per cent
ATM + Debit Card	13 per cent
Geographic Coverage	5.2 per cent villages are having a bank branch
Farmers Coverage	Out of 119 million farmers, small and marginal farmers are 97.7 million (82.1%)

Source: Chakrabarty 2009 D (Estimates based on various studies and Market Surveys).

Owing to several factors such as sharp increase in urbanisation, rural to urban migration as also the increase in urban poverty, the share of poor and the low-income households not having any access to finance in the urban areas is also increasing in several countries. Recent data shows that countries with large proportion of population excluded from the formal financial system also show higher poverty ratios and higher inequality. The financially excluded sections largely comprise marginal farmers, landless labourers, oral lessees, self-employed and unorganised sector enterprises, urban slum dwellers, migrants, ethnic minorities and socially excluded groups, senior citizens and women. While there are pockets of large excluded population in all parts of the country, the North-East, Eastern and Central regions contain most of the financially excluded population. There are a variety of reasons for financial exclusion. In remote, hilly and sparsely populated areas with poor infrastructure, physical access itself acts as a deterrent. From the demand side, lack of awareness, low incomes/assets, social exclusion, illiteracy act as barriers. From the supply side, distance from branch, branch timings, cumbersome documentation and procedures, unsuitable products, language, staff attitudes are common reasons for exclusion. All these result in higher transaction cost apart from procedural hassles. On the other hand, the ease of availability of informal credit sources makes these popular even if costlier. The requirements of independent documentary proof of identity and address can be a very important barrier in having a bank account especially for migrants and slum dwellers.

Causes for Lower Level Access to Financial Services

The major challenges in banks extending services to the excluded are large costs of covering the huge numbers (cost of enrollment), relative high maintenance costs for such accounts, small ticket size for each transaction, need for communication modes suited to the illiterate and in local language, affordability of the product or service, need for local acceptance and involvement of locally acceptable personnel, need for large scale coverage including difficult geographic terrain and areas with no electric power or normal telecommunication facilities. Further, as is now very obvious from the recent surveys by AIDIS and IIMS, the challenge also lies in offering to low income households and unorganized enterprises a simple loan product which is not based on or linked to the purpose of the loan, the collateral or assets held or income earned by the household, but is purely based on cash flow and credit record of the household (Thorat 2008).

Banks and financial institutions had been financially excluding poor people on the pretext that they have no or very little assets, they have nothing to offer as collateral; they have no business experiences, they cannot be trained for availing financial services, they have no credit history, and they cannot understand the nuances of banking due to illiteracy or less education (Chakrabarty, 2009). The main barrier to financial inclusion in rural areas is the great distances that rural residents must travel to reach a bank branch. Poor infrastructure and telecommunications, and heavy branch regulation, also restrict the geographical expansion of bank branch networks. In many developing countries there are fewer bank branches per rural resident than per urban resident (CGAP, 2009).

Using survey data from 209 banks in 62 countries, Beck, *et al.* (2008) develops new indicators of barriers to access and use of banking services around the world. The results show that barriers to access and use of banking services are correlated with existing measures of financial outreach, and explores their association with bank and country characteristics. In addition, those barriers are negatively correlated with aggregate indicators of financial outreach and access (such as branches, loans, and deposits per capita and the share of the adult population with access to financial services) and positively correlated with financing obstacles reported by firms. Some barriers seem to be more constraining than others. Specifically, minimum balances for checking accounts, annual fees, and document requirements associated with these accounts, the number of delivery channels for lending products, minimum amounts for consumer loans relative to GDP per capita, and days to process consumer loans are highly correlated with outreach measures and thus seem to constitute true hurdles to accessing formal banking services. Fees on consumer loans relative to GDP per capita are not consistently correlated with outreach. Similarly, the fees associated with international wire transfers and the use of automated teller machine (ATM) cards seem orthogonal to most other outreach indicators. Barriers to banking services could arise from banks' rational business decisions based on their business model, their market position, the level of competition they face, and the macro-economic, contractual, and regulatory environment in which they operate.

Access to financial products is constrained by several factors which include: lack of awareness about the financial products, unaffordable products, high transaction costs, and products which are not convenient, inflexible, not customized and of low quality. Financial inclusion promotes thrift and develops culture of saving and also enables efficient payment mechanism strengthening the resource base of the financial institution which benefits the economy as resources become available for efficient payment mechanism and allocation. The empirical evidence shows that countries with large proportion of population excluded from the formal financial system also show higher poverty ratios and higher inequality (Thorat, 2008).

Why Credit is Important for Rural India?

Access to financial resources enables the poor to exploit investment opportunities, reduces their vulnerability to shocks and promotes economic growth. But lack of credit at reasonable rates is a persistent problem reflecting the collapse of the cooperative credit system. The failure of the organised credit system in extending credit has led to excessive dependence on informal sources usually at exorbitant interest rates. This is at the root of farmer distress reflected in excessive indebtedness. The acceptance of the Vaidyanathan Committee report on co-operatives and the success of commercial banks to almost double the flow of agricultural credit after 2003 by the Government is a welcome step. Problems of the long-term credit structure have hardly been addressed and the large increase in commercial bank credit does not appear to have significantly improved access in either poorly banked regions or for small/marginal farmers and tenants. There is evidence that farm debt is increasing much faster than farm incomes and the larger issue of the overhanging debt stock, as distinct from credit flow, has not even been on the agenda except of a few State governments (GoI, 2006).

Table 3.14: Purpose of Loans

Purpose of Loan (All Sources)	*Rural*	*Urban*	*Rural (in%)*	*Urban (in%)*
Meeting Financial Emergency	20.2	4.7	26.3	31.0
Medical Emergency	12.5	1.8	16.3	11.7
Business Needs	7.1	2.1	9.3	14.0
Others	36.8	6.5	47.1	43.3
Total	76.6 mn	15.1 mn	100	100
From Non-Institutional Sources				
Meeting Financial Emergency	15.4	3.4	29.4	34.3
Medical Emergency	10.5	1.5	20.1	14.8
Business Needs	3.9	1.2	7.5	12.3
Others	22.6	3.8	43.0	38.6
Total	52.4 mn	9.9 mn	100	100
From Institutional Sources				
Meeting Financial Emergency	4.8	1.3	19.6	24.9
Medical Emergency	2.0	0.3	8.1	6.0
Business Needs	3.2	0.9	13.0	17.1
Others	24.2	5.3	59.3	52.0
Total	24.2 mn	5.3 mn	100	100

Source: Report on Currency and Finance 2006-08 (IIMS Survey, 2007).

An analysis by the Report on Currency and Finance (RCF) shows that the major reason for increase in the overall household debt and the increase in the share of households indebted to non-institutional sources between 1991 and 2002 was a significant increase in current farm expenditure and household expenditure, especially in rural areas (Table 3.14). The 'household expenditure' includes expenditure incurred on purchase of residential plot; purchase, construction, addition/alteration of building for residential purposes; purchase of durable households assets, clothes, among others and expenditure on medical treatment, education, marriages, and ceremonies. Thus, the 'household expenditure' includes many items for which households may find it difficult to obtain loans from institutional sources. The IIMS Survey also suggests that a large portion of loan is taken by the households for meeting financial emergency, medical emergency and social obligations. These three purposes accounted for about 53 per cent of the loans availed of by indebted earners. Furthermore, more than 60 per cent earners, indebted to non-institutional sources, took loans for the aforesaid three purposes. In the case of emergencies, people may find it convenient to approach non-institutional sources for their credit needs. Financial emergencies, for instance, include unplanned expenditure on business, consumption and marriage, among others, which may not be financed by banks and other institutional agencies (Thorat, 2008).

It will be wrong to classify all those who are not borrowing from the organized financial system as excluded. What is relevant is that whether those who need credit and who want credit from the organized system are included in the ambit of the financial system or not. The criterion for being bankable should not be interpreted narrowly to exclude the vast majority. Credit has to be integrated and made a part of an overall programme aimed at improving the productivity and income of small farmers and other poor households. Putting in place an appropriate credit delivery system to meet the needs of all marginal and small farmers must go hand in hand with the effort to improve the productivity of such farm households. So, it is extremely important that one should integrate the credit delivery system of the organized financial system with the programmes and policies being implemented by the government to improve the lot of the poor. Empathy with the poor, especially with those who need credit, must be established and here, perhaps, improved training will help. Also, rural branches must go beyond providing credit and extend a helping hand to farmers in terms of advice on a wide variety of matters relating to agriculture and other allied activities.

There are supply side and demand side factors driving inclusive growth. Banks largely are expected to mitigate the supply side processes that prevent poor and disadvantaged social groups from gaining access to the financial system. Apart from the supply side factors, demand side factors, such as lower income and /or asset holdings also have a significant bearing on financial inclusion. Owing to difficulties in accessing formal sources of credit, poor individuals and small and macro enterprises usually rely on their personal savings or internal sources to invest in health, education, housing, and entrepreneurial activities to make use of growth opportunities (Chakrabarty, 2009 B).

The Indian economy is growing at a steady rate of 8.5 per cent to nine per cent in the last five years or so. Most of the growth is from industry and services sector. Agriculture is growing at a little over two per cent. The potential for growth in the primary and small and medium enterprise (SME) sector is enormous. Limited access to affordable financial services such as savings, loan, remittance and insurance services by the vast majority of the population in the rural areas and unorganised sector is believed to be acting as a constraint to the growth impetus in these sectors. Access to affordable financial services especially credit and insurance enlarges livelihood opportunities and empowers the poor to take charge of their lives. Such empowerment aids social and political stability. Apart from these benefits, financial inclusion imparts formal identity, provides access to the payments system and to savings safety net like deposit insurance. Hence financial inclusion is considered to be critical for achieving inclusive growth; which itself is required for ensuring overall sustainable overall growth in the country.

Financial Inclusion: A Model Pathway for Full Coverage

The process of financial inclusion in India can broadly be classified into three phases. During the First Phase (1960-1990), the focus was on channelising of credit to the neglected sectors of the economy. Special emphasis was also laid on weaker sections of the society. Second Phase (1990-2005) focused mainly on strengthening the financial institutions as part of financial sector reforms. Financial inclusion in this phase was encouraged mainly by the introduction of SHG-bank linkage programme in the early 1990s and Kisan Credit Cards (KCCs) for providing credit to farmers. The SHG-bank linkage programme was launched by National Bank for Agriculture and Rural Development (NABARD) in 1992, with policy support from the Reserve Bank, to facilitate collective decision making by the poor and provide 'door step' banking. During the Third Phase (2005 onwards), the 'financial inclusion' was explicitly made as a policy objective and thrust was on providing safe facility of savings deposits through 'no frills' accounts.

It is widely accepted that financial inclusion is critical for achieving inclusive growth in the country. To achieve that, it is expected to increase the scope of financial inclusion initiatives to reach out to people at the grass-root level. It can be achieved in three ways, such as, (a) through State-driven intervention by way of statutory enactments, (b) through voluntary effort by the banking community by evolving various strategies to bring within the ambit of the banking sector the large strata of society, and (c) creating a demand by the people themselves to pull the banks, financial institutions and other service providers towards them to offer banking and financial services at a competitive and affordable rate (Chakrabarty, 2009). A major reason for failure to promote financial inclusion is the use of technology. Without technology it is not easy to reach out to the people. It is also clear that it is not possible to promote financial inclusion with a branch-based delivery mechanism (Kochhar, 2009). The idea of extending the reach of financial services to all sections of population through new technologies and simplified branch regulations gives a flicker of hope. Bringing financial services to rural clients is the biggest challenge in the quest for broad-based financial inclusion.

Non-bank financial institutions help fill this gap, with half the countries reporting more non-bank branches per rural resident than bank branches. Better geographic outreach can remove distance as a barrier to financial access for both lenders and borrowers, perhaps allowing banks to be more responsive and less intimidating to their customers. Simplifying the branch approval process can facilitate geographical expansion of branches. But the cost of building physical infrastructure or the combination of low income and low population density may make some areas unprofitable as branch locations. Allowing banks to operate through agents, including partnerships with postal networks and retailers, reduces the fixed costs associated with geographical expansion and holds great promise for improving access to financial services, especially in poor and remote areas (CGAP, 2009).

Initiatives towards the Path of Financial Inclusion

The institutions currently providing credit in the rural areas include the rural and semi-urban branches of commercial banks, regional rural banks, cooperative societies and micro-finance institutions. What is required is not to create any new institution for providing credit to the excluded, but to enable the existing institutions to extend their outreach. There is a need to find ways and means to effect improvements within the existing financial credit delivery mechanism and evolve new models for extending their outreach. The formal banking system, the rural cooperatives, and Non-Governmental Organizations (NGOs) must be strengthened organizationally to extend their outreach. The financially excluded sections require products which are customized to meet their needs.

The goal of inclusive growth can be achieve if all the available resources including technology and expertise available with the banks, the support of the government, the optimum utilization of the Micro-Finance Institutions (MFIs), NGOs and Self-Help Groups are geared towards including more and more people under the banking net. Initially, it may appear that taking banking to the sections constituting "the bottom of the pyramid" may not be profitable but various studies conducted reveal that even the relatively low margins on high volumes can be a profitable proposition. Banks therefore need to work out their appropriate business delivery models and financial products to cater to the needs of the people.

There are limits to the extent that banks can be expected to play a purely social role in today's more competitive environment. However, too conservative an approach on settling debt that has turned bad due to contingencies of poor weather or prices is not even prudential banking if this serves only to show bank balance sheets to be better than they are, and prevents profitable new lending. There are several suggestions, ranging from a Stabilisation Fund to be run by the Centre for automatic write-off under some specified conditions to the setting up by States of standing professional Debt Commissions to examine individual debt (including to non-institutional sources) on a case by case basis for one time settlement. The Eleventh Five Year Plan examines in detail the impediments which now stand in the way of social and developmental banking and suggest innovations that can improve access and speed up one-time settlements while maintaining credit discipline and financial prudence (Planning Commission, 2006).

The available statistics reveal that over 28.23 million no-frills accounts have been opened, but only less than 11 per cent of them are active. Opening no-frills accounts will not give any help to the poor if they do not conduct any transactions. Today, the number of rural bank branches is only 31,727 as against more than 6,00,000 villages in the country. Similarly, the number of ATMs is 44,857 with a majority of them being in metros and urban centres. Again, there are 4,70,237 points of sale (Kochhar, 2009). Financial inclusion unfortunately has become synonymous with the opening of bank accounts. It needs to be much more. We found a clear differentiation between bank accounts linked with livelihood and those just opened for the sake of opening a bank account. An analysis of 50 lakh individual, no-frill accounts revealed that the average balance in livelihood-linked accounts was about Rs. 11,000 while in the others, the average balance was just Rs. 176.

Table 3.15: Progress of 'No frills' Accounts in the Banking Sector in India

Category	*March 31, 2006*	*March 31, 2007*	*March 31, 2008**	*March 31, 2009**
Public Sector Banks	3,32,878	58,65,419	1,39,09,935	2,98,59,178
Private Sector Banks	1,56,388	8,60,997	18,45,869	31,24,101
Foreign Banks	231	5,919	33,115	41,482
Total	**4,89,497**	**67,32,335**	**1,57,88,919**	**3,30,24,761**

Note: *: Provisional.
Source: 1. Report on Trend and Progress of Banking India—2007-08.
2. Data for 2008-09 are received from banks.

To deepen and widen the financial services provided by banks particularly to the under-serviced areas and the rural poor, two Models are suggested, *viz.* the Business Facilitator Model and the Business Correspondent Model for providing non-financial support services and financial services as "pass through" agents respectively by leveraging MFIs/NGOs, Civil Society Organisations and other external entities (RBI, 2008).

Despite a wide network of bank branches spread across the length and breadth of the country, banking has still not reached a large section of the population. They are deprived of basic banking services like a savings account or minimal credit facilities. Banking penetration was not there because earlier technology was not available. But now, technology is available. Reserve Bank has taken measures to achieve increased financial inclusion through the "Banking Correspondent (BC)" model. The RBI also formulated a biometric access/smart card based scheme of Electronic Benefit Transfer (EBT) by banks to facilitate routing of social security benefits, National Rural Employment Guarantee Act payments and other government payments could be routed. The scheme, which involves subsidizing the cost of issue of the biometric access/smart cards by banks, was initially implemented in Andhra Pradesh in 2008 and has been extended across the country till June 30, 2010. I would also like to mention here that as per the annual report of India Post for the year 2008-09, there are over 1.55 lakh post offices in India, of which 89 per cent are in the rural areas. And post offices offer money transfer services through their Money Order and Instant Money Order schemes. One of the important concerns in any money transfer transaction is the bona fide of the underlying. This concern is not restricted to India, but it is felt across the globe.

The Bank Facilitators (BFs) were allowed to undertake facilitation services like identification of borrowers and fitment of activities; collection and preliminary processing of loan applications including verification of primary information/data; creating awareness about savings and other products and education and advice on managing money and debt counselling; processing and submission of applications to banks; promoting and nurturing Self-Help Groups/Joint Liability Groups; post-sanction monitoring; monitoring and handholding of Self-Help Groups/ Joint Liability Groups/Credit Groups/others; and follow-up for recovery (RBI, 2008).

Under the BF model, banks were permitted to use intermediaries such as, NGOs/Farmers' Clubs, cooperatives, community-based organisations, IT enabled rural outlets of corporate entities, Post Offices, insurance agents, well functioning Panchayats, Village Knowledge Centres, Agri Clinics/Agri Business Centres, Krishi Vigyan Kendras and KVIC/KVIB units, depending on the comfort level of the bank, for providing facilitation services. As these services were not intended to involve the conduct of banking business by BFs, no approval was required by banks from Reserve Bank for using the above intermediaries for facilitation of the services (RBI, 2009).

One of the preconditions for deepening of any process is the existence of a large number of participants. Hence, financial inclusion is a necessary condition for financial deepening. Barriers for poor people to access appropriate financial services include socio-economic factors e.g., lack of education-illiteracy, gender and age, low and irregular income, and geography, regulatory factors, e.g., mandatory requirements of identity documentation and product design factors. A major barrier cited to expand appropriate services to poor by financial service providers is the cost of providing those services including administering small loans. While transaction costs do not vary in direct proportion to a transaction's size and larger number of transactions brings down the costs, serving the poor with small value services is not viable using conventional retail banking or insurance approaches. We have to promote technological and institutional innovation as a means to expand financial system access and usage, including addressing infrastructure weaknesses.

The essence of financial inclusion is to ensure that a range of appropriate financial services is available to every individual and enabling them to understand and access those services. Apart from the regular form of financial intermediation, it may include a basic no frills banking account for making and receiving payments, a savings product suited to the pattern of cash flows of a poor household, money transfer facilities, small loans and overdrafts for productive, personal and other purposes, insurance etc. Micro-finance, by providing small loans and savings facilities to those who have been excluded from the formal financial services is viewed as an effective tool to reach the poor and the needy with timely and adequate credit facilities. At present, micro-finance institutions (MFIs) obtain finance from banks according to guidelines issued by RBI. MFIs provide small-scale credit and other financial services to low income households and small informal businesses. Government promoted MFIs in a big way.

A basic question that is raised frequently is: "Why are so many bankable people unbanked?"(UN, 2006). An inclusive financial sector would provide access to credit for all "bankable" people and firms, insurance for all insurable people and firms, and savings and payments services for everyone. Financial inclusion may be defined as the process of ensuring access to financial services and timely and adequate credit where needed by vulnerable groups such as weaker sections and low income groups at an affordable cost (RBI).

There is a division between financial services available to two groups in society—an increased range of personal finance options for a segment of high and upper middle income population and a significantly large section of the population who lack access to even the most basic banking services. This growing divide in the availability of formal financial services is termed "financial exclusion". Those who belong to the second group live on low incomes and cannot access mainstream financial products such as bank accounts, low cost credit, remittances, payment services, financial advisory services, insurance facilities, etc.

Indebtedness to the moneylender cannot be deemed a sign of financial inclusion. Rather, it has to be seen as a sign of exclusion, as a major part of those who access credit from non-institutional units like moneylenders would have been denied access to institutional credit. As per NSSO data,

45.9 million farmer households in the country (51.4%), out of a total of 89.3 million households, do not access credit, either from institutional or non-institutional sources. Only 27 per cent of total farm households are indebted to formal sources (of which one-third also borrow from informal sources). In other words, 73 per cent of farm households do not have access to formal credit sources. This shows that exclusion exists—to a large extent among specific occupational groups, specific social groups and in specific regions, either in isolation or in conjunction. It is, therefore, imperative to roll out an action plan to cover the highly excluded areas/regions in a very definite, time-bound manner, in order to get closer to the goal of 'financial inclusion'.

Micro-finance and Rural India

Since formal credit institutions rarely lend to the poor, special institutional arrangements become necessary to extend credit to those who have no collateral to offer. Micro-finance, the provision of a wide range of financial services to the poor on a sustainable basis, has proved to be immensely valuable. Access to financial services has allowed many families to make significant progress in their own efforts to escape poverty. The need for informality in credit delivery and easy access is demonstrated by the fact that Self-Help Groups (SHGs) and Micro-Finance Institutions (MFIs) constitute the fastest growing segment in recent years in reaching out to small borrowers. One can easily spell out five factors distinguishing micro-finance bodies from traditional banking institutions and they are: (a) client base (poor/low income); (b) lending methodology (no collateral, peer or character lending); (c) labour-intensive nature of work (with a cost structure reflecting it); (d) portfolio (small, short-term loans); and (e) institutional structure and governance.

Four important models have been tried out by the poor to help themselves in rural India:

1. *SHG Model*, where the promoters organise groups of five to twenty women, who save even up to Rs. 50 a week and deposit the amount in banks with the help of NGOs. Banks offer funds in the ratio of 1:1 (for every rupee deposited, the banks lend a rupee at around 13 per cent per annum) and there have been very little defaults;
2. *Grameen replicators* based on the concept of the Grameen Bank with four to five groups of five members each;

3. *Co-operative societies;* and
4. *NBFCs.* Some new generation development practitioners have registered as NBFCs. Examples are CASHPOR Financial and Technical Services, Mirzapur, Share Microfin and BASIX in Hyderabad.

Micro-finance is a recent development in which Indian institutions have acquired considerable expertise and where upscaling holds great promise both to expand the nature of financial services offered to micro-enterprises and to make these the springboard for entrepreneurial development (GoI, 2006).

Progress of Micro-finance

The SHG movement is bringing about a profound transformation in rural areas of India. MFIs play a significant role in facilitating inclusion, as they are uniquely positioned in reaching out to the rural poor. Many of them operate in a limited geographical area; they have a greater understanding of the issues specific to the rural poor, they enjoy greater acceptability amongst the rural poor and have flexibility in operations providing a level of comfort to their clientele. It is roughly estimated that there are about 1,000 NGO-MFIs and more than 20 companies facilitating the activities in all-over India. There are today over 22 lakh such groups linked with banks. The objective of the country is to enrol at least 50 per cent of all rural women in India as members of SHGs over the next five years and link these SHGs to banks. In the four years between 2003 and 2007, small borrower bank accounts (credit) i.e., up to Rs. 25,000 increased marginally from 36.9 million to 38.6 million, while SHGs' borrowing members grew from 10 million to 40.5 million and MFIs' borrowers grew from 1.1 million to eight million. In 2007-08, MFIs have added six million clients increasing their outreach to 14 million as per data brought out by Sa Daan.

An innovative scheme in rural delivery system launched by NABARD is the linking of SHGs of the poor with banks and bulk lending through NGOs. The SHG-Bank Linkage Programme implemented by commercial banks, Regional Rural Banks (RRBs) and cooperative banks has emerged as the major micro-finance programme in the country. Under the SHG-Bank Linkage Programme, as on March 31, 2009, 61,21,147 SHGs held savings bank accounts with total savings of Rs. 5,545.62 crore as against 50,09,794 SHGs with savings of Rs. 3,785.39 crore as on March 31, 2008. Thus, more than 8.06 crore poor households were associated with banking agencies under the SHG-Bank Linkage Programme. The number of outstanding micro-finance loans was 80 million. Some borrowers have multiple loans, so, net beneficiaries may total 60 million households. This is more than the 55 million poor households, and more than a quarter of India's 220 million households. Of course, many poor households are still left out, while non-poor households have got loans. MFIs have yet to reach or saturate large areas in India. But they are spreading fast across most States. The demand for micro-finance is enormous. According to the Tenth Plan document, in 1999-2000, 26.10 per cent of the population was living below the poverty line. Of the 260 million poor, 193 million were in the rural areas and the remaining 67 million in the urban areas.

Interest Rates: The Real Picture

The data from the Reserve Bank of India (RBI) show that over 53 per cent of loans are sourced from moneylenders. In Tamil Nadu, moneylenders account for 40 per cent of all borrowings. Moneylenders account for more than 30 per cent of all lending in four more States: Bihar, Manipur, Punjab and Rajasthan. MFIs borrow from banks at around 12 per cent and lend at anything between 25 per cent and 30 per cent. This can be very profitable. Most MFIs were started as NGOs. But NGOs had limited reach, being dependent on donor finance. So, many switched to a for profit model, which enabled them to raise money for expansion from equity investors and banks. Such MFIs expanded much reaching not just thousands, but millions.

Interest rates in the micro-finance sector have to be significantly higher than in the banking sector reflecting the much higher cost of doing business. Reserve Bank of India (RBI) has pulled up MFIs for their high interest rates—about 25 to 27 per cent. That is about double the rate at which they borrow from banks, but still lower than moneylenders. This attracts criticism but it is important to remember that most micro-finance institutions charge rates which are much lower than that of rates charged by moneylenders. Borrowers stand to benefit from the experience of micro-finance institutions as these provide competition to moneylenders (GoI, 2006).

MFIs started with loans of Rs. 3,000 in the first year, going up to Rs. 4,000 in the second year, and so on. But now some MFIs start with Rs. 10,000, go up to Rs. 15,000 the next year, and so on. They charge around 30 per cent interest. This looks usurious. But moneylenders lend at 50 per cent or more, seize the land of defaulters and make them bonded labourers. MFIs, by contrast, rely on group lending for repayment. If one member of a joint lending group defaults, the others cannot get credit, so they put social pressure on the defaulter to pay up. Credit card companies charge an annual fee plus interest at around 30 per cent. MFIs, like credit card companies, give small, unsecured loans, and their interest rates are no higher. In both cases, the interest rate reflects the high cost of handling very small loans.

The fact of the matter is that according to the State Sector Report 2009, out of about 230 MFIs that reported information, about one-third are making losses. Only about half of the smaller MFIs make profits. If the government is agitated about MFIs making supernormal profits, the right approach would be to control the spread (margin over cost of funds) rather than the rate at which an MFI lends. Incidentally, some companies in the financial sector (stock exchanges) have gross margins of 75 per cent because of a lack of competition. A global comparison shows that on average, return on assets of Indian MFIs was 0.7 per cent—considerably less than Brazil's 6.4 per cent, Mexico's three per cent and Indonesia's 3.1 per cent. So, while some larger, older MFIs in India are perhaps enjoying substantial profits, most of the others are not. Formulating public policies on the basis of a few outliers is fraught with a number of unintended consequences.

Financial Sustainability

Over the past two decades, institutions that make microloans to low-income borrowers in developing and transition economies have focused increasingly on making their operations financially sustainable by charging interest rates that are high enough to cover all their costs. They argue that doing so will best ensure the permanence and expansion of the services they provide. Sustainable (i.e., profitable) micro-finance providers can continue to serve their clients without needing ongoing infusions of subsidies, and can fund exponential growth of services for new clients by tapping commercial sources, including deposits from the public. MFIs on average have higher returns on assets than commercial banks do, but MFIs produce lower returns on equity for their owners. The median return on MFI owners' equity in 2006 was moderates—12.3 per cent, roughly four per cent lower than the return for banks (Rosenberg, *et al.*, 2009).

Why Micro-finance should be there in Rural Areas?

All these discussions make everybody to have a rethinking of the very notion of micro-finance. Many think that micro-finance has shot into the limelight of late, for entirely wrong reasons. In a country where only about 40 per cent of the population has access to banks, micro-finance institutions (MFIs), over the last decade and a half, have provided a lifeline to about 30 million households that are otherwise outside the banking system. Commercial banks, as they are structured today, are unable to service the requirements of micro-credit to those who have no collateral to offer as security.

MFIs have brought banking to the doorstep of the borrower, whereas commercial banks typically expect the borrower to come to their doorstep. Because of the activities of some MFIs, there is an attempt to strangle the entire sector. Onerous conditions are sought to be placed on their functioning. An impression is being created that rates of interest at which they lend should be capped as MFIs are earning profits of a high magnitude. The most extreme consequence will be that MFIs will vacate the credit space that will gratefully be reoccupied by the local moneylenders with all their associated ills. Another possibility is that MFIs will perforce have to borrow at a higher rate of interest from unconventional sources and therefore their lending rates would go up rather than come down. A third consequence will be that only the very large MFIs will survive.

It is actually a boon to moneylenders. For two decades, micro-finance institutions (MFIs) have spread fast in Andhra Pradesh, reaching millions of poor women and filling the space once dominated by moneylenders. But in the recent past, the State government issued an ordinance that temporarily shuts down and permanently maims MFIs in the State. This also threatens to maim MFIs across India, since equity investors and bankers will be reluctant to finance a sector with such political risks. But that will be an appalling loss for India. A globally acclaimed industry that employs thousands and benefits millions is at risk.

Finance is the lubricant, which oils the wheels of development. All economies rely upon the intermediary function of finance to transfer resources from savers to investors. In market economies, this function is performed by commercial banks, financial institutions and capital markets. In many developing countries, capital markets are at a rudimentary stage, and commercial banks are reluctant to lend to the poor largely because of the lack of collateral and high transaction costs. The poor would borrow relatively small amounts, and the processing and supervision of lending to them would consume administrative costs disproportionate to the amount of lending.

Micro-finance is now as important as mainstream banking. The present spread is 2.2 million SHGs covering 33 million poor families, and a cumulative disbursement of Rs. 11,400 crore. The annual growth rate is 51 per cent. The actual availability of funds is only a fraction of demand, leaving a huge gap. The robust banking sector of our country failed to provide integrated micro-financial services (including micro-credit and insurance) to the poorest sections. Hence, the economically active among the poor relied on NGOs, societies, trusts and cooperatives for micro-credit.

Table 3.16: Traditional Finance *v/s* Micro-finance

Area	*Traditional Finance*	*Micro-finance*
Lending Methodology	(1) based on collateral (2) more documentation (3) less labour intensive (4) Loans are usually serviced monthly, quarterly, or yearly	(1) based on character (2) less documentation (3) more labour intensive (4) Loans are usually serviced/ repaid in weekly or bi-monthly installments
Loan Portfolio	(1) fewer loans (2) loans larger in size (3) collateralized (4) longer maturity (5) more stable delinquency	(1) more loans (2) loans smaller in size (3) uncollateralized (4) shorter maturity (5) more volatile delinquency
Institutional Structure and Governance (of regulated financial institutions)	(1) Profit maximizing institutional and individual shareholders (2) Creation by spin-off from existing regulated institution (3) Centralized organization with branch offices located in cities	(1) Mainly non-profit institutional shareholders (2) Creation by conversion from NGO or formation of new entity (3) Decentralized set of small units in areas with weak infrastructure

Source: Rock & Otero, 1996; Behrenbach & Churchill, 1997.

There have been incidents of State governments imposing restrictions on micro-finance institutions in a manner which does not reflect an appreciation of the realities on the ground. Excessive regulation and control of this sector may be particularly dangerous as it can prevent the development of a healthy and competitive micro-finance sector which could compete with usurious moneylenders (GoI, 2006). The regulations should be good for the whole community. It should not be at the cost of the institutions which are already created and operated in rural India. A high degree of legitimacy, accountability and transparency will enable MFIs to source adequate debt and equity funds and also enable them to take and use savings as a low cost source for on-lending. MFIs can, thus, move into all areas of financial services including credit provision, savings facilities, and micro-insurance, financial services in times of emergency etc. The distinctive features of micro-finance as compared to traditional forms of finance are given in Table 3.16.

Remittance for the Poor

The poor need a remittance system to send money to their families when they migrate out of their villages or towns. Other cases of remittance could arise on account of transfer payments by Government or remittances of miscellaneous nature. As such the service they need should meet the criteria of accessible service; timeliness and certainty of service; cost-effectiveness; affordability and value for money; and, receipt of delivery. New technology and computerization of banking operations, new remittance products etc., have been introduced in the market. While these systems meet the needs of a modern economy, they leave the financially excluded sections of the population untouched. This calls for a conscious attempt to build a payment and settlement system that caters to the needs of the poor and excluded sections of society.

One successful example of suitable remittance product is the model adopted by Ahmednagar DCCB. It has implemented a system of low cost anywhere banking solution which has a facility of card to card transfer. Savings/current account holders at all its 280 branches have a choice to keep their savings bank account or a part thereof in a separate account at the bank's head office. Customers can have access to this account from all the bank branches. Each branch has been provided with two PoS devices which are connected through a dial-up telephone line to the head office. The customers can go to any branch and deposit or withdraw cash after authenticating access to their account. An account holder at a village can deposit cash in the village branch of the bank and her children studying in the city can withdraw cash from another card. The customer is charged only rupees four per transaction. Such experiments can be studied for replication. The e-kiosks in villages could be yet another source of operating a remittance system that is accessible to the poor.

Thus, while the financial inclusion through opening of no frills accounts with banks would improve the remittance facility for the poor, a conscious effort at devising a product within the existing payment and settlement system would enable the poor to benefit from the improvements in banking technology. Their needs have to be met by a multi-pronged strategy which uses the existing infrastructure optimally and in addition, new products should be introduced which leverage on technology.

Micro-insurance

Micro-insurance is a key element in the financial services package for people at the bottom of the pyramid. The poor face more risks than the well-off, but more importantly they are more vulnerable to the same risk. To combat these risks, the poor do proactive risk management—grain storage, savings, asset accumulation (especially bullocks), loans from friends and relatives, etc. However, the prevalent forms of risk management (in kind savings, self-insurance, mutual insurance) which were appropriate earlier are no longer adequate.

Poverty is not just a state of deprivation, but has latent vulnerability. Micro-insurance should, therefore, provide greater economic and psychological security to the poor as it reduces exposure to multiple risks and cushions the impact of a disaster. There is an overwhelming demand for social protection among the poor. Micro-insurance in conjunction with micro-savings and micro-credit could, therefore, go a long way in keeping this segment away from the poverty trap and would truly be an integral component of financial inclusion.

Micro-insurance is defined as "the protection of low income households against specific perils in exchange for premium payments proportionate to the likelihood and cost of the risk involved" (CGAP). Micro-insurance has, in no way, penetrated rural markets. Traditional insurers have not made much headway in bringing micro-insurance products to these markets. In fact, micro-insurance has not penetrated even among the urban poor. Studies show that 90 per cent of the Indian population are not covered by insurance and signify an untapped market of nearly US$2 billion (UNDP). This enormous "missing market" is in fact ready for customized life and non-life insurance, but first, serious mismatches between the needs of the insured and the insurers must be overcome, pitting priorities against profits.

At present, the Personal Accident Insurance Scheme (PAIS) which is being provided as a bundled offering along with the *Kisan Credit Card* (KCC) Scheme and the *Rashtriya Krishi Bima Yojana* (RKBY) for insuring crops, are, probably, the only borrowal-linked risk mitigation mechanisms available to rural households. Further, many State Governments are offering health insurance facilities to the rural poor (e.g., *Yeshaswini* Scheme of the Government of Karnataka) which have also generated considerable acceptance and awareness about insurance products in the rural areas. Most insurance schemes (66%) are linked with micro-finance services provided by specialised institutions or non-specialised organisations. 22 per cent of the schemes are implemented by community-based organisations and 12 per cent by health care providers (ILO, 2004).

The rural micro-insurance industry in India is characterized by limited and inappropriate services; inadequate information and capacity gaps; challenges in product design; mismatch between needs and standard products on offer; limited efforts at product development /diversification; difficulty in distribution; pricing problems; high costs of penetrating rural markets, combined with underutilization of available distribution channels; cumbersome and inappropriate procedures; and, contrasting perspectives of the insured and the insurers. Efforts must be made to reduce the demand-supply gaps, innovation of appropriate products and prices and provide distribution efficiencies for better outreach and remove procedural hassles facilitating easier renewals and claim settlements. Design of micro-insurance products to the rural poor must have the features of simplicity, availability, affordability, accessibility and flexibility. Partnership between an insurer and a social organisation like an NGO would be optimal, to promote micro-insurance by drawing on their mutual strengths.

Self-Help Groups in India

Self-Help Groups are based on groups formed endogenously in communities, sometimes facilitated by NGOs. The groups comprise 10 to 25 people, and groups gather regularly, typically every week, to pool their savings and lend from their accumulated pot to members at an interest rate designed to cover costs (Seibel, 2005). Usually, it is deemed that all SHG members must deposit regularly into compulsory savings accounts. These accounts have tight withdrawal restrictions: savings may only be withdrawn when a member leaves a group or if there are exceptional circumstances. This kind of forced saving aids the SHG by creating collateral that can be tapped in times of trouble, but it is of limited immediate value as savings for customers. Two-thirds of SHG participants usually have a loan; the interest rate charged by banks to SHGs is about 20 per cent annually; the interest rate for individual loans is at the discretion of SHGs and varies.

In India, SHGs represent a unique approach to financial intermediation. The approach combines access to low-cost financial services with a process of self-management and development for the women who are SHG members. Much of micro-finance in India is built upon the grassroots infrastructure of a SHG. They are small village-based groups, consisting of between 10 to 20 members, within which most micro-finance transactions are conducted. The vast majority of SHGs consist exclusively of women. Micro-finance transactions (including payments, loans, withdrawals, deposits, etc.) usually occur during monthly meetings of the SHG. During these meetings individual members deposit money into a common fund, which is in turn lent to other members at a mutually agreed interest rate, usually for some productive purpose, such as making an investment in their farm or business. Sometimes, SHGs also access larger loans from banks and other financial institutions, which is then lent as smaller loans to each member. No collateral is usually required, as the community liability among members of the same village is enough to enforce repayment. Also, repayment rates of these loans are often found to be higher than loans to the general populace.

SHGs also form larger structures by linking with other groups like themselves in their local geographic area. In some cases a set of 20 to 30 groups will come together to form a cluster, and a set of 20 to 30 clusters will come together to form a federation. These larger groupings allow SHGs to transfer funds between groups, and to attract larger sources of investment and institutional capital. SHGs and SHG Federations are often created and nurtured by a supporting micro-finance institution (MFI), often a non-governmental organization (NGO). This MFI helps create and support the SHGs, including providing training and capacity building, linkage to external sources of funds, linkages to other SHGs and to the formal banking sector.

SHG-Bank Linkage

Banks and SHGs work hand in hand by leveraging the strength of the formal banking system and the flexibility of informal SHGs in providing adequate financial services to the rural poor. Through NGOs, government agencies and banks, vast numbers of self-help groups have been established in recent years: as self-reliant autonomous local financial intermediaries. 85 per cent members of these SHGs are women; they have proven to be the better savers, borrowers and investors. Most of them are from the lowest castes and other disadvantaged groups.

The SHGs mobilize their own savings, transform them into loans to members and plow their earnings from interest income back into equity. On that basis, SHGs and banks enter into commercial relations of mutual benefit, with low bank and client transaction costs and negligible risks. In the absence of interest rate restrictions and with repayment rates >99 per cent, SHG banking is highly profitable—a message that has convinced hesitant bank managers in increasing numbers. SHGs are now forming local networks with their own cooperative financial institutions. The programme has turned into a social movement, with high expansion rates in recent years. Fuelled by competence and enthusiasm at all stakeholder levels, it has expanded rapidly throughout India, including marginal and tribal areas. It is probably the world's largest and most successful micro-finance programme for the rural poor—outstanding in its emphasis on self-reliance and local autonomy of the very poor.

Within its mandate of rural poverty alleviation, NABARD puts particular emphasis on:

- the poorest of the rural poor;
- women;
- empowerment through participation and ownership;
- marginal and tribal areas;
- outreach to large numbers;
- sustainability of impact; and
- sharing and dissemination of knowledge.

NABARD has chosen a two-pronged approach to poverty reduction, combining the principles of self-help and self-reliance with access to external human and financial resources:

(a) Establishing informal Self-Help Groups (SHGs) of the poorest of the rural poor with up to 20 members as local financial intermediaries: mobilizing their own savings, transforming these into loans to members, and financing their growth in the initial stage through both savings mobilization and retained earnings from interest rate income.
(b) Providing access, first to facilitating agencies and, once an SHG has proven its organizational and financial viability, to bank refinance.

NABARD makes a conscious effort of targeting the poorest of the rural poor. The face of poverty is too variegated in India for a standardized method such as the housing index. It, therefore, leaves the identification of the poor to its cooperating local partners and the people themselves. 85 per cent of the SHG members are women, and the women and men agree that women are better savers and more conscientious borrowers.

Loan sizes and periods are according to demand and creditworthiness as established by the group; they are no right of any member, nor are they standardized. The SHGs are autonomous in all their decisions, including the determination of interest rates. In the same vein, banks are free to participate and select SHGs as clients. With zero loan losses, the SHG linkage programme—in contrast to other programmes with high rates of non-performing assets—has been profitable to banks: far in excess of its share of their portfolio.

To the members, their SHG is first of all a financial institution. At the same time, it is an organization for mutual aid, which may pertain to all spheres of life:

(a) Emergency assistance and social welfare;
(b) Social development, e.g.: alphabetization, prevention of child marriage, prevention of bonded child marriage, sending all children to school, child care, nutrition, family planning, prohibition;
(c) Rural and agricultural development, e.g.: water conservation, irrigation; and
(d) Promotion of income-generating activities, e.g.: marble handicrafts, chair-making, vegetable vending.

Sustainability of SHGs

SHGs are established as local financial intermediaries with their own internal savings and credit business and access to bank refinancing. Sustainability will require:

(a) Effective implementation of the policy of complete freedom from interest rate restrictions.
(b) Continual encouragement to SHGs towards self-reliance and growth through retained earnings from interest income and savings mobilization, including eventually voluntary withdrawable savings and pygmy savings collected at doorsteps.
(c) Safekeeping of internal funds of increasing magnitude.
(d) Registration of SHGs as legal entities or as part of larger legal entities such as SHG federations or financial cooperatives.

(e) Auditing and supervision of SHGs by auditing services of SHG federations or banks.
(f) Legal registration of SHG federations and their financial service subsidiaries.
(g) An integrated accounting and reporting system for SHGs and federations, serving at the same time, as the basis for NABARD's monitoring system.
(h) A solution to the collateral problem of larger-size loans by SHGs and banks to women who are not legal holders of family property.
(i) A solution to the collateral problem of SHG federations when refinanced by banks, e.g., through a credit guarantee arrangement.

A paradigm, which emerged in the late 1980s and early 1990s, is a move from micro-enterprises as livelihood of the poor, often accompanied by charity, to micro-enterprises as business. From this perspective, size, not poverty, constitutes the defining characteristic of the micro-enterprise sector, although advocates of micro-enterprise development still argue that the sector is the key to reducing poverty in developing countries.

Micro-entrepreneurs are manufacturers, retailers and service providers that are an integral part of the economy as suppliers and purchasers. They not only create jobs, but also contribute to economic growth. In this view, micro-enterprises are related to small enterprises and it is at the centre of the economy in most developing countries. Along with this perspective comes a view of micro-enterprises as clients, as customers, of institutions providing services.

In the 1990s, governments and development donors have increased their support for micro-enterprises and have changed in line with the new paradigm. Micro-finance institutions are no longer funded through donations alone; they are receiving loans and "equity investments" from their traditional donors and tapping commercial financial markets, especially in their home countries.

Presently, we are in a world of competing paradigms: none of the views of micro-enterprises have disappeared. Each one colours the public policy debate about micro-enterprise development in a different way. However, the only view that envisions micro-enterprises, and consequently micro-finance, as "emerging markets" is the paradigm that casts micro-enterprises as businesses and customers. Whether this view is accurate or not, and to what extent it is compatible with the 'poverty reduction' views are yet to be researched on a wider scale.

4
Exploring Micro-finance Opportunities in Kerala

The Kudumbashree Impact

Kerala which lies on the South-western tip of India is one of the smallest States of India, accounting for nearly 1.18 per cent of its territory and 3.1 per cent of its population. Kerala forms a narrow strip of land along the Arabian Sea coast with the Western Ghats on its eastern border, sliding towards the west from the mountain ranges and having three distinct layers of land—the highlands, the midlands and the lowlands. Since, the formation of the State in 1956, Kerala has striven consistently to bring down the interregional disparities, has gone ahead with progressive legislation on land tenures and agrarian relations, has brought down mortality and fertility rates and has arrested population growth rate. The State has promoted educational growth with significant support to private sector initiatives and has expanded and modernized the healthcare sector.

In spite of the high degree of social development; unemployment, violence against women and poverty have cropped up as major issues. It is in this context that the importance of micro-finance arises, as a means of entrepreneurship, poverty reduction and a key to the empowerment of women. In the present chapter, we try to analyze the status of women in social sector and the role of micro-finance institutions in the context. Here we give an account of the development of micro-finance opportunities in Kerala through an evaluation of Kudumbashree.

Women in Kerala

Empowerment is a continuous process of realizing the goals of equality, human liberation and freedom. Women's empowerment implies equality of opportunity and equity between the genders, ethnic groups, social classes, age groups, collective participation in different spheres of life, etc. The two most commonly used gender related indices are the Gender Development Index (GDI) and the Gender Empowerment Index (GEM) of the United Nations Development Programme. The GDI is concerned with basic capabilities and living standards. It uses the same variables as the Human Development Index (HDI), but it focuses on the inequality between men and women and on the average achievement of all people taken together. The Gender Empowerment Index (GEM) is concerned with economic, political and professional participation. It uses the percentage of seats held in Parliament by women, the percentage of woman administrators and managers, and the percentage of woman professional and technical workers and the earned income share of women, as indicators.

Attempts are being made to construct HDIs within the country. It shows that among the major States in India, Kerala ranked at the top in the Gender Development Index. Even though the gender gap in terms of basic capabilities is much lower in Kerala than in other States of India, indicators of well-being in non-conventional terms such as mental health, crime against women, political participation and property rights have shown reverse trends. High rates of literacy and impressive levels of female education did not translate into rapid growth of paid employment for women, or into upward occupational mobility.

The popular understanding of the high status of women in the Kerala society is founded on conventional indicators of well-being such as education, health and employment. The less examined questions are the mental health of women, crime against women, and political and property rights of women. Evidences show rising rates of crime against women, growing practice of dowry, and declining property rights of women in Kerala. In the educational sector, women lag behind men in professional and technical streams except nursing. The preponderance of women is observed in stenography, dress making, cloth cutting and tailoring, secretarial practice and data preparation. Work participation rate of women in Kerala is the lowest in India, particularly in the rural areas. Educated unemployment of women is also quite high and it is rapidly rising. Nearly three fourths of the educated unemployed women have failed to find jobs of their preference. The younger generations among them are withdrawing from work in agriculture and other low status occupations. More than three fourths of the women workers in manufacturing units are found in the informal sector.

Women in Kerala have secured a higher share of employment in the organized sector than their counterparts elsewhere in the country. But the worker-sex ratio for women is higher in the private sector. The proportion of women in the public sector has been declining. The majority of women at work in the formal sector are located at the lower rungs of the employment hierarchy, as teachers, nurses and other paramedical personnel. In the service occupations, they are found as housekeepers, maids, cooks and beauticians. Occupational mobility is extremely low among women workers. Women are engaged also in unpaid work in household premises, such as tutoring children, kitchen gardening and poultry farming. Work participation rates of women among the poor including SCs and STs are higher, but are engaged in poorly paid and low status occupations.

Male migration has intensified women unemployment. Health achievements of women consequent on demographic transition are significant. But contraception has remained an exclusively women domain. The incidence of mental stress is quite high among women. Dowry-related issues are a major cause among the mentally stressed women. Violence against women, an atrocity rooted in patriarchal structure, is rapidly on the rise in Kerala. Poverty and employment status are factors for violence against women. Women's ownership of land is progressively on the decline. The growth of the practice of dowry has also led to the decline of the women's status in the household and in the society. Women's voices are not adequately heard and acted upon even in the new dispensation of decentralized planning. Ageing has added a new dimension to the travails of women particularly since women live longer than men; there are more widows among the aged than widowers in lower age groups; and women lack, more than men, own source of income. In this context, educational practices, work norms, employment opportunities, social security measures, property rights, marriage practice and behavioural patterns have to be duly modified to give respect and recognition to women's rights responsibility and legitimate status in society.

Serra (2001) studied sixteen Indian States in a comparative perspective and found that Kerala scored high on most counts making it the State having the highest stocks of social capital in the country. The study found Kerala exceptional. Kerala appears as the best Indian example of a society with high social capital. In a recent study of Kerala in the context of the people's planning programme, Veron (2001) says: "grass roots environmental action tends to meet favourable conditions in Kerala because of its richness in social capital; people are politically aware and experienced with collective action". A study done by Morris (1998) on the relationship between social capital and poverty also ranks Kerala's performance high on the basis of the existence of social capital.

Demographic and Health Indicators

Sex ratio is one of the most important social parameters indicating the balance between males and females in the society. The overall sex ratio in Kerala continues to be favourable to women, being 1058 compared to 933 for the country as a whole (Table 4.1). Among the major States in India, Kerala has the lowest Infant Mortality Rate (IMR). In Kerala, out of every 1000 children born, only 13 die before attaining their first birthday. The female IMR was 13 and the male IMR was 12 during 2008.

Table 4.1: Infant Mortality per 1000 live births in Kerala *vis-à-vis* India from 1961 to 2007

Year	*Kerala*			*All India*		
	Male	*Female*	*Total*	*Male*	*Female*	*Total*
1961	55	48	52	122	108	115
2005	14	15	14	56	61	58
2006	14	16	15	56	59	57
2007	12	13	13	55	56	55

Source: SRS Bulletin, October 2008, Registrar General, India.

Health achievements are reflected in life expectancy and infant and maternal mortality figures. Life expectancy of women in Kerala is much higher than that for India as a whole and also five years more than that of men in Kerala (Table 4.2)

Table 4.2: Life Expectancy at Birth in Kerala *vis-à-vis* India from 1997 to 2005

Year	*Kerala*		*All India*	
	Male	*Female*	*Male*	*Female*
1997-2001	70.8	76.2	61.3	63.0
1998-2002	70.8	75.9	61.6	63.3
1999-2003	70.9	76.0	61.8	63.5
2000-2004	71.0	76.1	62.1	63.7
2001-2005	71.3	76.3	62.3	63.9

Source: SRS Bulletin, October 2008, Registrar General, India.

Nutritional Indicators

The mean Body Mass Index (BMI) for women in the age group 15 to 49 in Kerala is 22.6 while it is 20.5 for the nation. Chronic energy deficiency is usually indicated by a BMI of less than 18.5. Eighteen per cent of women and 21.5 per cent of men in Kerala have a BMI below 18.5. Among the States in India, Kerala, Manipur, Goa, and Punjab have the lowest prevalence of anemia for both women and men. Only 2.55 per cent of women in Kerala have diabetes.

Pattern of Education

It is generally accepted that the basic problem of access to schools has been overcome in Kerala, which is evident from the fact that more than ninety per cent of children in the age group of seven and above are literate in Kerala. The pupil-teacher ratio in Kerala was 31 in 1991 and it declined to 28 in 2001. Gender gap is extremely low in school education (Table 4.3).

Table 4.3: General Educational Level for Kerala and India as on 2001

Level of Education	*Female of age 15 yrs and above per 1000 females*		*Male of age 15 yrs and above per 1000 males*	
	Male	*Female*	*Male*	*Female*
Not literate	129	491	53	253
Literate and up to primary	257	198	261	254
Middle	291	142	343	205
Secondary	151	79	164	126
Higher secondary	66	44	58	73
Diploma/certificate	34	4	50	14
Graduate and above	72	41	73	74

Source: NSS Report No. 522, Government of India.

A higher proportion of girls in the age group 5-29 have never attended schools; nearly twice that of men in Kerala. Also, the rate of discontinuing studies is higher among females in Kerala. The major reasons for either not attending or discontinuing/dropping out from the educational institution were to supplement household income (11% for female and 49% for male), and to attend domestic duties.

Employment and Unemployment

As against 51.6 per cent for males and 22.7 per cent for females in 2001 at the all-India level, the corresponding work participation rates in Kerala were 50.6 per cent and 15.3 per cent respectively. While the rate was not far lower in Kerala than at the all-India level for males, it was very much so, in the case of females. The factors that led to the decline in female work participation rate include the structural changes of employment in the State. Several labour-intensive activities such as rice cultivation and traditional cottage industries have been decreasing in Kerala—during the past three decades. These were the two areas in which most of the women workers found employment. The conversion for agricultural land to non-agricultural uses and of paddy fields to cultivation of commercial crops had reduced women workforce in the agricultural sector from 43.6 per cent in 1981 to 36.1 per cent in 1991. The crisis in the cottage industries led to a fall in women's workforce from 7.7 per cent to 5.9 per cent during the same period. It was also observed that while around 82 per cent of the educated men were employed, the corresponding proportion among women was only 71 per cent.

The educated unemployment rate was two and a half times higher among females than among males. Data from the 61st NSSO Round (2004-05) given in Table 4.4 also brings out much lower (than male) work participation rates of females in Kerala, even among the educated.

Table 4.4: Work Participation Rate in Kerala *vis-à-vis* India from 1993 to 2005.

Category	*Kerala*			*All India*		
	1993-94	*1999-2000*	*2004-05*	*1993-94*	*1999-2000*	*2004-05*
Rural male	53.7	55.3	55.9	55.3	53.1	54.6
Rural female	23.8	23.8	25.6	32.8	29.9	32.7
Urban male	55.9	55.8	54.7	52.1	51.8	54.9
Urban female	20.3	20.3	20.0	15.5	13.9	16.6

Source: NSSO Round (2004-05).

The average wage rate in India (for 2005-06) for regular wage/salaried employees was Rs. 138.74 for males and Rs. 87.71 for females (rural) and Rs. 205.81 for the males and Rs. 158.23 for the females (urban) and thus, male-female salary differential was around Rs. 50 in both rural and urban areas.

Women's Autonomy

Autonomy is the right of women to participate in public (political and civil society) as well as private life with an equal share in power and equal involvement in the decision making process. Autonomy in decision making, access to economic resources, mobility etc., are important components of this right. The ability of women to make decisions that affect the circumstances of their own lives is an essential aspect of empowerment. Percentage of women involved in decision making on their own health care and purchase of household assets, percentage of married women who do not require permission to go to the market or visit friends and relatives etc. are the indicators assessing the autonomy of women in decision-making. In decision-making, Kerala has 8th rank for decisions about own health care, 11th rank for decisions about making major household purchases, 13th rank for decisions about making purchases for daily household needs and 9th rank for decisions about visits to her family or relatives.

Poverty Reduction

Poverty is a multi-faceted sorry state of deprivation. Hence, by meeting disadvantage in the lives of the poor, poverty cannot be eradicated or mitigated. Naturally, the un-co-ordinated, income criteria based programmes implemented by different agencies did not come good. Moreover, though the delivery costs of such programmes were exorbitant, they were very much susceptible to under-reporting and manipulations. To accelerate the reduction in poverty and increase in employment, a number of poverty alleviation, employment generation and basic services programmes have been implemented in Kerala. Fully recognizing the centrality of the panchayats in effectively implementing poverty alleviation and most other social sector programmes, Government of India has set-up the Ministry of Panchayati Raj to carry forward the process of empowerment of Panchayati Raj Institutions (PRIs). A number of steps have been taken to devolve functions to PRIs in line with the Constitutional mandate. In Kerala, all these functions are entrusted to the Local Self-Government Department.

Various Phases of Poverty Reduction in Kerala

The poverty reduction strategies developed in Kerala can be divided into three prominent stages (Chathukulam, 2000) as given below:

First Phase: Land reforms, labour laws in favour of the poor and other pro-poor policies of the first communist government since 1957 had reduced poverty to a certain extent. The strategy was to increase the organisational and mobilisation capacity of the poor, which in turn acted as a powerful tool to reduce the incidence of poverty. Moreover, stress was laid on social security measures and public utility services for getting wider access to the poor.

Second Phase: The second phase of poverty reduction was started mainly with the support of financial assistance and policy package from the Centre. All the anti-poverty programmes started in late seventies have two approaches (self-employment approach and wage employment approach). In this phase, the Ministry of Rural Development, Government of India mainly undertook the poverty reduction programmes. In Kerala, as any other State in India, poverty reduction strategies were mainly confined to the administration of centrally sponsored programmes.

Third Phase: With the introduction of the 73rd and 74th Constitutional Amendments, the implementation of the Centrally Sponsored Schemes have been entrusted to the Panchayati Raj and Nagarapalika Institutions (Rural and Urban local bodies). Local bodies are also involved in distributing social security measures like pensions. Under the third phase, a participatory poverty reduction approach had been introduced in the poverty reduction strategies. This has been operationalised through two mechanisms—(1) decentralisation (schemes and programmes for poverty reduction have been decentralised), and (2) State poverty eradication mission (Kudumbashree).

Urban Basic Services for the Poor (UBSP) in Alappuzha Municipality

In 1992, an innovative programme introduced by the Local Administration Department of the Government of Kerala in Alappuzha Municipality was a fresh ray of hope. The programme created hierarchical community groups of urban poor women identified through objective parameters and empowered the groups to take up community based action in various sectors. This was an instant success and was extended to the other urban areas in the State. In 1994, the Government implemented a very ambitious replication of the programme in the whole of Malappuram District.

This anti-poverty programme had been evolved through a long phase of experimentation. The Urban Basic Services for the Poor (UBSP) implemented in Alappuzha Municipality in 1992 focused on a community based and participatory approach to planning and implementing poverty reduction programme. The new experiment took place in the early dawn of 1990s in seven wards of Alappuzha Municipality (1992) to come up with an alternative methodology to identify the poor and to redefine the nature and causes of poverty apart from the conventional methods based on income. The following nine indices were developed which later came to be known as the Alappuzha model.

P1 = Family living in a thatched hut (no *pucca* house)
P2 = Family with illiterate adults
P3 = Family with no or only one employed
P4 = Family with children below five years
P5 = Household with no sanitary facility
P6 = Household with no drinking water facility within 150 meters
P7 = Family with two square meals or less per day
P8 = SC/ST family
P9 = Family with alcoholic/drug addicts

Urban Model—From Seven Wards of Alappuzha Municipality to entire Urban Area of the State

The success of Urban Based Services (UBS)/Urban Basic Services for the Poor (UBSP) prompted the State Government to extend this project to all the Urban Local Bodies of Kerala. On 26th December, 1994, the State Government, through a special order, directed all Urban Local Bodies in the State to set-up Urban Poverty Alleviation Cells and to implement Poverty Alleviation Programmes with community participation as done in Alappuzha and Malappuram. The promise of the initiative prompted Government to pilot the approach in Malappuram district of Kerala, in November 1994 under the Community Based Nutrition Programme (CBNP implemented with UNICEF support). Almost simultaneously universal coverage of the programme was decided upon for urban areas in December 1994.

Rural Model—Malappuram CBNP

On 11th November 1994, a Community Based Nutrition Programme and Poverty Alleviation Project (CBNP & PAP) started functioning under UNICEF assistance with community participation in the entire area of the backward district, Malappuram. 4448 Neighbourhood Groups (NHG) of poor women were formed under this project. They started mobilising thrift, which touched Rs. 2.68 crores in August 2000. They were also able to channel financial assistance from RMK and NABARD. Around 700 NHGs were linked to various commercial banks under the Linkage Banking Programme of NABARD. Implementation of Government programmes for improving health and sanitation in the district was channelled through NHGs. Distribution of applications for old age pension and other social security measures were routed through Community Based Nutrition Programme and Poverty Alleviation Project (CBNP).

State UPA Cell—Urban Expansion Programme

The success of the Alappuzha and Malappuram Models prompted the Government to extend the CDS system to the rest of the towns (57) of Kerala. Most significantly, the bye-laws of the urban CDS were approved by the State Government through a Government Order, signifying official recognition of the CDS as a legitimate body of poor women, empowered to implement poverty eradication programmes and mobilise resources, including loans from financial institutions and other agencies.

People's Plan Campaign—Strengthening of Grass Roots Community Involvement

The big bang decentralization of Kerala came in two bursts in transfer of powers to local governments. First, in October 1995, the decision to transfer most of the development institutions to local governments along with staff was taken and the second in August 1996 the decision to transfer about a third of State Plan resources to local governments was announced and the People's Plan Campaign was launched. Alongside it was decided to universalize the Anti-Poverty Programme of the State under the name of "Kudumbashree". The concept of Kudumbashree sought to match the energy of the self help group movement with the need for a community platform to interface with local self-governments.

Another development, and the most crucial of them all, which led to Kudumbashree being conceived a community based organisation embedded in the local self-government, both rural and urban, was the 1996 People's Plan Campaign (PPC) for democratic decentralisation. The PPC set-up a framework for people's participation in local governance and development through the processes of resource allocation, consultative plan formulation and strengthening of people's participation like the *grama sabha* and the development seminar. The women's component plan and anti-poverty sub-plans helped to increase the access of women and the poor to the local development effort. The neighbourhood group which was meant to be a sub-set of the *grama sabha* morphed into an all woman community structure that got involved in development and social activities way beyond micro-finance. Community participation in *grama sabhas* was sought to be enhanced through the agency of the neighbourhood group. Exclusive women's groups for women capacitating for community participation culminated in Kudumbashree.

The Face of Micro-finance in Kerala—Kudumbashree

Kudumbashree is a multi-faceted women based participatory poverty eradication programme of the Government of Kerala. Kudumbashree was started on 1 April, 1998. It is a partnership between four major actors (Central Government, State Government, Local Bodies and National Bank for Agriculture and Rural Development—NABARD). The objective of the project is to eliminate absolute poverty from the State of Kerala within a decade. It is exclusively focussed on women, women in family and women in community. It is an organization of women from below poverty line. The core activity is women empowerment through micro-finance, micro-enterprise and convergent community action. Kudumbashree stands for organising the poor under a community based organization called Community Development Society (CDS).

Kudumbashree is a government programme for poverty alleviation of women experimented first in an urban setting in Alappuzha, which was later scaled up to selected panchayats. In this scheme woman representatives of all the neighbourhoods in a ward are grouped into an Area Development Society (ADS) chaired by the panchayat member. The ADS of all the wards in a panchayat are federated into a panchayat level development committee chaired by the panchayat president. In other words, this is a programme for poverty alleviation that seeks to bring all poor women organised for micro-credit under the governmental umbrella. Removal of poverty by the year 2007 is the declared goal of this programme. The programme looks upon the NHGs as similar to SHGs oblivious of the different contexts in which they arose.

The programme is a mechanism to bring the SHGs under the government umbrella and to give them access to a package of benefits that come in its wake including financial assistance. One of the panchayat staff is exclusively assigned for this purpose in each panchayat. The intention of this is to bring the SHGs under the regulatory control of the

State, because many of them have come into existence through NGO intervention. There has been resistance on the part of the SHGs created through the mediation of NGOs to such moves for incorporation. The Kudumbashree project is a strategy of the State to appropriate civic space and brings it under administrative surveillance capitalising on the general public faith in government institutions. The Kudumbashree was formally launched on May 18th, 1998. The Kudumbashree network developed across the State in three phases. By March 2002, the entire State was brought under the Kudumbashree network.

In Kerala, State Poverty Eradication Mission implements the Kudumbashree Programme by organizing the poor by creating community based structures of women below poverty line with focus on self-help, demand-led convergence of available services and resources under the leadership of the Local Governments. The key components of the programmes are:

- Enabling certain minimum needs of infrastructure, setting up of micro-enterprises and capacity building of the poor.
- Providing high quality support services for the design and implementation of self-employment ventures.
- Setting up of a challenge fund to support pro-poor policies of the local governments, a technology fund to support transfer of technology relevant for poverty reduction, an innovation fund to support path breaking innovations in poverty reduction and a common revolving fund to provide seed capital for micro-enterprises.
- Generating jobs for educated youth.

The Mission

The mission statement of Kudumbashree is:

> To eradicate absolute poverty in ten years through concerted community action under the leadership of local governments, by facilitating organization of the poor for combining self-help with demand-led convergence of available services and resources to tackle the multiple dimensions and manifestations of poverty, holistically.

Kudumbashree is envisaged as a Mission; also it functions as a process, a project and a delivery mechanism for the poor.

Specific Objectives of Kudumbashree

The specific objectives are:

1. Identification of the poor families through risk indices based surveys, with the active participation of the poor and the communities to which they belong.
2. Empowering the poor women to improve the productivity and managerial capabilities of the community by organizing them into CBOs.
3. Encouraging thrift and investment through credit by developing CDSs to work as informal bank of the poor.
4. Improving incomes of the poor through improved skills and investment for self-employment.
5. Ensuring better health and nutrition for all.
6. Ensuring basic amenities like safe drinking water, sanitary latrines, improved shelter and healthy environment.
7. Ensuring a minimum of five years of primary education for all children, belonging to risk families.
8. Enabling the poor to participate in the decentralization process through the CDS, as it is a subsystem of the local government, under which it works.

To achieve the specific objectives of the Mission, several auxiliary objectives are pursued methodically.

'Kudumbashree' for Social Capital Formation

Launched by the Government of Kerala in 1998 for wiping out absolute poverty from the State through concerted community action under the leadership of Local Self-Governments, Kudumbashree is today one of the largest women-empowering projects in the country. The programme has 37 lakh members and covers more than 50 per cent of the households in Kerala. Built around three critical components—micro-credit, entrepreneurship and empowerment—the Kudumbashree initiative has today succeeded in addressing the basic needs of the less privileged women, thus providing them a more dignified life and a better future. Literal meaning of Kudumbashree is prosperity (Shree) of family (Kudumbam).

Kudumbashree was born of the collective experience gained from the many anti-poverty programmes of the past. Most of the well conceived, centrally planned, rigid, individual-oriented anti-poverty programmes of the Central and State Governments failed to bring about the desired results, mainly because they did not allow for the involvement and commitment of the poor and viewed the poor as "resourceless" receivers of benefits.

Structure of the Organisation

Kudumbashree conceived of poverty as a basket of relative deprivations and vulnerabilities and developed an innovative methodology to identify the poor using non-economic parameters. The poor thus identified were organised under a well networked Community Based Organization (CBO). This methodology has since been incorporated into the policy framework of the State for identification of the poor.

The structure of the organisation has three tiers. Every 20 to 40 women from families under poverty line have a grassroots level association known as neighbourhood groups (NHGs). There are five organisers for every NHG; they are community health volunteer; community infrastructure volunteer; community income generation volunteer; secretary; and president. All the NHGs in a ward (electoral and spatial unit of the local body) are federated to Area Development Society (ADS) and all the ADSs are federated into Community Development Society (CDS) at the respective local body. CDSs have been legally recognised as NGOs, since they are registered under the Charitable Societies Act. As per the latest estimates, there are 1.94 lakhs NHGs, over 17,000 ADSs and 1061 CDSs in Kudumbashree.

The following are the community structures suggested for the rural side:

- Kudumbashree Ayalkoottam or Neighbourhood Group (NHG);
- Kudumbashree Ward Samithy or Area Development Society (ADS); and
- Kudumbashree Panchayat Samithy or Community Development Society (CDS).

Neighbourhood Group (NHG)

NHGs are forums for poor women. It is both a discussion and action group to share concerns, reflect on their State; analyse their situation, discuss issues and options, prioritize their needs and formulate a poverty reduction micro-plan. Plans proposed by NHGs are integrated at ADS level and is known as 'micro-plan'. These micro-plans are integrated at local body level, and is known as 'CDS plan'. The CDS plan is the anti-poverty sub-plan of the village panchayat or municipality. The CDS is empowered to identify beneficiaries of poverty reduction programmes and to take up community contracting of local level development work (Chathukulam, 2000).

For effective convergence of the programme, a three tier Community Based Organisation (CBO) is implemented. The lowest tier constitutes the Neighbourhood Group consisting of 10-20 women members selected from economically backward families. Meetings are convened on a weekly basis in the houses of NHG members. In the weekly meeting, all members bring their thrift, which will be collected and recycled, to the system by way of sanctioning loans. Micro-plans for addressing poverty issues are also prepared after taking stock of the situation. In each Neighbourhood Group from among the poor women five office bearers are selected for undertaking various functional activities:

1. Community Health-Education Volunteer;
2. Income Generation Activities (IGA) Volunteer;
3. Infrastructure Volunteer;
4. Secretary; and
5. President.

The paradigm shift in the approach is that any women who is residing in the Grama Panchayat can become a member of the Kudumbashree Ayalkoottam irrespective of the fact that she belongs to a Below Poverty Line (BPL) Family. Since, this aspect gives an opening for the APL families to enter into the community structures envisaged by Kudumbashree, it is further ensured that majority of the office bearers should belong to BPL families. These structures give added importance to women empowerment, both social and economic.

Area Develcpment Society (ADS)

The second tier is the Area Development Society, which is formed at ward level by federating all the NHGs in the ward. The activities and the decision in the ADS are decided by the representatives of the women elected from various NHGs. The Area Development Society consists of:

1. General Body—consisting of all Presidents, Secretaries and 3 sectoral volunteers of the federated NHGs.
2. Governing Body—consisting of seven member governing body elected from the general body. The seven member governing body consists of ADS chairperson, ADS vice-chairperson, ADS secretary.

The following are the ex-officio members of ADS general body and governing body:

1. ICDS/Anganvadi worker;
2. Saksharatha prerak;
3. Two experienced ex-ADS office bearers; and
4. Local Junior public health nurse.

There is also provision for proportionate representation of SC/ST members in the Committee.

Community Development Society (CDS)

Kudumbashree has organized Community Development Societies (CDSs) which act as a delivery system for the various Centrally Sponsored Urban Poverty Reduction Programmes. The physical and social developments and direct assistance to employment generation are the schemes taken up under these programmes. At the Panchayat/Municipal level, a Community Development Society (CDS), a registered body under the Travancore-Cochin Literacy Scientific and Charitable Societies Act is formed by federating all ADSs in the local bodies. The CDS consists of:

1. *General Body*: It consists of all ADS members and ADS Governing Body members.
2. *Governing Body*: The Governing Body consists of Chairperson, Vice-chairperson, Vice-President, Member-Secretary (Ex-officio member).

The CDS general body and governing body also consists of five women elected representatives and two experienced ex-CDS representatives as ex-officio members.

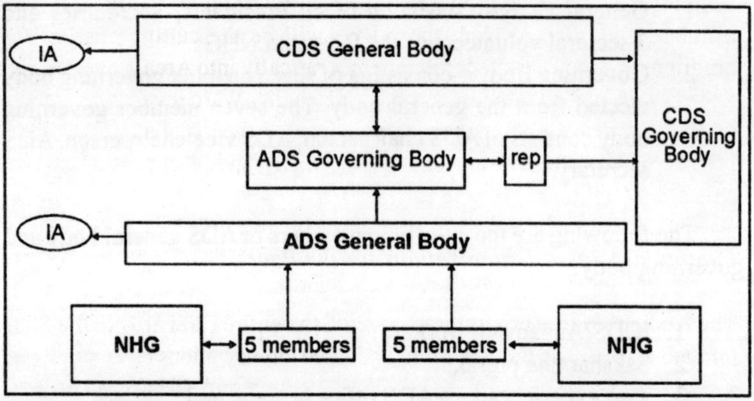

Fig. 4.1: CBO structure

Role of CDS

The CDS is the representative structure of the vast network of NHGs in the Grama Panchayat/Municipal areas. It works in close liaison with the Local Self-Government (LSG) and serves as both dissemination organ for government programmes and as enunciator of community needs in governance issues. A listing of its range of functions is attempted below:

1. LSG liaison at the level of CDS
2. Linkage Banking co-ordination
3. Information Dissemination
4. Community Network Strengthening Activity
5. Facilitating Income Generating Activity
6. Facilitating Identification of the Poor for the purpose of LSG led Development Programmes
7. Articulation of Community Demand for Development
8. Leadership of NHGs
9. LSG Plan Intervention
   - Anti-Poverty Sub-Plan,
   - Women Component Plan,
   - Local Economic Development
10. Legal Literacy

Programmes Undertaken by Kudumbashree

The poor women from identified families are organised into

Neighbourhood Groups (NHGs) representing 15 to 40 families. A five-member team elected from the NHGs will be the cutting edge of the programme. NHGs are federated democratically into Area Development Societies (ADSs) at the Panchayat/Municipality Ward level and then into Community Development Societies (CDSs) at the Panchayat/Municipal level. Their organizational structures will provide opportunities for collective public action.

Community Based Organizations for the Poor

The Kudumbashree programme covered the entire rural area in the State through 1,76,200 NHGs. Community Based Organizations have mobilized a sum of Rs. 940.0550386 crores as thrift fund and disbursed credit to the tune of Rs. 2,503.9394539 crores to their members. The Panchayat functionaries and CDS/ADS office bearers were given training for strengthening the CBOs.

Table 4.5: Community Based Organisation status in Rural Areas as on 30.09.2010

Sl. No.	*District*	*No. of GPs*	*Total NHGs*	*Families Covered (nos.)*	*Thrift (Rs.)*	*Thrift Loans (Rs.)*
1.	Thiruvananthapuram	78	20194	361446	1501419096	3658539664
2.	Kollam	71	12444	228392	889588235	1950223003
3.	Pathanamthitta	54	6753	136746	535537856	868532235
4.	Alappuzha	73	14351	252486	1052249533	2940517724
5.	Kottayam	75	11694	226257	724651960	1400149029
6.	Idukki	52	10840	175285	897969948	2042881733
7.	Eranakulam	88	13991	223909	967134118	4113435398
8.	Thrissur	92	16853	277378	889322513	3738809685
9.	Palakkad	91	20653	351134	1488423320	5963932108
10.	Malappuram	102	16607	340033	1214874855	1889552213
11.	Kozhikkode	78	15816	298844	1397395569	3887898654
12.	Wayanad	25	7837	117155	530213504	1788564016
13.	Kannur	81	12112	218962	856343835	3197848988
14.	Kasargode	39	6827	136075	641276981	2290747776
	Total	**999**	**186972**	**3344102**	**13586401323**	**39731632226**

Source: GoK, 2011.

CBO Strengthening Programmes

Kudumbashree is engaged in the implementation of various poverty eradication programmes and socio-economic developmental programmes of LSGs and Government Departments through community network in addition to Kudumbashree's own programmes. Therefore, it is necessary to augment and improve the Kudumbashree network leaders, office bearers, elected representatives, entrepreneurs, line department officials, resource persons, etc., for a better social engineering and development process. CBO strengthening programmes aim at achieving the annual targets and goals set by the Mission in a time bound manner by sensitizing every member of the community network system about Kudumbashree Programme. District-wise details of community based organization status in rural areas are given in Table 4.5.

Thrift and Credit Societies

Thrift and Credit Societies are set-up at the NHG level to facilitate the poor to save and to avail easy credits, which have now grown up to informal banks of the poor women at their doorsteps. Micro enterprise development which fosters the economic status of women is a powerful tool for poverty eradication. Canteens, catering units, IT units, group farming, units of solar dried fruits, etc. are some examples of micro-enterprise units initiated by the women entrepreneurs of Kudumbashree.

Kudumbashree promotes NHGs of 10 to 20 poor women members as an interface among poor women, banks and government agencies. NHGs are the instrument in thrift mobilization, encouraging the poor to save and to avail low cost formal credit. They facilitate easy and timely credit to the un-reached. The amount of loan to members and the purpose for which the loan should be utilized are decided by the NHGs. The repayment is collected weekly during the NHG meetings. It is estimated that the thrift mobilized is on an average Rs. 40 per month per member. The status of thrift and credit is given in Table 4.6.

Matching Grant to Thrift and Credit Societies

Ten per cent of the savings of the NHG subject to a maximum of Rs. 5000 is given as matching grant to each NHG as incentive to bank linkage for credit. The grant is released on the basis of their assessment rate using a 15 point criteria developed by NABARD. Interest subvention is being proposed, so as to make credit available to Kudumbashree on par with other SHG based organisations in the country. For the year 2008-09, Rs. 250 lakhs has been allotted under matching grant component and Rs. 315.61 lakhs has been spent. The excess amount was met from the surplus fund of previous years.

Table 4.6: District-wise Urban Thrift and Credit Operation as on 31.10.2010

Sl. No.	District	No. of NHG	No. of ADS	No. of CDS	Amount of Thrift (Rs.)	Amount of Loan (Rs.)	No. of families Started Thrift
1.	Thiruvananthapuram	2481	206	6	82551449	75119407	61616
2.	Kollam	1625	145	4	100642748	117351392	38774
3.	Pathanamthitta	427	68	3	19518108	13267100	17420
4.	Alappuzha	1080	102	5	140947331	137221946	33269
5.	Kottayam	449	61	4	27556036	30177349	12855
6.	Idukki	70	10	1	4716805	3653180	2100
7.	Ernakulam	1994	210	10	147062709	251398641	54636
8.	Thrissur	1324	183	7	61962488	99192778	24945
9.	Palakkad	1390	127	4	61456239	122083630	28201
10.	Malappuram	1005	152	5	59928714	48243411	27839
11.	Kozhikode	1400	73	4	56532663	66909817	28220
12.	Wayanad	79	11	1	4216650	4596602	2471
13.	Kannur	666	146	6	28464901	33420139	16588
14.	Kasargode	488	72	2	24181726	15786453	9186
	Total	**14478**	**1566**	**62**	**819738567**	**1018421845**	**358120**

Source: GoK, 2011.

24 Hour Banking System

Enabling women to realize their latent potential, strengthening them through self-help are the main objectives of Kudumbashree. Small savings generated at the families are pooled at various levels as thrift and used to attract credit from banks, which will operate as 24 hour bank for the poor, acting as a sub-system of the formal banks. Kudumbashree promotes Thrift mobilization by setting-up Thrift and Credit Societies at NHG level to encourage the poor to save and to provide them cost-effective and easy credit. Thrift and credit societies facilitate easy and timely credit to the un-reached. The amount of loan and the priority of disbursement are decided by the NHG. The repayment is collected weekly during the routine NHG meetings.

Table 4.7: Status Report of NHGs and Thrift & Credit under Kudumbashree as on March 2009

Sl. No.	District	No. of GPs	No. of NHG	No. of ADS	Families Covered	Families Started Thrift	Thrift (in crores)	Loan (in crores)
1.	Thiruvananthapuram	78	19012	1259	341874	341874	1254979660	2809896700
2.	Kollam	71	12443	1225	228392	228392	776276231	1744022331
3.	Pathanamthitta	54	6715	744	136746	136405	362848988	624894031
4.	Alappuzha	73	13727	1106	269131	269131	975949312	2150827504
5.	Kottayam	75	11122	1151	222691	222680	616540719	1180317906
6.	Idukki	52	9265	750	165949	165919	701607126	1722353347
7.	Ernakulam	88	13373	1352	215042	213513	801640460	2900047381
8.	Thrissur	92	15399	1415	259470	259470	718828496	2978546244
9.	Palakkad	91	20570	1437	349260	349260	1162311989	3085503785
10.	Malappuram	102	15210	1845	339874	339874	953364718	1556929323
11.	Kozhikode	78	14544	1309	298844	295718	1130600864	3075109145
12.	Wayanad	25	7482	434	120248	120248	388330373	1164780103
13.	Kannur	81	11378	1264	215053	215053	763025090	2516567786
14.	Kasargode	39	6031	646	126134	126134	429804458	1762629230
	Total	**999**	**176271**	**15937**	**3288708**	**3283671**	**11036108484**	**29272424816**
15.	Urban (58 ULBs)		13860	1429	355093	355093	659827280	791871377
16.	Tribal NHGs (9 Distt.)		2969		44000	42441	65154565	144941318
	Grand Total		**193100**	**17366**	**3687801**	**3681205**	**11761090329**	**30209237511**

Source: GoK, 2011.

The total thrift collected by NHGs in the State comes to Rs. 1,176 crore and the internal loans generated are to the tune of Rs. 3,020 crore (as of March 2009). For the year 2008-09, the total thrift collected by NHGs is Rs. 172.7 crores and the internal loans generated are Rs. 481 crores respectively.

Informal Banking System

The three-tier community based CDS system, envisaged for poverty alleviation in Kudumbashree approach, will take up the informal banking responsibility also. The poor women should be able to approach the informal banks whenever necessity occurs. The informal banks are formed with the active involvement of every member belonging to the NHG. An Informal Bank does not need an office building, furniture and other paraphernalia which is normally related with a formal bank.

The strength of an informal bank is the intimate relationship among the members of the NHG. The members know other's potential, weaknesses and problems. The members can deposit trifle amount in the thrift scheme of the banks. Informal bank always tried to encourage saving habit among poor women. An informal bank can provide collateral free loans with the terms and conditions decided by the group. The NHG behind the informal bank is free to fix market driven rates of interest for advances. Every operation of an informal bank takes place in the group level, including depositing of thrift amounts and sanctioning of thrift loans. The groups itself decide the eligibility of a member to get assistance from the bank after discussions and assessment of the need and repayment capacity.

The very existence of an Informal Bank brings about the homogeneity and affinity among members of the poor. Thrift savings of the members serve as the main bondage among members. The bank promotes regularity in savings and assures sufficient frequency for group meetings. The informal banks will instil collective decision-making capability among the poor women. This sublime quality will be of great support to them for their fight against poverty and their participation in planning process and economic development activities. Informal banks will slowly do away with the subsidy syndrome prevailing in the lowest stratum of the society. The poor women will begin to enjoy the unique pleasure of doing things with their own money. The financial empowerment of women achieved through thrift and bank accessibility will improve their status in their own families and society. Naturally, their confidence will increase. Above all, Informal Banks provide loans to the poor women at their own doorsteps without any hassle.

Once, the informal banks of the NHGs, ADSs and CDS reach a certain level of maturity, they can grant loans to the members for genuine needs. The poor need financial assistance for several purposes, falling under four major categories.

Linkage Banking

The Linkage Banking Programme was launched during 2002-2003 after proper grading of the NHGs as per NABARD norms. Up to September 2010, 1,22,877 NHGs were linked with banks. A sum of Rs. 1,08,294.71 lakhs has been made available to the NHGs as loan. The Bank Linkage Programme has helped NHGs to augment their existing resources collected through thrift. The efficiency and effectiveness of the NHGs are verified on the basis of some objectively verifiable and easily identifiable parameters.

Table 4.8: District-wise details of Linkage Banking as on 30.09.2010 (Linkage)

Sl. No.	*District*	*Cumulative*	
		NHGs linked	*Amount (₹ Lakh)*
1.	Thiruvananthapuram	14227	12081.34
2.	Kollam	11863	11972.14
3.	Pathanamthitta	3455	4670.27
4.	Alappuzha	13321	10876.02
5.	Kottayam	5757	5286.03
6.	Idukki	7773	13243.49
7.	Ernakulam	11875	6864.38
8.	Thrissur	10020	8714.10
9.	Palakkad	14806	10784.35
10.	Malappuram	6532	3247.35
11.	Kozhikode	7703	4727.56
12.	Wayanad	5991	6850.67
13.	Kannur	4988	6376.26
14.	Kasargode	4566	2600.75
	Total	**122877**	**108294.71**

Source: GoK, 2011.

NABARD has developed a 15-point index for rating NHGs on the basis of which they will be allowed to link with various banks under the Linkage Banking Scheme (Appendix III).

Table 4.9: Linkage Banking: Target and Achievement as on September, 2008

Sl. No.	*Name of District*	*NHGs Graded (Nos.)*	*NHGs Linked (Nos.)*	*Loan Disbursed (Rs. in Lakhs)*
1.	Thiruvananthapuram	13603	10969	8277.59
2.	Kollam	10216	9318	7115.48
3.	Pathanamthitta	4451	2697	3858.58
4.	Alappuzha	10277	10204	5916.12
5.	Kottayam	4641	4395	3080.67
6.	Idukki	5478	5333	5466.26
7.	Ernakulam	11219	9847	4992.98
8.	Thrissur	8574	7982	5116.54
9.	Palakkad	14984	12424	6457.00
10.	Malappuram	5558	5095	2080.80
11.	Kozhikode	10652	6174	4122.48
12.	Wayanad	7330	6755	4750.08
13.	Kannur	8345	1913	1518.78
14.	Kasaragode	4414	3224	1735.73
	Total	**119742**	**96330**	**64489.09**

Note: NHG—Bank linkage scheme is one of the flagship programmes of Kudumbashree. NHGs graded and linked has been presented in Table 4.9.

Source: GoK, 2011.

Micro-Finance Campaign

An Micro-Finance Campaign was conducted during April-May, 2008. The campaign brought together elected representatives of LSGs, banking officials, district mission officers and CDS members and provided forum for free and open discussions. ADS level discussions and reporting preceded the workshops conducted at panchayat and district levels.

The Micro-finance campaign focused on two areas—improvement in linkage banking and stabilization of *Bhavanashree* operations. The focus on linkage banking was to smoothen coordination with the banking system and to enhance the availability of affordable credit to the poor. *Bhavanashree* operations needed stabilization because the institutional gap in systems, guidelines and internal monitoring mechanisms had created sizeable problems in some areas. Operational guidelines of *Bhavanashree* were framed and monitoring made more sustained.

Facilitation of Centrally Sponsored Schemes

The State Poverty Eradication Mission is the State Level Nodal Agency for the implementation of major centrally sponsored Urban Poverty Reduction Programmes *viz.* Swarna Jayanthi Shahari Rozgar Yojana (SJSRY), Integrated Housing and Slum Development Programme (IHSDP) and Basic Services to the Urban Poor (BSUP). Table 4.10 shows programmes and schemes introduced and implemented under the initiative of the Kudumbashree.

Table 4.10: SJSRY-Status as on February 2008

	Fund Release	*Expenditure*
Unspent Balance of old UPA Programmes	863.700	—
1997-98	270.652	1070.930
1998-99	502.790	549.330
1999-2000	597.757	472.730
2000-2001	386.320	459.353
2001-2002	354.973	406.932
2002-2003	451.990	451.991
2003-2004	983.637	872.750
2004-2005	739.933	739.933
2005-2006	908.355	908.355
2006-2007	852.293	—
Total	**6912.400**	**5932.304**

Source: GoK, 2011.

Swarna Jayanthi Shahari Rozgar Yojana (SJSRY)

SJSRY is an ongoing centrally sponsored anti-poverty programme. It is shared 75:25 basis by both Central and State Governments. The scheme aims at reducing poverty from urban areas through self-employment programmes. The programme is being implemented at the Urban Local Body level through the Community Based Organizations (CBOs) of the poor (Table 4.10). Identification of beneficiaries, selection of projects for micro-enterprises, preparation of applications, implementation, monitoring, social audit, etc. are done through the Community Development Society (CDS) system of the respective Urban Local Bodies (ULB). The Special Livelihood Projects of Kudumbashree have been implemented under the aegis of SJSRY.

Integrated Housing and Slum Development Programme (IHSDP)

The IHSDP of the Government of India targets the poor living conditions of slums and clusters in cities and towns, and attempts to improve the housing stock and basic infrastructure and coverage service delivery to the poor. The programme runs on a project mode. 37 IHSDP projects worth Rs. 188 crore are operational in Kerala. Kudumbashree is the State Level Nodal Agency for the programme.

Basic Services to the Urban Poor (BSUP)

The Basic Service to the Urban Poor Programme is a centrally sponsored scheme tackling the suboptimal living conditions of the urban poor in the 54 mission cities (cities with over 1 million population, and cities housing the State capitals). It is a sub-project of the Jawaharlal Nehru National Urban Renewal Mission (JNNURM).

Table 4.11: Details of projects under BSUP-Thiruvananthapuram Corporation from 2006 to 2009

Sl. No.	*Project Components*	*Phase-wise split up*				*Total*
		I Phase (2006-07)	*II Phase (2006-07)*	*III Phase (2007-08)*	*IV Phase (2008-09)*	
1.	New Housing	218.71	3422.69	10628.95	2504.57	16774.92
2.	Housing Upgradation	26.75	0.00	0.00	83.50	110.25
3.	Community facilities	61.00	50.78	594.37	538.33	1244.48
4.	Roads	19.47	41.69	437.39	150.58	649.13
5.	Solid Waste Management	3.80	1.91	48.51	47.31	101.53
6.	Storm Water Drains	152.70	113.27	330.14	23.88	619.99
7.	Electrification	1.96	6.50	16.11	11.09	35.66
8.	Retaining wall	7.80	0.00	0.00	347.84	355.64
9.	Sewerage	2.75	9.14	2.31	81.03	95.23
10.	Water Supply	8.30	64.13	416.55	99.86	588.84
11.	Retaining wall/land scaping/others	0.00	19.29	112.45	67.21	198.95
	Total	**503.24**	**3729.40**	**12586.78**	**3955.20**	**20774.62**

Source: GoK, 2011.

The Kochi and Thiruvananthapuram urban agglomerations have been included as mission cities of JNNURM and their expenditure are given in Tables 4.11 and 4.12.

Table 4.12: Details of projects under BSUP-Cochin Corporation from 2006 to 2008

Sl. No.	*Project Components*	*Phase-wise split up*			*Total*
		I Phase (2006-07)	*II Phase (2006-07)*	*III Phase (2007-08)*	
1.	New Housing	72.02	60.83	33.8	12323.87
2.	Housing Upgradation	99.68	0	48.27	147.95
3.	Community facilities	26.7	54.15	25.6	106.45
4.	Roads	32.04	15.83	8.86	56.73
5.	Solid Waste Management	72.02	60.83	33.8	166.65
6.	Storm Water Drains	1.48	5.58	1.47	8.53
7.	Electrification	12.89	27.01	1.06	40.96
8.	Community Building	325.66	0	0.00	325.66
9.	Sewerage	83.03	75.87	41.21	200.11
10.	Water Supply	0	55.21	77.20	132.41
11.	Sanitation	0	0	56.84	56.84
	Total	**2661.24**	**10444.93**	**459.99**	**13566.16**

Source: GoK, 2011.

Better Living Conditions—Infrastructural Facilities

The needs identified at NHG level are shaped as micro-plans which are integrated into mini plans at ADS level and action plan at CDS level. This will be the anti-poverty sub-plan of the local body and this will facilitate convergent delivery of Government programmes meant for the poor. Kudumbashree promote self-help approach for building houses, latrines, access to drinking water, sanitary facilities etc., availing the minimum support from Government. Common infrastructural facilities in the community strengthen them further.

Power to the People Especially the Poor Women

The skill for identification of needs, fixing priorities, availing resources, bridging gap between needs and resources in a cost-effective manner etc., are taught to the poor women groups in various phases. In the decentralization of power to the local bodies and common man, Kudumbashree can act as a healthy sub-system facilitating participation of poor women in the planning, implementation and monitoring of the programme.

Leadership—Decision-Making Power

Interaction in women collectives will help them to have a better understanding, which will lead to the emergence of leadership. This will help to ensure efficient women leadership to elected governments in future.

Bala Sabha

Bala Sabha is a programme to organize the children of the poor families of the State as part of its approach to community development. The larger goal is recognizing and protecting child rights. Bala Panchayats have been formed in 998 Grama Panchayats with the support of UNICEF to support the children who hail from poor socio-economic background to have voice and visibility in the society. During 2004-05, *Bala Sabha* which intends to prevent intergenerational transmission of poverty, has been extended to the rural area also. The total number of *Bala Sabhas* formed is 49,423 with 8,46,875 children as members (Table 4.13). Bala Panchayats are apex level body of *Bala sabhas* in panchayats.

Strengthening of Bala Sabha/Bala Panchayat and Holistic Child Health Activities

Bala Sabhas are structured as grassroot level neighbourhood network of children in LSGs. The Mission organizes the children of poor families into *Bala Sabhas* as a part of its holistic approach to community development. Cultivating creative potential in children, by providing opportunities to express, learn and develop, identifying and nurturing innate talent, leads to the larger goal of recognition and protection of child rights. Each *Bala Sabha* consists of 15 to 30 children in the age group of five to fifteen years. The prime objective of constituting *Bala Sabha* is to prevent intergenerational transmission of poverty through capability enhancement of children. Bala panchayats are apex level body of *Bala Sabhas* in Panchayats. Kudumbashree has completed the formation of 51,086 *Bala Sabhas* across the State with membership of 8,85,301 children.

IT Enabled Services to the Poor

An innovative component in the Destitute Identification Rehabilitation and Monitoring project is an online monitoring system. As per the project,

Table 4.13: District-wise details of *Bala Sabha*—Children's NHG as on 30.09.2010

Sl. No.	District	No. of Gramapanchayat	No. of Bala Panchayats formed	2009		2010-11 (as on Sept. 2010)		Cumulative	
				No. of Bala Sabha	No. of Children	No. of Bala Sabha	No. of Children	No. of Bala Sabha	No. of Children
1.	Thiruvananthapuram	78	59	5896	94684	4	56	5900	94740
2.	Kollam	71	61	2264	46100	12	145	2276	46245
3.	Pathanamthitta	54	50	2216	38843	150	1304	2366	40147
4.	Alappuzha	73	72	4416	67487	196	3487	4612	70974
5.	Kottayam	75	48	3222	56967	51	430	3273	57397
6.	Idukki	52	46	2271	38630	6	126	2277	38756
7.	Eranakulam	88	87	4604	77437	611	17719	5215	95156
8.	Thrissur	91	46	1885	32331	401	11228	2286	43559
9.	Palakkad	91	66	4134	72120	51	918	4185	73038
10.	Malappuram	102	48	5905	111645	5	78	5910	111723
11.	Kozhikode	78	78	4848	85223	62	992	4910	86215
12.	Wayanad	25	17	2467	32835	3	51	2470	32886
13.	Kannur	81	81	2961	48423	58	1044	3019	49467
14.	Kasargode	39	39	2334	44150	53	848	2387	44998
	Total	**998**	**798**	**49423**	**846875**	**1663**	**38426**	**51086**	**885301**

Source: Kudumbashree, Government of Kerala.

* Bala Panchayats are apex level body of *Bala Sabhas* in Panchayats.

the CDS Office will be computerized in Panchayats where the destitute rehabilitation project is taken up for the benefit of the poor.

Gender Self-Learning Programme (GSLP)

Gender self-learning programme of Kudumbashree is a product of the improvisation of the strategies for both economic and social empowerment. It initiates capacity to fill the gap so as to achieve equity, equality, recognition, claim on governance, awareness on Domestic Violence Act, rights in decision-making process, and to induce ownership of assets through Kudumbashree networks. The process of gender self learning is routed through the larger networks of selected resource persons.

Kudumbashree serves as the pioneer organizational set-up to mobilize and equip women for poverty eradication through economic empowerment. Gender Self-Learning Programme is an outcome of the improvisation of the strategies for both economic and social empowerment. Gender Self-Learning modules are prepared by a participatory process and implemented through larger networks of women resource persons. The experiential learning of women is to be documented and analyzed for working further gender empowerment interventions and it addresses specific issues.

Bhavanashree

The micro-housing loan scheme for the poor called "*Bhavanashree*" was designed by Kudumbashree to meet the housing needs of the poor. Since, the start of the scheme, an amount of Rs. 18,622 lakhs has been disbursed by various banks under the *Bhavanashree* programme. An amount of Rs. 1,067 lakhs was disbursed and 2,405 houses were completed under *Bhavanashree* during the year 2008-09.

Ashraya

Ashraya, a sub-programme of Kudumbashree, is the first integrated programme for tackling the poorest of the poor who live at the margins of the economy, society and polity without a voice or the power of choice, with no capabilities to access entitlements—the really 'excluded'. It originated from the realization that even in a State like Kerala, the benefits of anti-poverty policies and programmes do not reach the absolutely poor, who constitute only about two per cent of the population. As of now, there are no schemes akin to *Ashraya* in India targeting the poorest of the poor. Thus, *Ashraya* is a pioneer, developing a model, which can be adapted by the rest of the country

Participation of Vulnerable Group

The modified bye-law provides for ensuring proportionate representation of the SC and ST communities as well as for special Area Development Societies (ADSs) to cater to the requirement of specific vulnerable groups.

Micro-enterprises

Kudumbashree views Micro-Enterprise development as an important tool for poverty reduction. When the concept of developing enterprises by poor women was planned in 1999, the response from various stakeholders including banks was far from encouraging. The previous experience of failures in group enterprises under various government programmes, perceived lack of entrepreneurial abilities of the poor and apathy of banks in associating with ventures of the poor were the prime reasons for this unfavourable environment.

Kudumbashree, from its very inception, has promoted micro-enterprises as a means of livelihood for the poor women both in the rural and urban areas under various Government schemes. Kudumbashree regularly sets-up monthly markets in each district on specified days and venues. The entrepreneurs are given opportunity to bring their products and efforts at standardization of product quality and presentation by entrepreneurs. Also, as part of its market development strategy, Kudumbashree exploits the opportunity of the Onam festival, by conducting State-wide Onam fairs.

The emphasis in the Kudumbashree enterprise programme was to encourage innovative business ideas rather than on the "tried and tested" ones. A simple and practical way for identifying enterprises was devised; any idea that could solve a problem existing in the society (Problem Solving), fill the gap that existed (Gap Filling) or cater to new opportunity (Emerging Opportunities) was converted into an enterprise. The fact that most of the entrepreneurs were first generation entrepreneurs from their families was kept in mind while implementing the Rural Micro-enterprises (RME) programme. The micro-enterprise development was seen as an emerging process, which will start with low capital, low risk and low profit in the initial stage that will gain momentum and later scale up to greater capital, risk and profit.

Providing skill upgradation trainings, self-employment opportunities and infrastructural development through wage employment schemes are the preparing grounds for further development of successful micro-enterprises. Kudumbashree is bent on giving necessary resource support and it facilitates forward/backward linkages, etc., to promote micro-entrepreneurship among poor women.

But the most crucial factor was the lack of any successful enterprises model, which was worth emulating. The task for Kudumbashree was simple and challenging, to create a model for enterprise development. Kudumbashree went about creating a model, and the results are for everyone to see. 18,969 enterprises across the State covering urban and rural areas, ranging from "traditional" enterprises like Goat rearing and Dairy, Catering units, Multi-Purpose job clubs, Health care enterprises, Computer hardware and data entry units, innovative enterprises like Clean Kerala Business in solid waste collection are a testimony to the resolve of women to succeed in enterprises.

The definition of Micro-Enterprise according to Kudumbashree is that, any enterprise that has:

- Investment ranging from Rs. 5,000 to Rs. 2.5 lakhs.
- Turnover ranging from Rs. 1 lakh to Rs. 10 lakhs.
- Potential to generate a net income of at least Rs. 1,500 per member per month.
- Fully owned, managed and operated by members themselves.

There are some common features in the funding of the various enterprise programmes. All Kudumbashree enterprises are bank linked and a minimum of 50 per cent of the project cost has to be through bank loans. The subsidy component is limited to 50 per cent of the total project cost and the entrepreneurs' share is to the tune of five per cent of the total project cost.

The district-wise details of micro-enterprise programmes, especially the status of group enterprises are given in Table 4.14.

Micro-Enterprises in Rural Areas

The State budget provides support to set-up micro-enterprises of women. It has been set-up in the pattern of the SGSY. So far 4,492 groups of

Table 4.14: District-wise details of Micro-Enterprises Programme—Status of Group Enterprises as on 30.09.2010

Sl. No.	District	2009-2010		2010-2011 (as on 30.9.2010)	
		No. of enterprises	Subsidy (Rs.)	No. of enterprises	Subsidy (Rs.)
1.	Thiruvananthapuram	432	25292500	126	14213750
2.	Kollam	149	7920000	30	700000
3.	Pathanamthitta	86	4382500	48	2512500
4.	Alappuzha	767	39125000	103	10430000
5.	Kottayam	159	8561625	15	337500
6.	Idukki	298	17860000	51	7325000
7.	Eranakulam	1095	57487650	12	3110000
8.	Thrissur	174	9075000	30	5340000
9.	Palakkad	144	20010000	18	760000
10.	Malappuram	352	19305000	202	10807500
11.	Kozhikkode	372	8093500	10	975000
12.	Wayanad	233	3730000	17	920000
13.	Kannur	162	12357250	55	3442500
14.	Kasargode	69	8690000	7	160000
	Total	**4492**	**241890025**	**724**	**61033750**

Source: GoK, 2011.

micro-enterprises of women (Table 4.15) have been set-up in the rural areas as on 30.09.2010. The activities are diverse and innovative in nature.

Kudumbashree has identified Micro-enterprise as a means for economic empowerment and employment opportunity to the poor women, with a view to reduce poverty. An amount of Rs. 16.04 lakh has been provided as subsidy to 215 individual enterprises and an amount of Rs. 610.34 lakh has been provided as subsidy to 724 group enterprises.

Market Interventions of Kudumbashree

Kudumbashree from its very beginning promoted micro-enterprises a means of livelihood for the poor women both in the rural and urban areas under various Government schemes. Kudumbashree decided to set-up monthly markets in each district on specified days and venue. The entrepreneurs are given opportunity to bring their products and efforts at standardization of product quality and presentation by entrepreneurs. 222 monthly markets were held from October, 2007 to July, 2008 and had a turnover of Rs. 1,92,06,804.

Table 4.15: District-wise details of Micro-Enterprises Programme—Status of Individual Enterprises as on 30.09.2010

Sl. No.	*District*	*2009-2010*		*2010-2011 (as on 30.9.2010)*	
		No. of enterprises	*Subsidy (Rs.)*	*No. of enterprises*	*Subsidy (Rs.)*
1.	Thiruvananthapuram	34	255000	21	152500
2.	Kollam	28	210000	14	105000
3.	Pathanamthitta	3	21000	0	0
4.	Alappuzha	40	300000	10	75000
5.	Kottayam	19	142500	0	0
6.	Idukki	105	787750	20	150000
7.	Eranakulam	14	105000	9	65000
8.	Thrissur	57	427500	50	375000
9.	Palakkad	327	2452500	34	255000
10.	Malappuram	227	1697500	0	0
11.	Kozhikode	145	1087500	12	88500
12.	Wayanad	2	15000	0	0
13.	Kannur	35	261300	30	225000
14.	Kasargode	140	1049500	15	112500
	Total	1176	8812050	215	1603500

Source: GoK, 2011.

Kudumbashree as part of its market development strategy exploited the opportunity of Onam festival, by conducting Onam fairs State wide during September 2008. A total 367 number of fairs were conducted all-over the State at District/Block/Taluk/Municipal/Grama Panchayat levels. The total turnover of the fairs which was really '*Janakiya Vilpanamela*' was Rs. 2,45,24,237.

More Information/Training

Weekly meetings of NHGs, sharing of experiences, discussions, organised/unorganized trainings etc., will broaden their outlook on better health, better education, better social and economic status.

Skill Upgradation Training

To facilitate economic development, suitable skill upgradation trainings will be given to women.

Table 4.16: List of Micro-Enterprises (District-wise) as on October, 2010

Sl. No.	Name of District	DWCUA	USEP
1.	Thiruvananthapuram	458	3320
2.	Kollam	119	2007
3.	Pathanamthitta	41	1164
4.	Alappuzha	196	2977
5.	Kottayam	105	1304
6.	Idukki	17	139
7.	Eranakulam	609	3729
8.	Thrissur	253	1747
9.	Palakkad	137	2588
10.	Malappuram	127	1330
11.	Kozhikode	201	2264
12.	Wayanad	21	162
13.	Kannur	202	2350
14.	Kasargode	61	995
	Total	2547	26076

Source: GoK, 2011.

Lease Land Farming

The Lease Land Farming programme, initiated in the rural areas during the year 2002-03, has been successfully extended to 855 Grama Panchayats. Through this programme 67,655.2 acres of land have been brought under cultivation.

Collective farming is one of the major initiatives undertaken by Kudumbashree to enhance livelihood of the poor families in NHGs by utilizing mainly fallow lands. In turn this results in increased agricultural production. Based on the NABARD JLG concept and guidelines, these groups are organized as joint liability groups from 2010. The area and production incentives under this programme are directly provided to the groups. Lease land farming programme was initiated in the rural areas during the year 2002-03. This programme has been extended to 855 Grama Panchayats benefiting 2,32,220 families through 46,444 NHGs. Through this programme, 67,655.20 acres of waste land have been brought under cultivation. The district-wise details of lease land farming as on September, 2010 is shown in Table 4.17.

Table 4.17: District-wise details of Lease Land Farming as on 30.09.2010

Sl. No.	*District*	*No. of GPs*	*No. of NHGs*	*Covered families*	*Area in acres*
1.	Thiruvananthapuram	55	1773	8865	6652.00
2.	Kollam	71	1204	6020	1093.40
3.	Pathanamthitta	49	2872	14360	617.50
4.	Alappuzha	69	2504	12520	1121.30
5.	Kottayam	68	1773	8865	2688.80
6.	Idukki	48	9805	49025	20313.00
7.	Ernakulam	80	3988	19940	5265.00
8.	Thrissur	55	4979	24895	2440.20
9.	Palakkad	72	3812	19060	3255.00
10.	Malappuram	81	5004	25020	8701.50
11.	Kozhikode	69	2090	10450	2928.80
12.	Wayanad	24	1316	6580	4619.50
13.	Kannur	75	2308	11540	6540.00
14.	Kasargode	39	3016	15080	1419.20
	Total	**855**	**46444**	**232220**	**67655.20**

Source: GoK, 2011.

Achievements: An Encouraging Signal for the State

In contrast to the previous poverty eradication programmes there are no specific financial and physical targets set for Kudumbashree. In Kudumbashree, we practice a process approach and not a project approach. For effective monitoring of the programme, the following milestones are adopted:

- The largest women movement in Asia with a membership of 36 lakhs representing equal number of families.
- 36 lakh poor families brought under the community based organisations (CBOs) consisting of 1.87 lakh Neighbourhood Groups (NHG), 17,000 Area Development Societies (ADSs) and 1,058 Community Development Societies (CDSs) rural and urban.
- Mobilized a sum of Rs. 1,105 crores as thrift and disbursed loans amounting to Rs. 2,818 crores to the members of Neighbourhood Groups.
- 1,14,761 NHGs were graded under Linkage Banking Programme, out of which 96,330 NHGs were linked with banks and an amount of Rs. 645 crores mobilised as credit.

- 25,050 individual enterprises and 1,757 group (with minimum 10 members) enterprises of women were developed in urban areas.
- 1,430 individual enterprises and 4,578 group (with minimum 10 members) enterprises of the poor women were formed in rural areas.
- 2,55,270 families participated in lease land farming and 63,560 acres (257.2 km^2) of land were brought under cultivation.
- 376 group enterprises and 319 individual enterprises were started under the Special Employment Programme (*Yuvashree*).
- *Ashraya*—Destitute identification and Rehabilitation Project was implemented in 745 Local Self-Governments and 58,389 destitutes identified.
- 44,586 houses were constructed under the *Bhavanashree* housing loan scheme (without subsidy) for the poor in rural areas.
- 235 entrepreneur groups (Thelima) were formed for the municipal solid waste management in urban areas.
- 'Buds'-10 special schools for physically and mentally challenged children were set-up under the leadership of the Local Self-Government.
- 45,262 *Bala Sabhas* (Children's Neighbourhood Groups) with 7.9 lakh children were formed in urban and rural areas.
- Formation of 1.87 lakh NHGs all over Kerala.
- Formation of 17,000 ADSs at Ward level.
- Formation of 1,058 CDSs at Panchayat/Municipality/ Corporation level by federating various ADSs.
- Linking at least 20 per cent of NHGs with NABARD's scheme for linkage banking every year.
- Aim to provide shelter to all poor.
- Aim to provide safe drinking water within 300 meters of their residence.
- Aim to provide sanitation facility in all the families within next five years.
- Aim to establish at least one sustainable micro-enterprise in each NHG leading to large-scale employment.
- Aim to establish an Informal Bank of Women in the model of Bangladesh Grameen Bank.
- Implementation of special package programme for the development of SC/ST and traditional fishermen.

Kudumbashree covers 991 panchayats and 58 municipalities. Through this network women have the freedom to demand, and to receive money without red tape. Abraham and Johnnykutty (2006) conducted a study on the viability of Kudumbashree in Kerala. They found that Kudumbashree movement has promoted women empowerment and improved situation of the poor families. This project has evolved a new strategy in Kerala that enables the successful operationalisation of anti-poverty programmes by the poor themselves. It offered ample opportunities to the poor, who are neglected by the formal banking sector, to avail of financial services in the form of thrift and credit and promoted economic empowerment of the poor women. Through their involvement in the activities of the project, their social and political empowerment is also ensured.

5
Outlier Communities of Kerala Society

Study Area

> "We live in a most diverse country, and in many spheres our records are extremely disparate. In respect of certain variables like average levels of literacy, life expectancy, infant mortality etc. conditions in India are enormously adverse compared with China, and yet in all these respects, Kerala does significantly better than China."
>
> (*Amartya Sen* while delivering the first D.T. Lakdawala Memorial Lecture entitled 'Markets, Social Opportunities and Economic Development' in June 1994)

Kerala is a small State in the southern part of India. But it has gained international acclaim due to its development experience during the second half of the twentieth century. The basic characteristic of Kerala's experience is that it has gained high levels of social development despite low levels of per capita income. In Kerala, 96 per cent of the males and 92 per cent of females are literate. The corresponding figures for all-India are 82.2 per cent and 65.46 per cent for men and women respectively. The sex ratio in Kerala (1084/1000 males in 2001) is higher than that of most countries in South Asia. The infant mortality rate is also one among the lowest in the country with 12 per 1000 live births. The female life expectancy of 73.62 years is the highest among all the Indian States. The male life expectancy stood at 71 years which is two and a half years lesser than women's.

In the present chapter, an attempt is made to look into the status of outlier communities in Kerala by way of different districts of the State. In the first section, the significance of Kerala model of development in the context of marginalisation of the vulnerable sections of the society is made. In the subsequent sections, a discussion was held on the districts of Alappuzha, Idukki, Kozhikode, Malappuram, Thiruvananthapuram and Wayanad, which have been selected for the survey as a representation of the outlier communities such as agricultural labourers, plantation workers, marine fisherfolk, Muslim population, urban poor and tribal population respectively.

The Kerala Model: Its Central Tendency

The State of Kerala has been highlighted by its positive achievements in health, education and standard of living. The public action which took place in the State has been cited as the major factor in its achieving a relatively high quality of life despite relative economic backwardness. While elaborating on the 'Kerala Model', Sen pointed out that "there are great many things we can learn from within the country by using the diversity of our experiences, particularly in the use of public action-involving the public itself as well as the government. Despite the fact that economic growth of Kerala has been sluggish, it has been able to achieve tremendous results in important areas such as literacy, life expectancy and mortality rates. The existence of a paradox—high human development and low economic development—is visible in the entire State of Kerala, and is often dubbed as the *Kerala phenomenon* or the *Kerala Model* of development. When people allude to the 'Kerala Model', they refer to the 'average' situation. The much referred work of Centre for Development Studies (CDS) on Kerala model of development too emphasized the central tendency of the distribution of the indicators to establish the point. However, as in all distributions, the 'Kerala Model' also has its 'outliers'—communities that seem to have been left out of the domain of public action."

The history behind the statistics of the 'Kerala Model' is replete with a wide variety of forms of public action. These start intensively from the era of British colonialism in India had its influences on the region which presently constitutes Kerala State. The reform movements among many of the lower castes and communities were matched by actions of the native rulers of the region who responded to these demands by providing basic social services to a wider section of the population.

The Maharani of Travancore declared thus in 1817: "the State shall defray the entire cost of the education of its people in order that there may be no backwardness in the spread of enlightenment among them, that by the diffusion of education they become better subjects and public servants". Later in 1865, the Maharaja of Travancore made the following statement at the opening of the Trivandrum civil hospital, "I take this opportunity earnestly to impress this fact on the minds of all my native subjects and to urge them to seek for themselves, for their children, for their friends and their servants the great protection of vaccination. They will see the strength of my conviction in the fact that there is no member in my family who has not had this protection conferred at an early age". These two pronouncements show that the rulers of pre-independent Kerala, at least in the parts ruled over by native princes, had made valuable contributions in the field of social development. The social movements led by various community leaders laid the foundation for the emergence of more secular movements along class lines among the peasants and workers which were led by radicals with leftist leanings. In the post-independence period this led to the creation of political history when the world's first democratically elected communist government came to power in Kerala State in 1957. The public action measures which this government initiated in the agrarian sector were land reforms, abolition of tenancy and granting of homestead rights.

Marginalized and Vulnerable

As the economy grows, certain sections of the society get naturally marginalized. They are left out of the mainstream economic development and social reform agenda. In the case of Kerala, even though the State is much forward in the area of social development, some of the social and economic groups are still found as outliers in the society. From the available evidences, it is found that the Kerala society has its outliers all over the State. Some of them are marginalized historically (for example, the SC/ST population), some others are marginalized culturally or religiously (for example, the Muslim population), some others locationally (for example, the urban poor in the slums), and yet others are occupationally (plantation workers). The overriding peculiarity of these people would be underlying poor economic and social status. The backwardness in social arena makes them economically stagnant or vulnerable too. The type of work assigned to these people by the society, wages given to them, public utility services rendered to them are accentuating their status.

Fig. 5.1: Political Map of Kerala.

Kerala, a State renowned for social sector development witnessed the emergence of several margnialised sections. They live in remote places (the mountainous tracts, protected forest areas), make a livelihood from nature (fisher folk) and so they are open to the vagaries of the nature for their livelihood. Resourcelessness is their major problem. The ownership of land would be a problem for many of them. The land ownership issues prevailing among tribal, plantation workers, marine fisher folk and alienation from their present dwellings are the major problems faced by them. Lack of assets such as physical, social, human, financial and economic make them more vulnerable.

The advent of Globalization, Liberalization and Privatization (GLP) has a major impact on the economy. Indian economy is showing a robust growth, but the faceless teeming population has been forgotten due to various reasons. Withdrawal of State machinery from various social sectors like education, health and infrastructural development has an adverse impact on these people.

Alappuzha

Alappuzha district is located at 9.54°N 76.40°E. Alappuzha covers an area of 1,414 square kilometres (546 sq mi) and is flanked by 2,195 square kilometres (847 sq mi) of Vembanad Lake, where one can witness a magnificent union of six major rivers which spread out extensively before joining the 80 km coast line of the district.

Demographics

According to 2011 Census, Alappuzha district has a population of 21,21,943 with 10,10,252 men and 1,111,691 women with a population density of 1492 persons per km^2. There are 1,86,022 persons under six years of age in Alappuzha district. The literacy rate of Alappuzha stands at 96.26 per cent out of which 895,476 are males and 9,68,082 are females. Alappuzha has a decadal population growth of 0.61 per cent. Alappuzha has a sex ratio of 1,100.

Table 5.1: Basic facts on Alappuzha

Area (in sq.km)	1,414
Population	21,21,943
Males	10,10,252
Females	11,11,691
Sex ratio: Females/1000	1,100
Density of Population	1,492
Literacy rate	96.26%; Male 96.27%; Female 90.82%

Economy

The economy of the district is predominantly based on agriculture and marine products. Though the district is industrially backward, some traditional industries based on coir and coir products, marine products, handlooms, different types of handicrafts, toddy tapping, have been dominating the scene from the very early times. The district is known as the traditional home of coir industry in Kerala. From the district of Alappuzha, two Panchayats are selected for conducting the survey—Kavalam and Pulinkunnu (Figure 5.1). The reason behind selecting the two Panchayats is that agricultural labourers are predominantly residing in these localities.

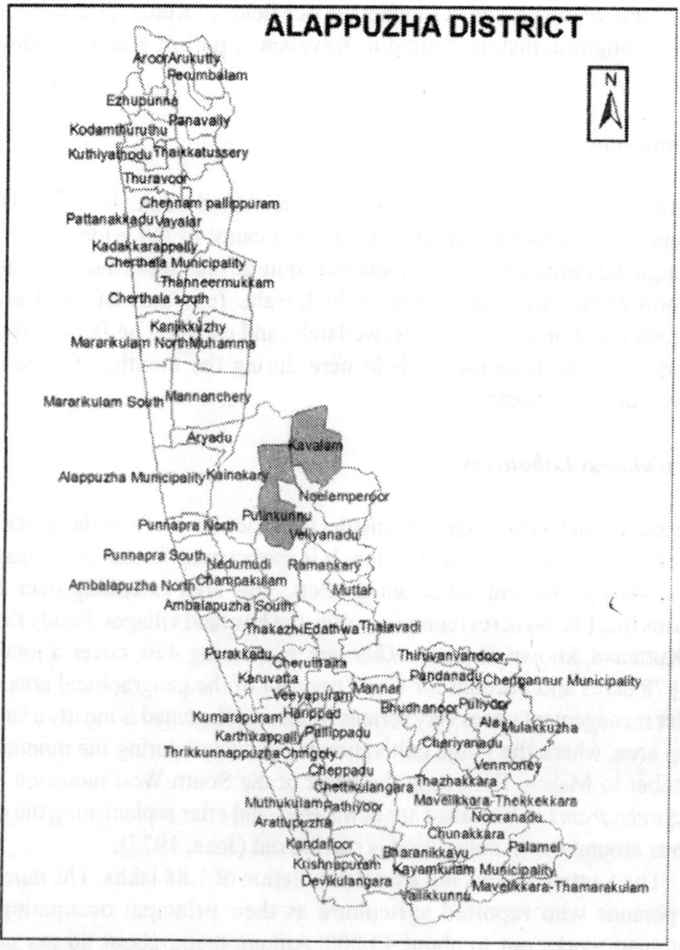

Fig. 5.2: Map of Alappuzha District
Source: Land Use Board, Government of Kerala.

Kavalam

Kavalam is a village in Kuttanad. This backwater village in Kerala is situated on the borders of Alappuzha and Kottayam Districts, on the banks of Vembanad Lake. The Pampa River flows through the Panchayat to merge into the famed Vembanad Lake. Relatively untouched by modernity, Kavalam is a green haven. Interspersed with the *kayals* (canals) and lakes, this belly of Kerala's backwaters is serene. The lakes and *kayals* are filled with flocks of ducks, and in summer the rice fields of Kuttanad turn golden. With a longtime history behind it, Kavalam is part of Kerala's cultural folklore.

Pulinkunnu

Pulinkunnu Panchayat is located in the Kuttanad taluk. It is an island village in Alappuzha district. The scenic beauty of the wide river ride through the Pampa River has made this route as one of the most favoured by houseboats tourism operators in Kerala. It is part of the Kerala backwaters, a network of lakes, wetlands, and canals. The famous Rajiv Gandhi Trophy boat race is held here during the months of October-November every year.

Agricultural Labourers

Kuttanad which is in Alappuzha district is the rice bowl of Kerala. Kuttanad is not a part of any revenue division. It is spread over 76 low land villages in the Alappuzha and Kottayam districts. This area extending over 265 sq.kms (65,172.60 acres) comprises only the low land villages. Paddy fields in Kuttanad, known as *padasekharams*, numbering 429, cover a total of 56,878 acres and account for 87.27 per cent of the geographical area. As water management poses very serious problems, Kuttanad is mostly a single crop area, where the Punja cultivation is conducted during the months of October to March. Following the onset of the South-West monsoon, the *padasekharams* in Kuttanad are dewatered, and after replenishing the ring bunds around them, cultivation is carried out (Jose, 1977).

The Kuttanad taluk has a total population of 1.88 lakhs. The number of persons who reported agriculture as their principal occupation in Kuttanad works out to about 43,000. Among them, about 86 per cent, that is, 37,000 are agricultural labourers: the breakup being 20,000 male and 17,000 female. Thus, agricultural labourers form about 60 per cent of the workforce in Kuttanad. Kuttanad taluk also has the highest proportion of female participants in agricultural operations. More than 87 per cent of the women in the labour force have been reported as agricultural labourers. Wage employment during the Punja cultivation is the single most important source of income to the agricultural labourers in Kuttanad. In fact, there is very little employment opportunity outside agriculture; and within agriculture it is mostly in rice cultivation, as about 87 per cent of the entire geographical area is under rice cultivation.

The paddy lands reclaimed out of the lakes are the base for rice cultivation of the State. The nature plays an important role on the lives of the people, they are sometimes affected by it. The farmers are at woes when the crops are destroyed by rainfall. This 'water water everywhere' phenomenon surely attracts tourists from all parts of the world. The farmers always have pathos to sing. Traditionally, the agricultural activities are conducted by agricultural labourers of the area. They mostly belong to the SC community. When the agricultural activities are in loss, naturally their livelihood is affected. Many labourers left the traditional activity and went for construction work and eventually to Gulf countries.

Idukki

The name of the district is derived from the Malayalam word Idukki, meaning narrow gauge. Idukki has an area of 5,105.22 km^2 (1,971.14 sq. mi) and is the second largest District of Kerala. Rugged mountains and forests cover about 97 per cent of the total area of the District. Idukki is bordered by the districts of Pathanamthitta to the south, Kottayam to the south-west, Ernakulam to the north-west and Thrissur to the north and Coimbature, Dindigul and Theni Districts of Tamil Nadu to the east.

There are eight Community Development Blocks in Idukki district—Devikulam, Adimali, Nedumkandom, Azhutha, Kattappana, Idukki, Elamdesom and Thodupuzha. There are 51 Panchayats in the district. Thodupuzha is the only Municipality and Idukki is the only township in the district. Munnar Panchayat of Devikulam block is the largest in the district with an area of 557 km^2 and Karimkunnam in Thodupuzha block is the smallest Panchayat of the district with an area of only 22 km^2. The district headquarters was originally located at Kottayam and moved to Painavu in June 1976.

Demographics

According to the 2011 Census, Idukki district has a population of 11,29,221. The district has a population density of 254 inhabitants per square kilometre (660/sq mi). Its population growth rate over the decade 2001-2011 was 1.93 per cent. Idukki has a sex ratio of 1006 females for every 1000 males and a literacy rate of 92.2 per cent.

Agriculture is the main resource of the district and over 50 per cent of the revenue of the district is from this sector. From the district of Idukki two Panchayats—Munnar and Mattuppetty—are selected for the study

Fig. 5.3: Map of Idukki District.
Source: Land Use Board, Government of Kerala.

Table 5.2: Basic facts on Idukki

Area (in sq.km)	4476
Population	11,29,221
Males	5,66,682
Females	5,62,539
Sex ratio: Females/1000	1006
Density of Population	254
Literacy rate	92.2%; Male 92.11%; Female 85.04%

(Figure 5.3). From these two localities, the Tamil migrant plantation workers have been selected.

Munnar

Munnar Panchayat is a hill station in Kerala and it is located on the Western Ghats in the Idukki district. The name Munnar is believed to mean "three rivers", referring to the town's strategic location at the confluence of the Madhurapuzha, Nallathanni and Kundaly rivers. The town has shared a strong cultural link with Tamil Nadu and over 70 per cent of the population of the town are Tamils. The Munnar town is in Kannan Devan Hills (KDH) Village in Devikulam taluk and is the largest panchayat in the Idukki district having an area measuring nearly 557 km².

Mattupetty

Mattupetty Panchayat is cradled by the undulating plantation hills of Munnar, and it is not far away from the Anamudi peak. Mattupetty which is 13 km away from hill town of Munnar is situated at a height of 1700m. Mattupetty offers many fascinating sights to relish. Besides the lush green tea plantations, and the rolling grasslands, the Shola forests in and around Mattupetty are ideal for trekking and are habitat to a variety of birds.

The Plantation Workers

The history of tea plantations in Munnar goes back to the middle of the nineteenth century when an Englishman John Daniel Manro intended to start tea plantations there. He got permission from the Maharaja of Poonjar for acquiring 588 square kilometres of land. Manro was assisted by the local chief Kannan Thevar in setting up of the plantations. It is said that in his honour, the region was called Kannan Devan Hills and the company was Kannan Devan Tea Company. Later in 1878, Finlay Company took over the plantations. In the year 1964, the Tatas in collaboration with the United Kingdom based James Finlay and Company, established Tata Finlay. Tata Tea in its real sense originated in the year 1983, when James Finlay sold their shares completely to Tatas. The Tata Tea Group of Companies consisting of Tata Tea and Tetley Group—which were merged in the year 2000 with Tatas—is the second largest branded tea operator, spread across 40 countries. Tata Tea, Tetley, Kannan Devan, Chakra Gold and Gemini are their five brands dominating Indian market. Their distribution network caters to around 1.7 million retail outlets in the country. The tea estates of Tatas in the north through their North Indian Plantations Operations (NIPO) are spread over the States of West Bengal and Assam. Their plantations in the south are spread in the Western Ghat regions, the major ones located in the Idukki district in Kerala known as the Kannan Devan Hills. These are clustered around the town of Munnar; a charming tourist destination situated 1,300 to 1,900 metres above the sea level (www.tatatea.com/history.htm).

A full-time labourer earns a wage of Rs. 124.03 per day in the estate and Rs. 126.43 in the factory. The history of tea plantation in Idukki as in other parts of the country dates back to British era. It was the British entrepreneurs who got hold of the nature and started planting cash crops in the eighteenth and nineteenth centuries. The raw materials, foodgrains and cash crops had been cultivated commercially in the Indian mainland to feed the British factories and markets. The tea cultivation in Kerala is also the result of this uprising. Though Munnar was a part of Madras Presidency and though it became a part of Kerala during reorganization of States, it still has an affinity to Tamil Nadu. It borders the Tamil Nadu border from Dindikal. The plantation workers are Tamil migrants from poor and backward parts of Tamil Nadu like interior Thirunelveli, Dindigul, Madurai and surrounding areas. They live in the plantation estates and own no land. As Munnar has been elevated as an international tourist destination, the land prices shoot up and a lot of problems started coming up. Both men and women work in the plantations.

By the end of eighteenth century British rulers found an immense opportunity in the cultivation and trade of plantation crops in Western Ghats region. In this region, they planned to cultivate tea, coffee, cardamom and almost all spice items. In the Western Ghats region, especially in the Nilgiri mountains, for the purpose of cultivation they used a lot of skilled labourers. They brought these skilled people from the Southern part, mostly from Tirunelveli district in Tamil Nadu. The people had been brought to Western Ghats region in different batches not only to Nilgiri, but to Peremedu and Wayanad regions also. Geographically, these are the places situated in the highest mountain regions of Kerala and Tamil Nadu. In this way, the people living in Idukki are from different places of Tamil Nadu. They bought the people to some specific places such as Munnar, Valpara, Perimadu, etc. The British entrepreneurs made them work hard to clear the thick forest. In the earlier days, they had cultivated tea and coffee in these places. In the early nineteenth century, Munnar was known for heavy rainfall and it was inaccessible to people. In 1920, James Finlay, a British man established a Tea company in Munnar. He too brought people from southern parts of Tamil Nadu. They made huge profit from the tea plantations. They have constructed build schools, hospitals, road, bridges, dams and even railways.

During those days, they used horses for transportation/commuting. The supervisors too used horses to visit the plantation for managing people. The living conditions of the people there were dreadful, because the climate was extreme. They had a hard living in these places with unhygienic living conditions. They survived there without heaters, electricity, water etc. Nowadays, the workers have changed a lot. The reasons for the change are due to little education and tourism. Income has been improved because of the tourism activities. Even the plantation workers are engaged in tit and bit jobs in order to increase their income. This helped them to improve upon their overall development.

Kozhikode

The name Kozhikode is thought to be derived from *koyil* (palace) + *kota* (fort), meaning "fortified palace". The place was also referred to as *Chullikkad*, meaning "shrubby jungle", probably referring to the marshy nature of the land.

Geography

Kozhikode district is bordered by the districts of Kannur to the north, Wayanad to the east, and Malappuram to the south. The Arabian Sea lies to the west. It is situated between latitudes 11°08′ N and 11°50′ N and longitudes 75°30′ E and 76°8′ E. The district is divided into three taluks; Vadakara, Koyilandy, and Kozhikode and there is one Revenue Division, Kozhikode.

Demographics

Kozhikode has an average literacy rate of 92.24 per cent wherein male literacy rate is 96.6 per cent and female literacy rate is 90.6 per cent. According to the 2011 Census, Kozhikode district has a population of 30,89,543. This gives it a ranking of 115th in India (out of a total of 640). The district has a population density of 1,318 inhabitants per square kilometre (3,410/sq mi). Its population growth rate over the decade 2001-2011 was 7.31 per cent. Kozhikode has a sex ratio of 1,097 females for every 1000 males, and a literacy rate of 95.24 per cent.

Economy

Kozhikode occupies a nodal position in the Malabar Coast and has an undisputed economic standing of its own being the trade centre for a large and resourceful hinterland. It is the market place of hill products like pepper, cardamom, etc. It also has large timber yards along the banks of the Kallayi River. Kozhikode District with eight per cent of the State population makes a 12 per cent contribution to the State's income. With a coastline of 71 km from Chaliyar to Azhiyoor, the district of Kozhikode offers enormous natural resources for the development of fisheries. The major fish landing centres are Beypore, Vellayil and Puthiyappa in the city limits and the average annual landing is estimated to about 1 lakh metric tonnes. There are about 614 registered mechanized boats and 2,657 motorized country crafts in this district. The District has an intermediate port at Kozhikode (including Beypore) and a minor port at Vadakara. In coast line of the Kozhikode port extends from Elathur cape to the south bank of Kadalundi river and treads roughly in straight line. From the district of Kozhikode, two wards of Kozhikode district are selected for the study—Marad and Beypore (Figure 5.4). From these two localities the marine fisherfolk have been selected.

Table 5.3: Basic facts on Kozhikode

Area (in sq.km)	2,206
Population	30,89,543
Males	14,73,028
Females	16,16,515
Sex ratio: Females/1000	1,097
Density of Population	1,318
Literacy rate	92.24%; Male 96.6%; Female 90.6%

Marad

Marad is a part of Kozhikode Municipal Corporation. The place has come into media attention due to the riot that occurred on 2nd May, 2003 at the Marad beach.

Beypore

Beypore is a small coastal village in Kozhikode district. The place was formerly known as Vaypura. This place also has a small port and a beautiful beach. *Beypore port* is one of the oldest ports in Kerala from where trading

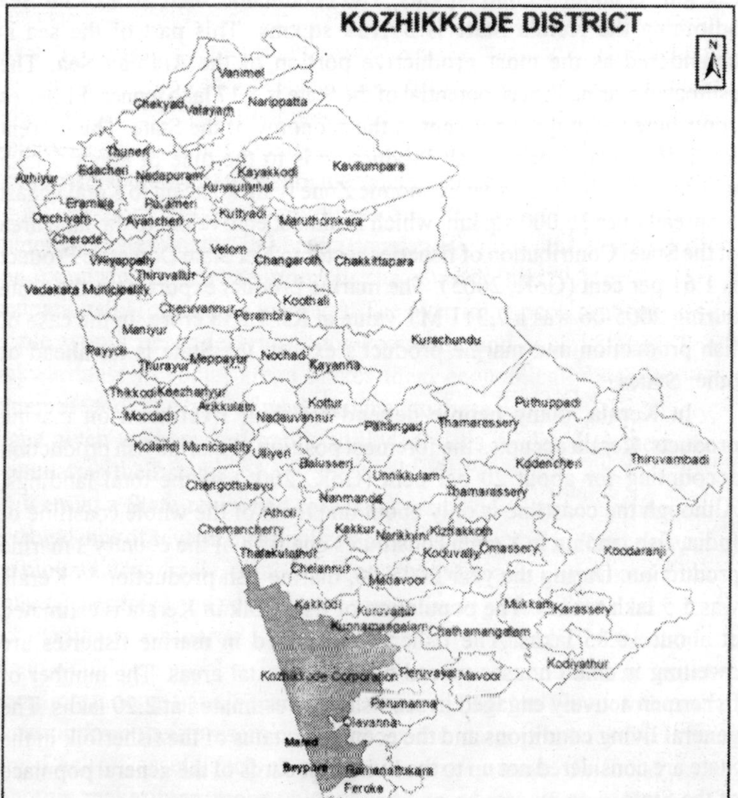

Fig. 5.4: Map of Kozhikode District.
Source: Land Use Board, Government of Kerala.

was done to the Middle East. Beypore is also famous for building wooden ship, it is called *Dhows* or *Urus* in Malayalam language. These ships are usually bought by Arab merchants for trading, fishing and now they are used as tourist ships.

The Marine Fisherfolk

Kerala is bordered by a range of mountains *viz.* the Western Ghats on the eastern side and the Arabian Sea on the western side. The coastal line of the Arabian Sea sprawling on the western part of the State is 590 kms in length. The inshore sea area falling within the territorial limit of the State (22 km) is about 13,000 sq.kms. The continental shelf area of the sea adjoining the Kerala State is 39,139 sq.kms. This part of the sea is considered as the most productive portion of the Arabian Sea. The estimated marine fishery potential of the State is 5.17 lakh tonnes. Fisheries contribute about three per cent to the economy of the State. The current level of annual Marine Fish Production is to the tune of about 6 lakh tonnes/year. The Exclusive Economic Zone lying adjacent to Kerala coast is spread over 36,000 sq. km. which is almost equivalent to the land area of the State. Contribution of fisheries sector to Net State Domestic Product is 1.61 per cent (GoK, 2005). The marine product export from the State during 2005-06 was a 7,311 MT value at Rs. 1,258 crore. In the case of fish production and marine product's export, the State is far ahead of other States.

In Kerala, many people depend for their livelihood on marine products. Kerala occupies the foremost position of marine fish production accounting for about 20 per cent (GoK, 2006) of the total landings. Although the coastline is only about one tenth of the whole coastline of India, fish landing in Kerala constitutes one fifth of the country's marine production. During the year 2005-06, marine fish production in Kerala was 5.5 lakh tonnes. The population of fisherfolk in Kerala is estimated at about 10.85 lakhs. The fisherfolk engaged in marine fisheries are dwelling in small houses spread over the coastal areas. The number of fishermen actively engaged in sea fishing is estimated at 2.20 lakhs. The general living conditions and the economic status of the fisherfolk in the State are considered not up to the living standards of the general populace of the State.

The socio-economic conditions of the fishing communities in Kerala have passed through vicissitudes an improving phase during 1956 to 1975, fisheries development without fisherfolk development from 1975 to the mid-1990s and positive changes in the economic conditions of fisherfolk thereafter. Though per capita income of fisherfolk increased, it always lay behind the State per capita income of the general population. The widening of the difference during the 1990s was mainly due to rising fixed capital costs caused by mechanization and automation of fishing crafts and gears and the use of non-renewable sources of energy such as kerosene or petrol, for propulsion. While costs were rising, the economic outcomes were dismal.

Density of population is the highest in areas of the coastal tract along the Arabian Sea, near the high-tide line where fisherfolk live. Housing conditions have marginally improved for the fisherfolk since the 1980s. The number of household livings in huts declined from 48 per cent in 1980 to 27 per cent in 1990. Health conditions of fishers' households remain quite poor. Cases of cholera, malaria, dengue fever and tuberculosis outbreaks are often reported from coastal areas. Porous soils and lack of land make construction of sanitary toilets difficult; supply of potable drinking water is also problematic. The levels of food intake of the fishing population are also found extremely low, deficient and unbalanced.

One of the paramount reasons for the poor standard of living and the substandard conditions of habitat of the marine fishing communities in Kerala State is the crowding of the whole community on a narrow strip of land along the length of Kerala's coastline. Fishing and fish processing are the important occupations of the marine fishing villages. Export of fish products has an important role in their earning potential. But the socio-economic status of fishermen is very low, with high morbidity and mortality. A study of the health status of Kerala State highlights that respiratory and skin infection, diarrhea disorders and hook worm infestations are much prevalent in the coastal areas of the State.

It is observed that occupation of marine fishing is subject to relatively higher levels of risks. Many cases of accidental deaths and loss of property are being reported every year. Every fisherman prefers to live on the sea front near the point from where he can observe the sea. Floods, storms and waves of the sea are very frequent in these areas. One difficulty of providing sanitation facilities in coastal villages is that septic tanks do not function effectively because of the high water table in sandy soil and the risk entails of leaching of sewage into wells used for drinking purpose.

Malappuram

The word Malappuram ("terraced place atop the hills") came to represent the present region only after the formation of the district, before it was called Eranad or Valluvanad. The district of Malappuram was formed on 16th June, 1969 with four taluks, Eranad taluk, Perinthalmanna taluk, Tirur taluk and Ponnani taluk, four statutory towns, fourteen developmental blocks and 95 Panchayats. Two more taluks, namely Tirurangadi taluk and Nilambur taluk, were formed later by bifurcating Tirur taluk and Eranad taluk.

Table 5.4: Basic facts on Malappuram

Area (in sq. km)	3,550
Population	41,10,956
Males	19,61,014
Females	21,49,942
Sex ratio: Females/1000	1,096
Density of Population	1158/sq.km
Literacy rate	93.55%, Male 95.78%; Female 91.55%

Geography

The district lies in northern Kerala and is bounded on the north by Wayanad and Kozhikode districts, on the north-east by Tamil Nadu, on the south-east and south by Palakkad District, on the south-west by Thrissur District, on the west by the Arabian Sea, and on the north-west by Kozhikode District. At present Malappuram District consists of 2 revenue divisions, 6 taluks, 135 villages, 15 blocks, 7 municipalities and 100 Panchayats.

Economy

The people of Malappuram depend mainly on agriculture for their living. Timber industry, fishery, tourism and spice trading also contribute much to the economy of the district. The foreign money remitted by the migrants from the Middle East is another significant revenue to the district. The small-scale industries in the district which are agricultural and textile based also adds revenue to the district. Wood related business is widely common in the district with more than hundred industries dealing with wood. Saw mills, furniture manufactures and timber sales are the most important business in Malappuram district.

Demographics

The total population of Malappuram is 41,10,956 as per the census report of 2011. The number of male in the total population is 19,61,014, whereas the number of female in the district is 21,49,942. The population density of Malappuram is 1096 per square kilometer.

Malappuram district in Kerala is predominantly dwelled by the Muslim population. In the present study, the State is obviously the choice to study the Muslim women population. From the district, the Panchayats of Chokkad and Edakkara are selected.

Chokkad

Chokkad Panchayat is situated in south-east of Nilambur in Malappuram district. It is 13 km from Nilambur railway station and seven km from Kalikavu. The village is on the bed of two rivers—Kottappuzha and Chokkadanpuzha and the hills near it have tribal settlement made by the government, rehabilitating the native hill tribes. Adjacent to the tribal colony, native people groups such as, Ernadan, Muthan, and Paniyan are settled.

Edakkara

Edakkara Panchayat is a mountainous area in Malappuram district. The nearest town is Nilambur, about 15 km away. A vast component of the population has relatives working abroad in the Gulf countries or USA. Edakkara is emerging as one of the main townships in the East Eranad region under Nilambur taluk and Malappuram district itself. Agriculture is the primary occupation with rubber and pepper as the main crops cultivated. Edakkara is very close to Nilagiri District of Tamil Nadu.

Muslim Population

The core of the Muslim population in the district is poor and has a backward social and economic status. Most of the houses visited are women headed. The girls study up to the 10th standard before they get married. Many of the women are having three or four children. In many cases, their husband are in gulf countries. In some households though the men have gone to gulf countries for gainful employment, they could not succeed in getting gainful employment there and they returned to India.

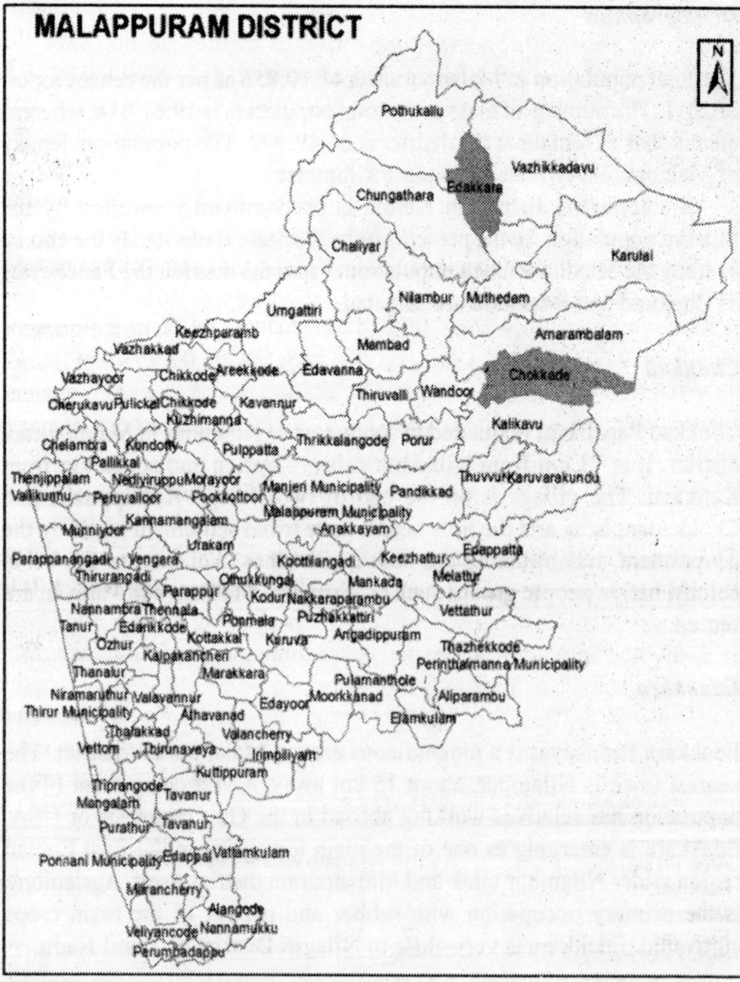

Fig. 5.5: Map of Malappuram District.
Source: Land Use Board, Government of Kerala.

But the debt which they have to repay on account of the travel and visa expenses is a real burden to those families. Most of the women are staying at home due to religious and social reasons. Even if they would like to go to work, the restrictions, child care burden, low skill and education hinder them to do so. The older women who are free to do work outside the house participate in Mahatma Gandhi National Rural Employment Guarantee Programme (MGNREGP). The younger women are reluctant to initiate any income generating activities as they do not have the confidence in running the enterprise and marketing the products.

Thiruvananthapuram

Thiruvananthapuram is the southernmost district of Kerala. It came into existence in the year 1957. The headquarters is the city of Thiruvananthapuram (Trivandrum) which is also the capital city of Kerala. Thiruvananthapuram district is situated between north latitudes 8°17′and 8°54′and east longitudes 76°41′and 77°17′. The southernmost extremity, 'Parasala', is 56 kms away from Kanyakumari, the "land's end of India". The district stretches along the shores of the Arabian Sea for a distance of 78 kms. The district has an area of 2,192 square kilometres (846 sq mi)

Demographics

The district has a population of 33,07,284 (as per the 2011 Census), the second-most populous district in Kerala after Malappuram district. It is the densest district in Kerala with 1,509 people per square kilometer. It is divided into four taluks—Thiruvananthapuram, Chirayinkeezhu, Neyyattinkara, Nedumangadu. The urban bodies in the district are the Thiruvananthapuram Corporation, Varkala, Neyyattinkara, Attingal and Nedumangad municipalities.

Table 5.5: Basic facts on Thiruvananthapuram

Area (in sq.km)	2192 Square Kilometers
Population	33,07,284
Males	15,84,200
Females	17,23,084
Sex ratio: Females/1000	1088
Density of Population	1509 per sq.km
Literacy rate	92.66%; Males 94.60%; Females 90.89%

Economy

The economy of Thiruvananthapuram district mostly consists of tourism and leisure, information technology, agriculture and education. The modern economy of Thiruvananthapuram is dependent on the media and IT sector. India's first animation park, The Kinfra Animation Park, is situated in the district.

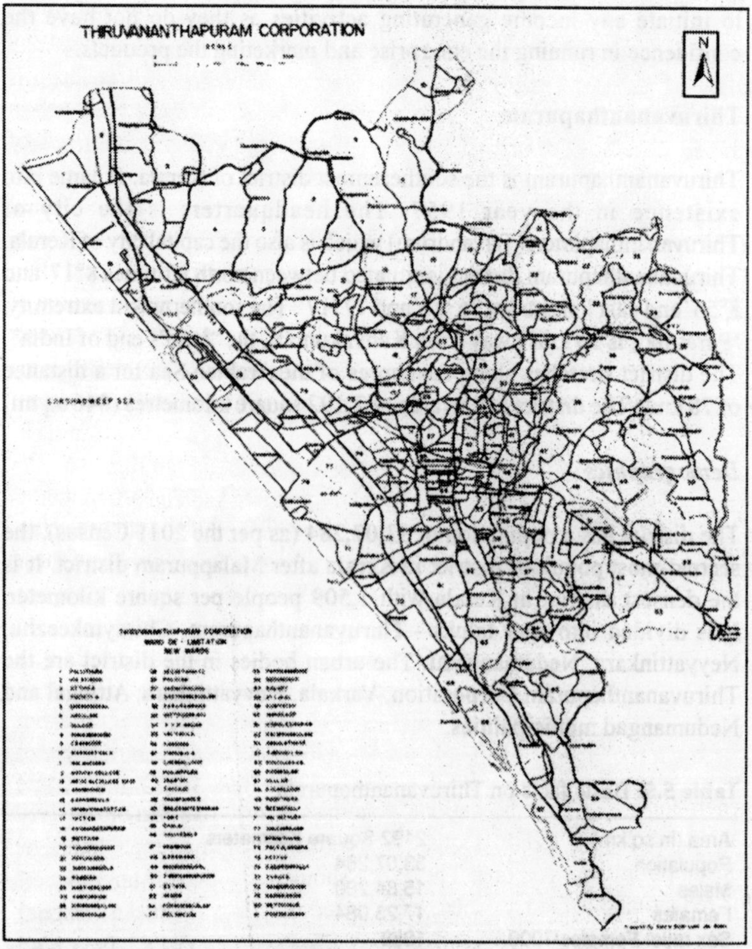

Fig. 5.6: Map of Thiruvananthapuram Corporation.
Source: Land Use Board, Government of Kerala.

For the purpose of study, two slums—Rajeev Nagar of Kannanthura ward and Chithravilasam of Pound Kadavu ward—of Thiruvananthapuram Corporation (Figure 5.6) are selected.

Thiruvananthapuram Corporation

Thiruvananthapuram is the capital of Kerala and the headquarters of the Thiruvananthapuram District. It is located on the west coast of India near the extreme south of the mainland. The city is characterized by its undulating terrain of low coastal hills and busy commercial alleys. With nearly 1,000,000 (one million) inhabitants as per the 2011 Census, it is the largest and most populous city in Kerala; the wider urban agglomeration has a population of more than 1 million. It is an IT hub of the State with over 80 per cent of the state's software exports. Thiruvananthapuram is built on seven hills by the sea shore and is located at 8.5 N 76.9 E on the west coast, near the southern tip of mainland India. The city is situated on the west coast of India, and is bounded by Arabian Sea to its west and the Western Ghats to its east. The city spans an area of 214.86 km^2 (82.96 sq mi) and the greater metropolitan area spans an area of 250 km^2 (96.53 sq mi). The average elevation of the city is 16 ft (4.9 m) above sea level. In October 2010, the area of the city was increased from 86 wards to 100 wards by adding Sreekaryam, Vattiyoorkavu, Kudappanakunnu, Vizhinjam and Kazhakuttam panchayats into the corporation. The city has now an area of 214.86 km^2 and a population of 9,57,730 inhabitants with 4,67,739 males and 4,89,991 females. BPL survey indicated the urban poor population at 1,20,367. Majority of these populace live in slums and coastal fishing areas.

The Slum Dwellers (Urban Poor)

Urban poverty is a multi-dimensional phenomenon. The urban poverty is characterized by nutritional deficiency, lack of basic needs of housing, water, sanitation, medical care, education and opportunity for income generation also. As per the National Commission on Urbanization, poverty cannot be characterized adequately in terms of income, expenditure or consumption pattern alone. The focus should be a human upgradation for reduction of poverty. Thus, what is required is a multi-dimensional concept inclusive of the environment, access to services, social and psychological supports.

In spite of the tremendous development achieved in several areas like literacy and health care, poverty refuses to leave the State. More than fifteen lakh families of the State, *alias* 'gods own country' are still in the clutches of poverty. High density of population in urban areas of Kerala has contributed to urban poverty. This manifests in many forms, such as slums, unemployment, lack of social services, and increasing violence and crime. The National Sample Survey Organization (NSSO) in its 61st round survey (2004-05) estimates that in Kerala the poverty ratio was 20.6 per cent in urban areas. The magnitude of urban unemployment is also increasing due to the weaknesses of the economy. In particular, due to stagnation in manufacturing industry in Kerala, sufficient employment opportunities are not available for the urban dwellers. National Sample Survey data show that urban unemployment in Kerala is the second highest in India, at ten per cent in 2000 (only after Goa). Due to the rapid increase in land price and construction costs, a small section of the urban population in Kerala is forced to live in slums. The living conditions of slum dwellers are very pathetic. Availability of drinking water and sanitation facilities is grossly inadequate. Only one-fourth of households in slums have electricity. The composition of the poor has been changing. While rural poverty is getting concentrated in the agricultural labour and artisan households, urban poverty is found in the casual labour households.

Rapid growth of urban population, expansion of existing towns and cities and low investment in urban development have created deficiencies in basic amenities especially in the urban areas. The shortages are serious for the urban poor due to inequality in the access to these amenities. A well coordinated approach is necessary to reduce urban poverty for which the following aspects are suggested for serious consideration: (i) Employment opportunities of a permanent nature need to be made available to the poor both by macro strategies aimed at labour intensive growth and micro-strategies to enable the poor to attain the skills needed by the formal and semi-formal sectors. (ii) Self-employment, product development, and marketing. (iii) With the support of urban local bodies and State Government, basic urban infrastructure related to housing, water supply, sanitation, electricity and roads are to be provided at a minimum standard. (iv) The access of the poor to quality health and education facilities needs to be ensured, which again calls for improving the services available through hospitals and schools. (v) Finally, the most vulnerable groups need to be identified through a transparent index. A robust social protection system has to be set-up for them, with a much higher level of support than at present.

Wayanad

Wayanad District is situated in the north-east of Kerala. It was formed on November 1, 1980 as the twelfth district by carving out areas from Kozhikode and Kannur districts. Kalpetta is the district headquarters as well as the only municipal town in the district. The region was known as Mayakshetra (Maya's land) in the earliest records. Mayakshetra evolved into Mayanad and finally to Wayanad. The Folk etymology of the word says it is a combination of *Vayal* (paddy field) and *Naad* (land), making it 'The Land of Paddy Fields'. There are many indigenous tribals in this area. It is set on the majestic high Western Ghats with altitudes ranging from 700 to 2,100 m.

Geography

Wayanad district stands on the southern tip of the Deccan plateau and its chief glory is the majestic rugged terrain of the Western Ghats, with lofty ridges interspersed with dense forest, tangled jungles and deep valleys. Quite a large area of the district is covered by forest but the continued and indiscriminate exploitation of the natural resources point towards an imminent environmental crisis.

Demographics

According to the 2011 census, Wayanad district has a population of 8,16,558. This gives it a ranking of 482nd in India (out of a total of 640). The district has a population density of 383 inhabitants per square kilometre (990/sq mi). Its population growth rate over the decade 2001-2011 was 4.6 per cent and Wayanad has a sex ratio of 1,035 females for every 1000 males, and a literacy rate of 89.32 per cent.

Table 5.6: Basic facts on Wayanad

Area (in sq.km)	4,358
Population	7,80,619
Males	3,19,273
Females	3,89,346
Sex ratio: Females/1000	1,035
Density of Population	383
Literacy rate	89.32

Economy

Wayanad is 3.79 per cent urbanised. Agriculture is the main stay of the economy. Coffee, tea, cocoa, pepper, plantain and vanilla are the main crops. Besides these cash crops, the most important crop in the district is rice. Dams and aqueducts have been constructed to take water to the otherwise dry areas in the district. Price of land is going up even after the agrarian crisis phase. In 2006, the Ministry of Panchayati Raj named

Wayanad one of the country's 250 most backward districts (out of a total of 640). It is one of the two districts in Kerala currently receiving funds from the Backward Regions Grant Fund Programme (BRGF).

From Wayanad district, two Panchayats were selected—Thirunelli and Panamaram (Figure 5.7). They are dwelled predominantly by the tribal population.

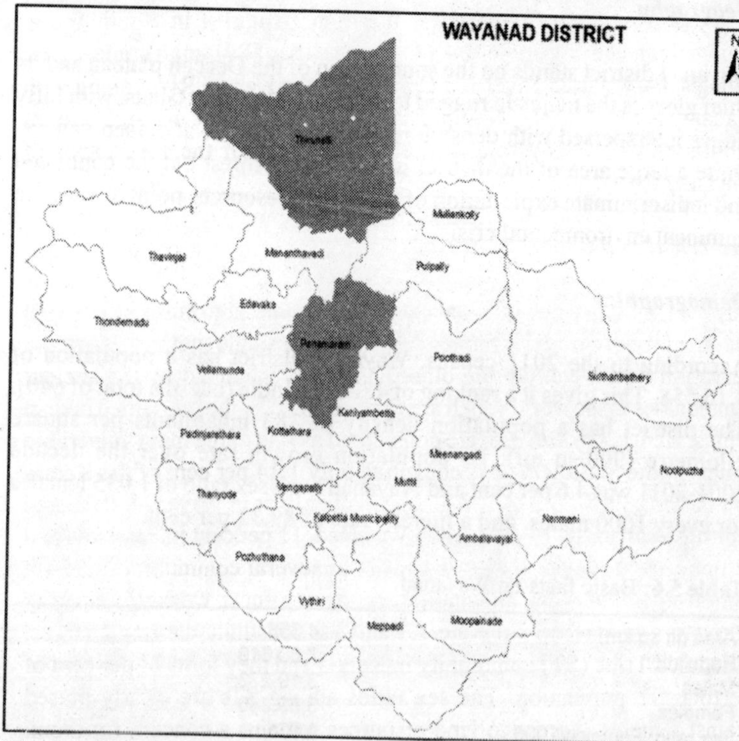

Fig. 5.7: Map of Wayanad District.
Source: Land Use Board, Government of Kerala.

Thirunelli

Thirunelli is situated 29 km north-east of Mananthavady under the Brahmagiri hills in the reserve forest. The temple at Thirunelli is often called '*Thekkan Kasi*'. It is believed that a bath in the holy water of '*Papanasini*' will wipe off all sins. Apart from the temple, Thirunelli is a place of scenic beauty. Pakshipathalam, an interesting trekking centre, is 7 km away from the temple.

Panamaram

Panamaram has great significance in the history of Indian freedom struggle as it witnessed one of the first freedom struggles in South India. Panamaram had a population of 11,651 with 5891 males and 5,760 females. Panamaram River is a tributary of the Kabani River along with Mananthavady, Babali, Noolpuzha and Nugu Rivers. Kabani and its tributaries play a key role in the enhancement of the landscapes of Wayanad District.

The Tribal Population (Adivasis)

Wayanad, the tribal hub of Kerala State often comes into public discussion due to a lot of reasons. It ranges from poverty, single mother, desertion, starvation death, etc. On the other hand, it is inhabited by the ancient communities in the world which are characterized by the pre-settled human beings. Hence, the *adivasis* are considered as one of the main vulnerable groups in the State. *Adivasis* constitute only 1.14 per cent of the Kerala population. About 37 per cent of this number lives in Wayanad, Palakkad and Idukki districts, 14 per cent in Wayanad, 11 per cent in Palakkad and 12 per cent in Idukki. *Adivasis* consist of several communities and are composed of hunters and gatherers, agricultural workers, shifting cultivators and settled cultivators. Paniyans constitute the single largest Scheduled Tribe (ST) community in Kerala and they form 21 per cent of the total ST population. The sex ratios among STs are clearly biased against females. Access to land resources remains a concern for them. Literacy among *Adivasis* in Kerala is the highest, 57.22 per cent in 2001. In terms of the quality of housing and the access to basic education also, the tribals of Kerala are much ahead of their counterparts elsewhere in the country.

The level of poverty among *Adivasis* have declined among STs in the State, to only about half the percentage for all India, thanks to agrarian reforms and numerous poverty alleviation programmes. But in comparison with the rest of the State population, the poverty level among *Adivasis* is about two-and-a-half times higher. Their access to medical facilities is also poor. Starvation deaths and sickle cell anemia are rampant among them. Though work Participation rates are high among *Adivasis*, the incidence of poverty is also paradoxically higher. They do unskilled work and are lowly paid. *Adivasis* lands are alienated through lease, mortgage and downright unauthorized occupation. The average extent of land cultivated by tribal household came down heavily from 0.8 hectares in 1987-88 to 0.2 hectares in 1992-1994. All the promises made by successive governments in Kerala about restoration of tribal land have gone unfulfilled. Efforts made by *Adivasis* to assert their land rights have been crushed and defeated. In the new dispensation of neo-liberal agenda of globalization, the miseries of the tribals have increased manifold. The numerous development programmes for advancement of education among STs, have not yielded much positive results; the *Adivasis* continue to get marginalized and deprived. Unless the society at large is seriously concerned with questions of redistributive justice, the marginalized sections are unlikely to empower themselves for a struggle for identity.

In many of the tribal households, the men folk are not found. They would be away for work or they would have deserted the household. Naturally, the burden falls on the women who have to look after the children. In Bhaveli, one of the survey areas, the women go to Kurg, located in the neighbouring State of Karnataka, to work in the ginger fields. They get meagre income. Some women are sexually exploited. One of the women visited here has five children from such sexual abuses. The male members in the settlement areas do not give much importance to education and social development. Many children are seen dropped out from the schools and are roaming here and there. A school which is inside the settlement is in a deplorable State. Altogether 20 pupils are studying in all classes there and one teacher comes to teach them. The teacher does not turn up on all working days. The children who are studying in the primary schools (I standard to IV standard) roam around the settlement with no clue. These things bring dejection in the minds of locals and they are not concerned about the social development. It has an impact not only on them but also on the future generation which causes intergenerational transfer of poverty. As soon as the male children attain the age of 13 or 14, they go in search of job in nearby places like Kurg and other parts of Wayanad. There are recruiting agencies that come and collect the boys for their respective areas. As they start getting money in a very young age, they get trapped into a lot of anti-social activities like drinking, drug addiction, etc. It is a tradition that both male and female get married at early age, the boys and girls who get married would be of the same age group. A boy may marry more girls or desert the girl soon after her giving birth to children. The woman's life is full of struggle to keep her life and body together. The Kudumbashree movement has reached the doorsteps of these settlements and the people are engaged in various activities. They have got houses under EMS *Bhavana Padhathi* (EMS Housing Scheme), a State run programme. The electricity is yet to come to their settlements. They have to get special permission as the settlements are bordering the forest area.

A brief account of the outlier communities in Kerala comes up with a lot of questions on their vulnerability and the ways to remove the poverty among them. In the subsequent chapters, an attempt is made on this direction.

6

Social Capital Formation and Effectiveness of Micro-finance Mechanism

Social capital is the quality and quantity of relationships, networks, and norms among people and organizations that facilitate collective action. It can increase productivity (both individual and collective), so social contacts affect the productivity of individuals and groups. Collective action is thus an indicator of increased social capital. The resurgence of interest in "social capital" as a remedy for the cause of today's social problems draws directly on the assumption that these problems lie in the weakening of civil society.

Micro-finance, by providing small loans and savings facilities to those who have been excluded from commercial financial services, has been promoted as a key strategy for reducing poverty in all its forms by agencies all-over the world. Access to these facilities is seen as a way of providing the poor with opportunities for self-reliance through entrepreneurship, cushioning the poor against economic shocks and providing a means of social empowerment for poor women in their communities. In most cases, micro-credit programmes offer a combination of services and resources to their clients in addition to usual credit for self-employment. Also, this is an effort to provide a bridge between formal financial markets and the informal groups in the formal micro-finance initiatives.

The present chapter attempts to examine whether the tool of micro-finance is effective in forming social capital among women and thereby enhancing the capacity building process for the larger development of the country. As explained in Chapter Five, altogether six districts, each representing a particular social group have been selected for the purpose of the present study. From each district a separate social group has been selected. From Alappuzha district agricultural labourers, predominantly dominated by Scheduled Castes (SCs) population have been selected.

From Idukki district, Tamil migrant plantation workers have been selected. The marine fisher folk population has been selected from Kozhikode district. The northern district of Malappuram has a concentration of Muslim population and the poor Muslim women have been selected from there. The capital city of the State, Thiruvananthapuram has been selected for representing slum dwelling population of the State. As the district of Wayanad has more tribal population, it was selected for the same.

In the present chapter, a detailed analysis of the NHGs in the study area has been attempted. The profile of NHGs in study area, status of group meetings, membership in NHGs and drop-out, micro-financing activities, activities besides micro-financing, rules, regulations and enforcements are discussed in the subsequent sections.

Profile of NHGs in Study Area

The neighbourhood groups (NHGs) are the basic units of micro-finance activities under Kudumbashree movement. In this section, the profile of the NHGs selected in the study area is explained.

Group Formation

Since, the inception of Kudumbashree in 1998, the NHGs had been initiated all-over the State in different periods. The groups selected for the study had been started in different periods of time.

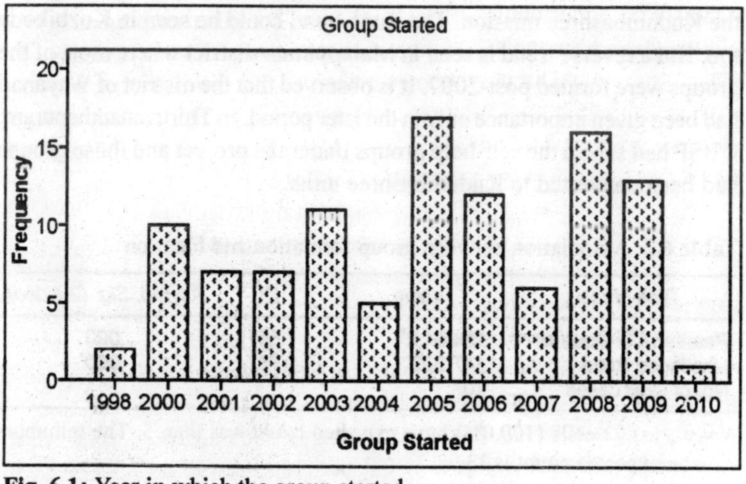

Fig. 6.1: Year in which the group started.

Figure 6.1 shows that a good number of NHGs had been formed post-2005 only. The reason for this was that the focused action towards this direction had been made during this period. Another reason was that the earlier groups had withered away due to lack of enthusiasm.

Table 6.1: Profile of group formation in sample districts

Name of the district	*Class Interval of Group Started*				*Total*
	1998-2001	*2001-2004*	*2004-2007*	*2007-2010*	
Alappuzha	6 (31.6)	8 (42.10)	2 (10.50)	3 (15.80)	19 (100)
Idukki	0	0	14 (100)	0	14 (100)
Kozhikode	6 (33.30)	8 (44.40)	2 (11.10)	2 (11.10)	18 (100)
Malappuram	2 (9.50)	1 (4.80)	2 (9.50)	16 (76.2)	21 (100)
Thiruvananthapuram	2 (11.80)	4 (23.50)	8 (47.10)	3 (17.60)	17 (100)
Wayanad	3 (16.70)	2 (11.10)	7 (38.90)	6 (33.30)	18 (100)
Total	19 (17.8)	23 (21.5)	35 (32.7)	30 (28.0)	107 (100)

Source: Figures in brackets show percentages.

A closer look at the various districts shows a clearer picture. In the case of Idukki, all the groups taken up for study had been started during the same period, i.e., between the period 2004 and 2007 (Table 6.1). In the case of Alappuzha, the groups have been spread almost evenly across the periods. The Urban Basic Services for the Poor (UBSP) project which had its advent in this district shows the trend that most of the groups (73%) were formed before 2004. In later periods, they were merged to the Kudumbashree mission. The same trend could be seen in Kozhikode too. But a reverse trend is seen in Malappuram district where most of the groups were formed post-2007. It is observed that the district of Wayanad had been given importance only in the later period. In Thiruvananthapuram, UBSP had set-up the self-help groups under the project and those groups had been converted to Kudumbashree units.

Table 6.2: Association between group formation and location

Type of test	*Value*	*Df*	*Asymp. Sig. (2-sided)*
Pearson Chi-Square	154.611[a]	55	.000
Likelihood Ratio	147.303	55	.000
No. of valid cases	107		

Note: (a) 72 cells (100.0%) have expected count less than 5. The minimum expected count is 13.

Chi-square value indicates a significant association between the group formation and the districts. Since, in the present context more than 72 per cent cells had an expected frequency count of less than five, it is better to look at the likelihood ratio of chi-square. Here also the value shows significant association between the two variables. So, we can conclude that the group formation and the locality (here districts) have a strong association (Table 6.2).

Membership in NHGs

It is stipulated by the National Bank for Agriculture and Rural Development (NABARD) that each self-help group should have 20 members. The Kudumbashree mission also insisted on it. The field data show the same trend (Table 6.3). Majority of the NHGs (51.4%) are having members in between 15 and 20, while another 31.8 per cent are having members in between 10 and 15. Yet another 10 per cent have a membership of 20 to 25. Some of the groups are still having membership of more than 25 (about 6.5%).

Table 6.3: Number of members in NHGs

Number of members	*Frequency*	*%*
10-15	34	31.8
15-20	55	51.4
20-25	11	10.3
25-30	4	3.7
30-35	2	1.9
35-40	1	.9
Total	107	100

The reason was that many of the groups had been formed even before the advent of the mission in 1998. At that time, the membership was allowed at 40 per group. For the purpose of bank linkage and other administrative purposes, the group membership had been fixed at 20. So, many of the groups have been reorganised and made into groups of 20 members each. But many groups have a membership even less than 15. In due course of time, some members would wither away from the NHGs.

Total Number of Members in Each District

Of all the groups surveyed in selected districts, a total of 1880 members were there. The distribution of the members in the respective NHGs is given in Table 6.4. It is observed that the districts of Kozhikode and Malappuram have the highest number of members while in districts like Thiruvananthapuram and Alappuzha the membership is less.

Table 6.4: Number of Members in NHGs

District	*Number of Members*	*%*
Alappuzha	217	11.5
Idukki	324	17.2
Kozhikode	432	23.0
Malappuram	389	20.7
Thiruvananthapuram	200	10.6
Wayanad	318	16.9
Total	1880	100.0

Age Structure of Members in NHGs

Of the total members, sixty per cent of them belong to the age group of 30 to 50 years (Table 6.5). As far as these women are concerned, they are the homemakers and always they are keener in what is happening around them. The majority of the members belong to the age group of 30 to 40 (32.1%) and another 27.6 per cent belong to the age group 40-50. Younger women, less than the age of 30 years have less representation, forming about 19 per cent. The unmarried ladies under the age of 20 years form only 1.6 per cent of the total. Women above the age of 50 years represented comparatively lesser than the younger generation. While the women in the age group of 50-60 years have a representation of 14.6 per cent, much lesser representation is with women of 60-70 years, i.e., 6.1 per cent. A miniscule representation of women from older cohort (age of 70-80) is observed, i.e., 0.4 per cent only (Table 6.5).

Table 6.5: Age structure of members

Age	*Frequency*	*%*
<20	30	1.6
20-30	332	17.7
30-40	603	32.1
40-50	518	27.6
50-60	275	14.6
60-70	114	6.1
70-80	8	0.4
Total	1880	100.0

The age structure of all the members present in all the groups is given in Table 6.6. The age of the members in all the NHGs surveyed ranges between 18 and 80. The mean age is 41.64 and the median age is 40. The standard deviation is 11.76.

Table 6.6: Mean age of members in NHGs

Mean	41.64
Median	40
Mode	45
Std. Deviation	11.76
Variance	138.34
Range	75

Marital Status

The universalization of marriage in the Kerala society is reflected in Table 6.7. About 97 per cent of the women in the NHGs are married and the rest of the women are unmarried. The majority of the unmarried women belong to younger age group.

Table 6.7: Marital status of members in NHGs

Marital status	*Frequency*	*%*
Married	1820	96.8
Unmarried	60	3.2
Total	1880	100.0

From the field, it is observed that the married women are more active in these types of financial institutions as they have to shoulder a lot of responsibilities in the family. They have children to get educated, they have husbands to be self-employed, and they too have a dream about livelihood in the form of micro-enterprises. In many of the cases, the women are said to be currently married. But, many of them are female headed households. They have to take care of their own survival and of their families, especially their children. The benefits they reap from the Kudumbashree help them meet atleast some of their needs.

Religion

Religion is an important institution in every society and it performs certain important functions. Religion acts as an agency of social control and maintains social order. The religion's influence on society is varied in many walks of life. Majority of the respondents (67.4%) who are the members in the NHGs are Hindus. The remaining 25.2 per cent belong to Muslim population and 7.3 per cent belong to Christianity (Table 6.8).

Table 6.8: Religion of members in NHGs

Religion	*Frequency*	*%*
Hindu	1268	67.4
Muslim	474	25.2
Christian	138	7.3
Total	1880	100.0

Community

The community of the members in different NHGs in the various districts of Kerala is presented in Table 6.9. It is found that the Other Backward Castes (OBCs) are the majority community which takes part in the groups surveyed. About 14 per cent of the members who have membership in the groups belong to general category. Another 17 per cent belong to Scheduled Caste (SC) and yet another ten per cent belong to Scheduled Tribe (ST) population. Only a small percentage belongs to Other Economically Backward Castes (OEC) category.

Table 6.9: Community of members in NHGs

Community	*Frequency*	*%*
SC	328	17.4
ST	198	10.5
OEC	105	5.6
OBC	991	52.7
General	258	13.7
Total	1880	100.0

The present study focussed on the backward regions of Kerala State and the above result has been obtained. Most of the members in the NHGs belong to backward and marginalized sections of the society. In another way one can view the result in such a manner that the organization could reach out to various sections of the society in Kerala and the extent of its penetration is not small.

Education

The present set of population has an interesting pattern of education. A good number (30.5%) of women who are members of the NHGs reached up to the education level of Secondary School Leaving Certificate (SSLC). Another 28.8 per cent reached up to the high school level. Still a substantial number of women in the NHGs is illiterate, i.e., 10.7 per cent (Table 6.10). Another four per cent is literate; but they do not have any formal education. The higher education in the tertiary level is less; the percentage of persons who attained the degree level is only 2.5 per cent; Post Graduate (PG) level is only 0.2 per cent (Table 6.10).

Table 6.10: Educational status of members in NHGs

Educational status	*Frequency*	*%*
Literate	76	4
Illiterate	201	10.7
LP -	207	11
UP	107	5.7
HS	541	28.8
SSLC	573	30.5
PDC	119	6.3
Diploma	1	0.1
Degree	47	2.5
PG	4	0.2
Professional	4	0.2
Total	1880	100.0

Kerala is a State which gives utmost importance to education. But these figures show that the status of backward women coming from socially and economically backward sector is still lagging behind. One of the indicators of poverty among women is the lack of human asset.

The theoretical suggestion can be clearly visible in the field also. The peculiar disadvantages faced by women are due to relative lack of assets—human, natural, physical, social and financial. Distribution of human assets such as the capacity for basic labour, skills and good health is heavily biased against women. In developing countries like India, ownership of natural assets such as land has tended to be heavily biased in favour of the male members of the family. Access to physical assets such as infrastructure is restricted by institutional barriers. Social assets, such as networks of contacts and reciprocal obligations that can be called on in time of need, and political influence over resources are also low for women. Lack of access to financial assets such as savings and formal credit is another stumbling block to their progress.

Table 6.11: Association with educational status of members in NHGs

	Value	*df*	*Asymp. Sig. (2-sided)*
Pearson Chi-Square	338.143[(a)]	55	.000
Likelihood Ratio	320.047	55	.000
Linear-by-Linear Association	7.885	1	.005
No. of Valid Cases	1860		

Note: (a) 25 cells (34.7%) have expected count less than 5. The minimum expected count is .11.

A striking feature which one can observe in the field is that, whatever be the educational status, the women are so keen to send their wards to school and for higher education. They are ready to spend any amount of money for the purpose. Exception to this trend was seen only in Wayanad where the mothers in many cases are managing the entire affairs of households and where the facilities available to them for sending their children to schools are very limited. The chi-square test result shows (Table 6.11) a significant association between educational status of members in NHGs and the district surveyed.

Total Savings of Members

Savings of members are the key element in the micro-finance industry. It is a central part in the SHG model too. Only on the basis of savings amount, the loans are sanctioned to the members. In short, the basic function of the SHGs is to mobilize own savings in order to create its own fund to rotate among the members.

The data shows that the level of savings is not evenly spread across the districts (Table 6.12). A good percentage (29.5%) of members still has savings ranging between Rs. 1000 and 2000. A quarter of the respondents have savings below Rs. 1000. Another 30 per cent have savings between Rs. 2000 and Rs. 4000. Only 15 per cent of the members have savings ranging from Rs. 4000 to Rs. 9000. It is an astonishing fact that for a small percentage, amount of savings is greater than Rs. 5000.

Table 6.12: Total savings of members in NHGs

Amount	*Frequency*	%
<1000	463	24.6
1000-2000	554	29.5
2000-3000	285	15.2
3000-4000	290	15.4
4000-5000	85	4.5
5000-6000	74	3.9
6000-7000	38	2
7000-8000	28	1.5
8000-9000	20	1.1
>9000	43	2.3
Total	1880	100

In order to have a deeper feeling of the savings size of the members, the mean value of savings is computed (Table 6.13). It is observed that among the members the mean savings is Rs. 2517.69. The standard deviation is 2251.27.

Table 6.13: Mean savings

Mean	2517.69
Median	1840
Std. Deviation	2251.27
Variance	5068193
Skewness	2.553
Kurtosis	10.52
Range	20640

Even though many of the NHGs were constituted more than a decade ago, the level of savings is very low. As the area of study is confined only among the women in the poorer sections of the society, it is evident that the inability of the poor to save is the major problem. The other problem they have raised is that, they are not allowed to withdraw a portion of their savings when they have an emergency. The micro-finance industry usually keeps the savings and rolls it as loan among the members. They are not aware of those principles upon which the industry works, namely pooling the micro-savings and providing credit to the needy out of it. Unfortunately, many of the members are not participating in saving mobilization of the respective units.

Table 6.14: Total credit of the members in NHGs

Amount	Name of District						Total
	Idukki	Alappuzha	Kozhikode	Malappuram	Wayanad	Thiruvananthapuram	
Nil	61 (11.0)	48 (8.7)	104 (18.8)	170 (30.7)	48 (8.7)	122 (22.1)	553 (29.4)
100-1000	32 (14.9)	12 (5.6)	52 (24.2)	36 (16.7)	27 (12.6)	56 (26.0)	215 (11.4)
1000-2500	46 (13.3)	26 (7.5)	92 (26.6)	76 (22.0)	45 (13.0)	61 (17.6)	346 (18.4)
2500-5000	69 (15.0)	82 (17.8)	115 (25.0)	85 (18.5)	47 (10.2)	63 (13.7)	460 (24.5)
5000-7500	6 (9.2)	17 (26.2)	20 (30.8)	5 (7.7)	13 (20.0)	4 (6.2)	65 (3.5)
7500-10000	3 (1.8)	83 (50.9)	41 (25.2)	10 (6.1)	15 (9.2)	11 (6.7)	163 (8.7)
10000 Above	0 (0)	56 (72.7)	7 (9.1)	7 (9.1)	6 (7.8)	1 (1.3)	77 (4.1)
Total	217 (11.5)	324 (17.2)	431 (22.9)	389 (20.7)	200 (10.7)	318 (16.9)	1880 (100)

Source: Figures in brackets show percentages.

Total Credit of Members

One of the most important functions of the micro-finance industry is to render credit to the poor sections of the society. It is found that out of the total 1880 respondents, about 30 per cent of the people have not availed any loans at all (Table 6.14).

About 40 per cent of the members availed loans less than Rs. 5000 while a small percentage of people (15%) availed a loan more than Rs. 7500. It is observed that even a number which is equal to four per cent has availed a loan greater than Rs. 10000. Although the credit given to the poor is very low, it is observed that some of the groups could give out an amount more than Rs. 10000. One of the reasons for the high amount of loan disbursed by the MFI nowadays is that the bank linkage programme is providing the NHGs with higher amount. Moreover, the groups which were started some years ago could disburse more money.

Table 6.15: Arithmetic mean of credit among NHGs

Mean	3248.89
Median	2000
Std. Deviation	4332.46
Variance	18770243
Skewness	4.29
Kurtosis	46.90
Range	75000

When looking into the mean it is Rs. 3288.89 and the median is Rs. 2000 (Table 6.15). The standard deviation of the data is Rs. 4332.46.

Training

Nowadays, SHGs are not only giving credit and collecting savings, but also they are imparting training to their members. Training which the members receive through micro-finance is an asset for them as many of them are undereducated or unskilled. They cannot find a place in the job market with their level of education. That is the reason why many of the poor women are confined to their households and are content with their present situation. But the advent of micro-finance gives a new avenue to the women in the rural areas. In this background, they are given financial support along with the required training for starting enterprises.

Table 6.16: Training to the members

Training	*Frequency*	*%*
Yes	1088	57.9
No	792	42.1
Total	1880	100.0

It is observed that the Kudumbashree mission has rendered the micro-finance services in the right spirit among the women, especially to those who are underprivileged in the society. About 58 per cent of the women have admitted that they have received some kind of training from the micro-finance organization while about 42 per cent have not received any kind of training (Table 6.16). On enquiry, it is observed that many of the members have been offered with different types of training. But due to the traditional settings (as in Malappuram) very poor background (as in Wayanad) and other engagements (as in Idukki), the women could not participate in these kinds of training (Table 6.16).

Motivation

Motivation behind the facilitation of the group formation is very important. It is not an easy task to facilitate and initiate the group activity. The facilitator has to perform many tasks such as carrying out field-work, meeting the prospective members, educating them what the group is for, how the groups has to function, the duties and responsibilities of members, and other institutional preconditions.

Table 6.17: One who motivate the members to start the group

Facilitators	*Frequency*	*%age*
Other NHGs in the locality	4	3.7
Friends	7	6.5
Others	96	89.8
Total	107	100.0

The survey results show (Table 6.17) that only 3.7 per cent of the total groups were started due to self motivation or the initiative of the other NHGs in the locality. The friends helped in the formation of 6.5 per cent of the total groups. 89.8 per cent of the groups were started under the initiative of others in the locality. They include the office bearers like

ADS president, ADS secretary, Panchayat member, Ward Councillor, CDS chairperson, etc. In addition to their normal services, Block Panchayat Members, Scheduled Tribe promoters in the case of Wayanad, Welfare officer of plantation in the case of Idukki district, etc. too played a crucial role. An important thing one can observe is that the local politicians and Kudumbashree leaders play a major role in initiating groups.

Group Meetings

Development programmes can create social ties and enhance social capital among the members of a highly localised community in a strikingly shorter span of time. Close neighbours from similar socio-economic backgrounds come to know one another through micro-finance meetings.

Periodicity of Group Meetings

Group meeting is one of the innovations in the field of micro-finance. The idea of group formation and weekly meeting of members owes to the Grameen Bank founder Prof. Muhammed Yunus. The regularity of meeting by the members, frequency of meetings and participation in group meetings are important catalyst for social capital formation. They come together for a cause, many mobilizing savings and disbursing loans.

The group should decide the periodicity of the meetings, i.e., weekly, fortnightly or monthly. In the case of Kudumbashree, it is stipulated that the group should meet regularly on a weekly basis. The groups should also decide on the timing of the meeting. The groups plan the timing and periodicity of group meetings in consultation with the members for regular conduct of it. The regularity in the holding of meeting and attendance during meeting gives an indication about groups' functioning. Therefore, a financier (in the present context, the bank who links up with the NHG) usually sees whether the meetings are being held regularly; whether the members attend the meetings punctually and stay till the end of the meeting, there are any sanctions being initiated against delinquent members.

Table 6.18: Periodicity of group meeting

Period	*Frequency*	*%*
Monthly	6	5.6
Monthly twice	4	3.7
Weekly	97	90.7
Total	107	100.0

The direction from the authorities of Kudumbashree insisted the members to have a group meeting every week. 90.7 per cent of the groups strictly follow the instruction (Table 6.18). But a percentage less than ten does not follow the instruction. While 5.6 per cent of the total groups meet only once in a month, another 3.7 per cent meet twice a month.

Table 6.19: Association between frequency of group meeting and districts

	Value	*Df*	*Asymp. Sig. (2-sided)*
Pearson Chi-Square	81.444[(a)]	20	.000
Likelihood Ratio	56.329	20	.000
No. of Valid Cases	107		

Note: (a) 24 cells (80.0%) have expected count less than 5. The minimum expected count is .13.

Since the cells having less than five count is higher, we resort to the likelihood ratio chi-square to test the association between group meetings and districts. It is seen that there exists significant relationship between the group meetings and districts with the likelihood ratio value of 56.329 and the significance level is less than 0.05 (Table 6.19).

Periodicity and Regularity of Group Meeting

Everybody claims that the members meet regularly. But some of the groups opine that not all groups meet regularly. About 99 per cent of the NHGs witnessed that they meet without fail. Only less than one per cent of NHGs admit that they do not meet regularly.

Place of Group Meeting

It is instructed that the place at which group meetings are conducted should be changed on a weekly basis. This would help to have visitation to other households. When fellow group members come to one's house, it will help them to discuss the problems faced by the family and they make sympathetic enquiry about the issues. This often lead to a healthy discussion on the issues and the group attempts to resolve the same.

Even though the theory seems to be excellent, the reverse is seen in the field. Only 62.6 per cent of the groups conduct their group meeting on rotational basis, while the rest of the 37.4 per cent groups still have a permanent place to conduct their group meetings (Figure 6.2). In

Alappuzha, it is found that all the groups conduct their group meetings on rotational basis while in Kozhikode, 15 groups have rotational locations, and only three groups have permanent places. On the other hand, Malappuram has the highest number of groups meeting in permanent place (i.e., 12) and only eight groups are meeting on rotational basis.

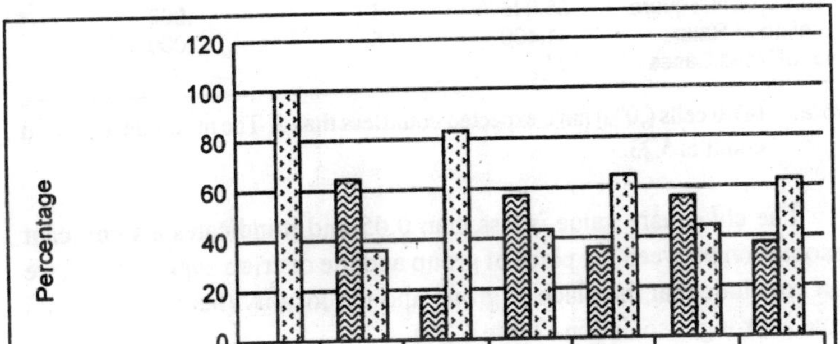

	Alappuzha	Idukki	Kozhikode	Malappuram	Thiruvanantha-puram	Wayanad	Total
Permanent place	0	64.3	16.7	57.1	35.3	55.6	37.4
Rotational basis	100	35.7	83.3	42.9	64.7	44.4	62.6

Fig. 6.2: Place of group meetings

The question that naturally arises is why permanent place is selected though it is being instructed otherwise. Usually in a meeting, on an average of 15 members are expected. To accommodate them, small dwelling units of the members are not sufficient. Most of the poor people live in very small spaces and it may be difficult for them to share their own spaces for others to convene meetings. For example, slum dwellers in Thiruvananthapuram stay in rental buildings; plantation workers in Idukki live in company allotted lines and tribal people dwell in settlements. As they have very limited space for them and their families, it would be difficult for them to open their own houses for convening the meetings. So, there is a little chance for having the group meetings on rotational basis.

The permanent places which are referred to here, in most cases, would be public places like *Anganwadi* or open spaces which are selected for the purpose of meeting. In other cases, it would be the house of a prominent member like president, secretary or a person possessing a house which is spacious enough to accommodate all members.

Table 6.20: Association between place of group meeting and districts

	Value	*df*	*Asymp. Sig. (2-sided)*
Pearson Chi-Square	25.046[(a)]	5	.000
Likelihood Ratio	31.490	5	.000
No. of Valid Cases	107		

Note: (a) 0 cells (.0%) have expected countless than 5. The minimum expected count is 5.23.

The chi-square value is less than 0.05 and it indicates a significant association between the place of group and the districts surveyed. So, we can conclude that the place of group and the locality (here the districts) have a strong association (Table 6.20).

Duration of Weekly Meetings

Weekly meetings are one of the major functions of self-help groups all-over the world. In Kudumbashree, groups meet usually on Saturdays and Sunday afternoons. But there are groups that meet on weekdays also. Weekly meetings on weekends help women to come together, after attending their household chores to discuss various issues—personal, political, social and cultural matters. The members remit their weekly savings to the secretary of the group at the meeting. Moreover, decisions are taken on matters relating to sanctioning and repayment of loans and calculation of interest on loan amount.

For performing all these functions, a group has, on an average, to meet for more than one hour. The majority of the groups (78.5%) meet for less than one hour a week, while 21.5 per cent groups (i.e., 23 groups) take more than one hour for meeting (Figure 6.3).

Many members in the group felt that the time they spend for group meetings gives them exposure to the world of friends and fellows for sharing experiences and gaining insights. Housewives from lower middle class families have a lot of time to attend the meeting. But the poor people give more importance for their livelihood and survival. They can hardly spare time for this purpose. In the districts of Malappuram and Wayanad, all the groups meet for less than one hour, while in districts like Alappuzha and Idukki one can see that more groups are engaged in meeting for more than one hour.

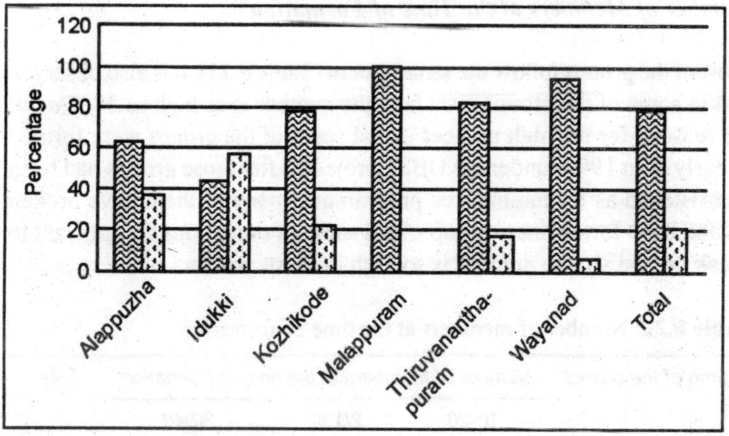

Fig. 6.3: Duration of weekly meetings

Table 6.21: Association between duration of group meeting and districts

	Value	*df*	*Asymp. Sig. (2-sided)*
Pearson Chi-Square	21.809[(a)]	5	.001
Likelihood Ratio	24.608	5	.000
No. of Valid Cases	107		

Note: (a) 6 cells (50.0%) have expected count less than 5. The minimum expected count is 3.01.

Chi-square value indicates a significant association between the duration of group meeting and the districts. In the present context, as more than 50 per cent cells had an expected frequency count of less than five, it is better to look at the likelihood ratio chi-square. Here, also the value shows significant association between the two variables. So, we can conclude that duration of group meeting and districts have a strong association (Table 6.21).

Membership in NHGs and Drop-out

The number in a neighbourhood group is fixed at 20 by the Kudumbashree. This is for the ease of forming the group and having meetings among the members.

Number of Members at the Time of Formation

Most of the groups follow the same pattern (Table 6.23). It is also observed that in some of the groups even now the number is as high as 38. One of the reasons for the high number is that some of the groups were formed as early as in 1990s under the UBSP project. After those groups had been rechristened as Kudumbashree programme, many of them have broken up and have formed new groups. Still some of the groups do not want to break up and so, the number is so high in those groups.

Table 6.22: Number of members at the time of formation

Name of the district	*Number of Members at the time of Formation*			*Total*
	10-20	*20-30*	*30-40*	
Alappuzha	15 (78.90)	4 (21.10)	0	19 (100)
Idukki	14 (100)	0	0	14 (100)
Kozhikode	5 (27.80)	10 (55.6)	3 (16.70)	18 (100)
Malappuram	17 (81.00)	4 (19.00)	0	21 (100)
Thiruvananthapuram	16 (94.10)	1 (5.90)	0	17 (100)
Wayanad	18 (100)	0	0	18 (100)
Total	85 (79.40)	19 (17.8)	3 (2.80)	107 (100)

Source: Figures in brackets show percentages.

Chi-square value indicates a significant association between the number of members and the districts. Since in the present context more than 66 per cent cells had an expected frequency count of less than five, it is better to look at the likelihood ratio chi-square. Here also the value shows significant association between the two variables (Table 6.22).

Table 6.23: Association between number of members and districts

	Value	*df*	*Asymp. Sig. (2-sided)*
Pearson Chi-Square	44.702[(a)]	10	.000
Likelihood Ratio	43.325	10	.000
No. of Valid Cases	107		

Note: (a) 12 cells (66.7%) have expected count less than 5. The minimum expected count is 39.

The number of members of a group plays a very important role in disbursement of loan, waiting period between different loan cycles, distribution of capital, and distribution of bank loans among members. So, even if a member drops-out, the groups are reluctant to include new person. The major reason is that the new person has to raise the savings because in many of the groups, savings play a major role in sanctioning and distribution of loans. Loans are sanctioned on the basis of the savings of the respective members. Many groups feel that when they take new members, it takes time for them to be accustomed with the tradition and rules of the groups. So, they desire to be smaller. In many cases, the groups prefer to be exclusive. Hence, they are hesitant to entertain new members. (Table 6.23)

Number of New Members

Many of the NHGs do not have stipulated membership of 20 members. In 79 per cent of NHGs, there is no new enrolment of new members after the formation of the groups. In some of the groups, the number of new members is two to six, but in some groups, 15 to 16 new members are added (Table 6.24).

Table 6.24: Number of new members in NHGs

Number of new members	*Frequency*	*%*
0	85	79.4
1	11	10.3
2	7	6.5
4	1	.9
6	1	.9
15	1	.9
16	1	.9
Total	107	100.0

Homogeneity of the Groups

It is stipulated that the members of the NHG should be residents of the same area and must have an affinity towards their unity. The theory of group lending always emphasizes the point that the groups must be homogeneous. The homogeneity of relationship could be in terms of caste/occupation/gender or economic status, whichever is critical in the specific local settings. In other words, homogeneity in this context means that the members should be from same social and economic status, so, that the functioning of the groups becomes smooth and effective.

Social capital explains a chance of having exclusions by other groups. Some level of reluctance to accept new members or incorporate people from other social groups can be seen in some areas. Formation of tribal groups in Wayanad or SC group in Thiruvananthapuram has been given emphasis by the authorities. This may be done on the basis of benefits given to them collectively.

Debate of Non-poor Inclusion in MFIs

Micro-finance is basically meant for the poorest sections of the society. Yet a worldwide phenomenon is that the non-poor are also included in the sphere of micro-finance activities. There is an ongoing and elaborative discussion as to whether non-poor can be allowed in the MFIs. Many argue that the non-poor should also be in the groups in order to sustain the groups in a viable manner. On the other hand, those who are in the borderline naturally get attached to the realm of the groups. It is observed in the field, the Kudumbashree mission has instructed that the members in a neighbourhood should be the members of the NHGs irrespective of their economic background. In general, the Kudumbashree NHGs incorporate both poor and non-poor into their NHGs. They have their own reasons for following this kind of a broad targeting.

Possession of BPL Ration Card

Only in 23 per cent of groups, all the members hold Below Poverty Line (BPL) ration cards. In majority of groups (76.6%) not all members hold BPL ration cards (Figure 6.4). This suggests that in majority of the groups, the presence of non-poor members is evident. The districts in which more number of non-poor present are Kozhikode (94%), Idukki (92.9%), Malappuram (90.5%) and Alappuzha (89.5%) (Figure 6.4).

A striking example is seen in the case of Idukki where the plantation workers are sampled. As the plantation workers are permanent employees of the tea estates, they are not provided with the BPL cards. But the living standards of these people are in no way better than the rest of the poor population (BPL) of the State. They are living in residential quarters provided by the estate, with low living standards. They are presumably poor but hey are excluded from the BPL list. The NHGs found that the people living in the tribal areas of Wayanad are predominantly poor and they possess BPL ration cards.

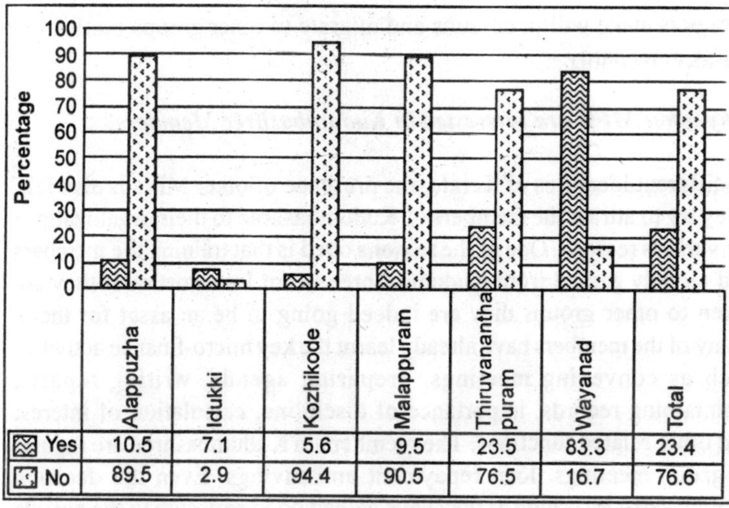

Fig. 6.4: Possession of BPL ration card by all members

Drop-out

One of the main problems of Micro-Finance Institutions (MFIs) is the issue of drop-out of the members from their SHGs. It is a major concern to the micro-finance movement all-over the world. The foremost reason for this is that stiff competition exists among micro-finance institutions formed under various organizations. Hijacking and kidnapping of members from one MFI to other are also commonly seen here. It is interesting to observe that it is not much prevalent in Kudumbashree. The major reason is that it is a government programme. Most of the benefits from the Government are channelized through the programme over some years. Those who are poor take more interest in availing the benefits; so, they do not move out of Kudumbashree in normal course.

Multiplicity of Promoting Agencies

Nowadays in Kerala, many other organisations and government programmes have also emerged to support SHGs of poor women. These 'promoting' agencies try to hijack the existing self-help groups in a particular area. It is now noted that some of the members of Kudumbashree are also joining groups formed by other 'promoting' agencies. This creates problems for the existing groups as some of the members make willful defaults and migrate to other groups putting the SHGs in jeopardy.

Why other MFIs are Interested in Kudumbashree Members?

In different localities of Kerala, the presence of other MFIs is also felt. They try to attract the members of Kudumbashree to their organizations for various reasons. One of the reasons cited is that training the members had already gained from Kudumbashree is not less worthy. If they are taken to other groups they are indeed going to be an asset for them. Many of the members have already learnt the key micro-finance activities such as convening meetings, preparing agenda, writing reports, maintaining records, importance of discipline, calculation of interest and other related functions. The members in Kudumbashree are regular in group meetings, loan repayment and savings. Even the decision making capacity is high as they have gained good exposure to the outside world.

Multiple Membership means Split Loyalty

The field experience revealed that even though the authorities are giving strict instructions, Kudumbashree members are taking part in other micro-finance institutions/organizations. They have membership in Nair Service Society (NSS), Sree Narayana Darma Paripalana Yogam (SNDPY), church organizations and other private micro-finance organisations. They are very much active in those organizations too. Obviously, when the respective communities start the self-help groups (SHGs), the women who are already in Kudumbashree movement would be an automatic choice for them. The members too enjoy their multiple memberships. They hold key positions like secretary or president in such groups. Some of them have been identified for acting as facilitators to other MFI/Ps too.

Janashree

As a strong wave of the Congress party funded Janashree came up, confusion arose among the minds of the people. They target everybody irrespective of his financial position. As a result, there is a shift in loyalty from Kudumbashree in favour of Janashree and other micro-finance organizations.

Private MFIs

Private MFIs like ESAF, Muthoot, etc. have been found working among the beneficiaries of Kudumbashree. These NBFC-MFIs have spread their tentacles even among the poorest of the people. Their prevalence is seen more in Thiruvananthapuram and Kozhikode where the members are having affinity to city area.

The mode of activity is entirely different from the traditional micro-finance activities. While the traditional micro-finance institutions try to raise the savings of the poor as seed capital and rotate the savings among the members as credit, the new generation micro-finance institutors do the reverse. For example, one of the MFIs is seen working among the fishing villages of Kozhikode, ESAF has another mode of operation. It grants loan of Rs. 10,000 to each member. There is no need of a meeting or any other informal gatherings. They collect ten members in the locality and disburse the loans to all the members. In many cases, the husbands offer guarantee for wives and *vice versa*. The interest rate is apparently high. It is a reemergence of moneylenders in new forms in local area.

It is observed that even if the interest rates are high and the conditions are strict, many members fall prey to it. One of the major reasons cited is that the average loan size from Kudumbashree is small compared to the loan which the members can get from other MFIs. But they do not want to quit Kudumbashree. They know that it is a government programme and the conditions are less stringent here and loans are available at lower rate of interest. There are many instances of multiple memberships, but many such members have not disclosed the same.

Loan Repayment and Drop-out

Poor repayment history of some members may invite sanctions and enforcements. When one member does not repay her loans, naturally the other members become alert as the loan may turn bad. The peer pressure works in these cases, and the result would be promp payment. But at times, some members make willful default. This affects the solidarity of the groups. In most of the areas of study, where very poor people are living, they really feel it difficult to repay it. In such situation, they silently leave the group.

Lack of Time and Drop-Out Relationship

Time is a major factor behind the participation of group meetings and other activities. As people are busier, they do not find time to participate in these kinds of groups. Time is also a commodity for modern people having alternative uses for it, if participation in these groups is not found to be fruitful; they may quit and give more preference to other things.

For poverty stricken people, the things are entirely different. For them, it is the time they spend for making their livelihood. For example, if a member is a housemaid or a canteen worker any time in a weekday may be inconvenient for her. Getting leave from her income earning activity would be a difficult proposition. They prefer to stick to their livelihood rather than attend group meetings. When the micro-finance is only an appendage for their lives, they give more importance to their own livelihood than the organisation. This may be one of the reasons why poor women are found to keep away from these kinds of organisations.

The problem with several SHGs is that members leave them when some problems crop up in the group. Many groups have lost their cohesion due to internal strife and personal rivalry. Some members left the groups for their failure to obtain loans on demand. In other cases, members left the groups when they shifted residence consequent to their marriage. In such cases, the groups have endeavoured to take new members who are not much experienced in taking part in MFO. This creates some problems of cohesion and instability. Another problem is that these new members are often women from not-so-poor strata of society.

Reasons for Drop-Out

Many questions are posed to the secretary or president of the NHGs; but their problems inside the NHGs won't come out. The major reason cited was marriage or migration or death. Some have cited their inability to repay loan and money problems as the major reasons. Lack of time is also mentioned as another reason by some respondents. Some blame the conditions and reluctance on the part of the members to have an effective participation in the meetings. Some others felt that they do not get any benefit in continuing in the group (Table 6.25).

Micro-financing Activities

Micro-savings and micro-credit are the major activities of any MFI/Ps

Table 6.25: Reasons for drop-out

Reasons	*Frequency*	*%*
Not dropped out	65	60.7
Marriage	9	8.4
Migration	13	12.1
Shifted to other MFIs	2	1.9
Unable to repay loans	1	.9
No time	3	2.8
Others	14	13.1
Total	107	100.0

around the world. Incidently, Kudumbashree also gives very much importance to these activities.

Regularity of Savings

It is found from the study that all the members are aware of the importance in the regularity of savings. There is some delay in remitting the savings with the NHGs, but it is mandatory that all the members should remit their savings. Another reason for the regular saving pattern of the members is that the credit disbursement in most of the groups is linked with the savings of the group members.

Many of the members are asking about the choice of withdrawing their saving. The controversy of non-withdrawal status of savings invites a lot of discussion/criticism. Savings is a cushion for so many people. On the strength of savings as collateral, they draw credit. Savings is the major component of micro-finance.

Table 6.26: Members savings regularly without fail

Name of the District	*What Percentage of members savings regularly without fail*			*Total*
	50%	50-75%	>75%	
Alappuzha	7 (36.8)	12 (63.2)	0	19 (100)
Idukki	0	11 (78.6)	3 (21.4)	14 (100)
Kozhikode	6 (33.3)	12 (66.7)	0	18 (100)
Malappuram	6 (28.6)	15 (71.4)	0	21 (100)
Thiruvananthapuram	5 (29.4)	11 (64.7)	1 (5.9)	17 (100)
Wayanad	2 (11.1)	15 (83.3)	1 (5.6)	18 (100)
Total	26 (24.3)	76 (71.0)	5 (4.7)	107 (100)

Source: Figures in brackets show percentages.

Only 4.7 per cent of the groups stated that more than 75 per cent of the members are making their savings regularly. 76 per cent of the group members said that in their respective groups 50 to 75 per cent members are saving regularly, while in another 26 per cent of the groups told that 50 per cent of the members are saving regularly without fail (Table 6.26).

Operating Bank Account and Other Dealings with Bank

One of the major aims of having micro-finance activity at the grassroot level is to give training in the banking operations. The poor people who were once away from the doorsteps of banks are now invited to its premises through the arm of micro-finance. It is the method through which the poor women are taken to the banks by giving training in the operation of the bank account and other dealings with banks.

Table 6.27: Person responsible in operating the bank account

Name of the District	Person Responsible in operating the bank account						Total
	Elected members	Everybody on rotation basis	Secretary	President	Secretary and President	Secretary and everybody on rotation basis	
Alappuzha	2 (10.5)	1 (5.3)	7 (36.8)	1 (5.3)	8 (42.1)	0 (.0)	19 (100)
Idukki	0	0 (.0)	8 (57.1)	5 (35.7)	1 (7.1)	0 (.0)	14 (100)
Kozhikode	0 (.0)	0 (0)	8 (44.4)	3 (16.7)	7 (38.9)	0 (.0)	18 (100)
Malappuram	2 (9.5)	0 (.0)	8 (38.1)	10 (47.6)	0 (0)	1 (4.8)	21 (100)
Thiruvanantha-puram	0 (0)	0 (0)	6 (35.3)	4 (23.5)	7 (41.2)	0 (0)	17 (100)
Wayanad	0 (.0)	0 (0)	10 (55.6)	7 (38.9)	0 (0)	1 (5.6)	18 (100)
Total	4 (3.7)	1 (.9)	47 (43.9)	30 (28.0)	23 (21.5)	2 (1.9)	107 (100)

Source: Figures in brackets show percentages.

In the field, one could observe different trends. In some of the groups, an elected member take care of the responsibilities, while in a small number of NHGs everybody share the responsibility on a rotational basis, while in 44 per cent of the groups secretary does the same and in an another 27 per cent of NHGs president does the work (Table 6.27).

Awareness about Loan Rules and Bank Loan Details

Only 42 per cent of the NHGs say that 50 per cent of the members in their respective NHGs are aware of the loan rules and bank loan details. The leaders of the rest of the groups (58%) hold the opinion that 50 to 75 per cent of the groups have the awareness about the loan rules and bank loan details. It is striking to notice that the district of Wayanad has a higher proportion (83%) with low awareness level. The literacy level as well as mobility from their local areas is low among the tribal women (Table 6.28).

Table 6.28: Members' awareness about loan rules and bank loan details

Name of the District	Members' awareness about loan rules		Tulal
	50	50-75	
Alappuzha	5 (26.3)	14 (73.7)	19 (100)
Idukki	8 (57.1)	6 (42.9)	14 (100)
Kozhikode	2 (11.1)	16 (88.9)	18 (100)
Malappuram	6 (28.6)	15 (71.4)	21 (100)
Thiruvananthapuram	9 (52.9)	8 (47.1)	17 (100)
Wayanad	15 (83.3)	3 (16.7)	18 (100)
Total	45 (42.1)	62 (57.9)	107 (100)

Source: Figures in brackets show percentages.

Repayment of Bank Loans

Most of the NHGs are already linked with the banks in the locality. Many of the NHGs have enjoyed the facility and they are in a position to get more money than that they can disburse using their own fund. They are to repay it to the bank and it is carrying low interest. As the government is subsidizing the interest, they are very much interested in repaying the bank loans.

It is observed that, 10 per cent of the groups have not yet received any kind of bank loans. They are meeting their needs with their own funds or by other available sources. On the other hand, the groups which availed the loans said that they are very prompt in repayment of their loans. 83 per cent of the groups are of this opinion. A small number of NHGs confessed that they have either delayed their payment or defaulted the payment (Table 6.29).

Table 6.29: Repayment of bank loans

Name of the District	Repayment of bank loans				Total
	No Loan at all	Paid on time	Default time	Delayed payment	
Alappuzha	0	17 (89.5)	1 (5.3)	1 (5.3)	19 (100)
Idukki	0	14 (100)	0	0	14 (100)
Kozhikode	0	17 (94.4)	1 (5.6)	0	18 (100)
Malappuram	0	18 (85.7)	0 (.0)	3 (14.3)	21 (100)
Thiruvananthapuram	11 (64.7)	6 (35.3)	0	0	17 (100)
Wayanad	0 (.0)	17 (94.4)	0 (.0)	1 (5.6)	18 (100)
Total	11 (10.3)	89 (83.2)	2 (1.9)	5 (4.7)	107 (100)

Source: Figures in brackets show percentages.

Default in Loan Repayment

The problem of mounting defaults has begun to emerge in the field of micro-finance. Default is found both in the case of remittance of savings and repayment of loans. When default occurs, recycling of funds gets interrupted. This would in turn affect the sustainability of the micro-finance organisations.

Since, the poor avail larger loans, they find the burden of monthly repayment too heavy. It is also noticed that the funds borrowed by them

Table 6.30: Default the loan repayment

Number of Members	Frequency	%
2 to 3 Members	2	1.9
4 to 5 Members	3	2.8
5 to 6 Members	1	.9
8 to 10 Members	1	.9
Nil	99	92.5
Some Members	1	.9
Total	107	100.0

are not always spent for remunerative activities. They find, therefore, repayment is all the more difficult. Hence, recycling process is often affected and the sustenance of the groups becomes difficult.

Some of the members in the NHGs default repayment of loans. In majority of groups (92%) defaults are not reported. But in some groups up to 10 members defaulted their repayment (Table 6.30).

Decisions on Loan Taken during Meeting

Decisions on loan are taken at the group meetings of NHGs. From the field study, it is found that in 95 per cent of the groups the decision is taken by all the members in the NHGs. Only less than five per cent of the NHGs said that it is taken by other people including the elected members or others inside the NHGs (Table 6.31).

Table 6.31: Decisions on loan taken during meeting

Name of the District	*Decisions on loan taken during meeting:*			*Total*
	By all	*By elected members*	*By leaders or others*	
Alappuzha	19 (100.0)	0	0	19 (100)
Idukki	14 (100)	0	0	14 (100)
Kozhikode	18 (100)	0	0	18 (100)
Malappuram	21 (100)	0	0	21 (100)
Thiruvananthapuram	12 (70.6)	4 (23.5)	1 (5.9)	17 (100)
Wayanad	18 (100.0)	0	0	18 (100)
Total	102 (95.3)	4 (3.7)	1 (.9)	107 (100)

Source: Figures in brackets show percentages.

Auditing

It is mandatory on the part of the Kudumbashree to audit the accounts of the NHGs on a regular basis. It is found that auditing was done by all the groups under study. It has been done under the aegis of different persons in the locality. They include bank manager, CDS chair person, Kudumbashree auditors, corporation authorities, Panchayat members, etc. (Table 6.32).

Table 6.32: Person conducted auditing

Person conducted auditing	*Frequency*	*%*
Bank Manager	2	1.9
CDS Chair	36	33.6
Kudumbashree	68	63.6
Nil	1	.9
Total	107	100.0

Loans for Production Purposes

Even though the micro-credit given to the members is meant for productive purposes, it is a well known fact that the micro-credit is largely being used for consumption smoothing purposes. The evidence is seen from the result of 42 per cent of groups who are denying the claim that there is misutilization of the loan for purposes other than productive purposes for which loans are sanctioned (Table 6.33). 62 per cent of the groups said that there is a steady increase in the loans for productive purposes.

Table 6.33: Increase in loans for production purposes

Name of the District	*Increase in loans for production purposes*		*Total*
	Yes	*No*	
Alappuzha	18 (94.7)	1 (5.3)	19 (100)
Idukki	0	14 (100)	14 (100)
Kozhikode	13 (72.2)	5 (27.8)	18 (100)
Malappuram	8 (38.1)	13 (61.9)	21 (100)
Thiruvananthapuram	7 (41.2)	10 (58.8)	17 (100.0)
Wayanad	16 (88.9)	2 (11.1)	18 (100.0)
Total	62 (57.9)	45 (42.1)	107 (100)

Source: Figures in brackets show percentages.

One of the major reasons for this state of affairs is the poor background of the members in the NHGs in the study area. Lack of education, skill and lack of entrepreneurial capacity among the people, lack of mobility, laxity of marketing avenues, social taboos, and weak monitoring mechanism on the part of the MFI and livelihood issues are the reasons for this problem.

Table 6.34: Reasons for not going for productive purposes

Reasons	*Frequency*	*%*
Apply for the Loan	2	1.9
Didn't Get loan from the bank	26	24.3
New Group Applying Loan	1	.9
Nil	64	59.8
Plantation Workers with Salary	14	13.1
Total	107	100

While enquiring about the reasons for lower spending for productive purposes, different replies were received. Some have said that they did not get a loan from the bank for such unproductive purposes. For others availing SHG assistance for using it as a stop gap arrangement till the loan applied for is sanctioned by the financial institutions (Table 6.34).

Group Members Possessing a Resource/Skill Asset for Regular Income

The major concern of micro-finance is to make a micro-enterprise to generate sufficient income for people. For that purpose, the members of the NHGs should possess some kind of resource or skill as an asset for generating a regular income.

Table 6.35: Group members possessing a resource/skill asset for regular income

Name of the District	*Members Possessing a resource/ skill asset for regular income*		*Total*
	<50	50-75	
Alappuzha	12 (63.2)	7 (36.8)	19 (100)
Idukki	12 (85.7)	2 (14.3)	14 (100)
Kozhikode	15 (83.3)	3 (16.7)	18 (100)
Malappuram	18 (85.7)	3 (14.3)	21 (100)
Thiruvananthapuram	10 (58.8)	7 (41.2)	17 (100)
Wayanad	15 (83.3)	3 (16.7)	18 (100)
Total	82 (76.6)	25 (23.4)	107 (100)

Source: Figures in brackets show percentages.

According to the opinion of the leaders in 77 per cent of NHGs, less than 50 per cent members in their respective NHGs possess resource or skill assets for generating regular income. On the other hand, 23.4 per cent of the NHGs said that about 50 to 75 per cent of their members have some sort of resource or skill for creating regular income (Table 6.35).

Activities besides Micro-financing

The success of any micro-finance institution is to have more activities other than micro-financing. This section is meant to enquire into those details.

Activities Other than Loans and Savings

Along with the micro-finance activities such as dealing with loans and savings, some NHGs are engaged in other activities. From the results, it is found that 77 per cent of the NHGs are not engaged in any other activities other than savings and loans. Only 23 per cent of the groups are said to have been engaged in some kind of activities (Figure 6.5).

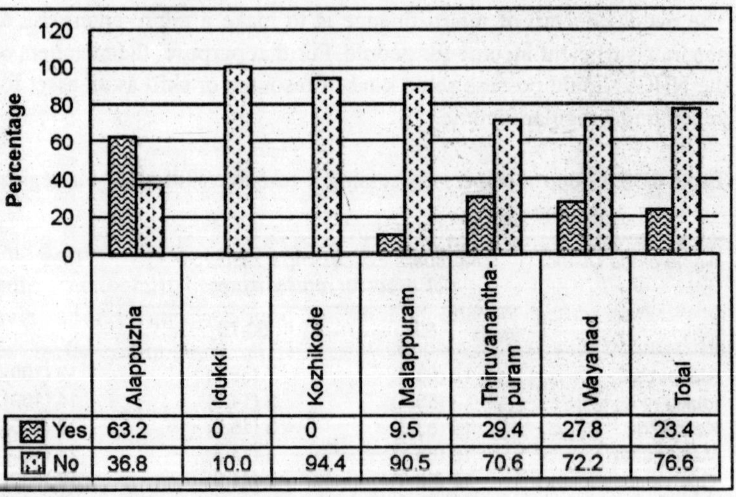

	Alappuzha	Idukki	Kozhikode	Malappuram	Thiruvanantha-puram	Wayanad	Total
Yes	63.2	0	0	9.5	29.4	27.8	23.4
No	36.8	10.0	94.4	90.5	70.6	72.2	76.6

Fig. 6.5: Any other activity besides Micro-finance

Type of Activities

Besides dealing with loans and savings, NHGs take up other activities—financial, economic and cultural. Conduct of *chitti* (rotating credit) is the major financial activity done by these groups among the members. One group conducts *chitti* with the non-members. This activity fetches additional income for the group. The extra economic activities conducted by SHGs include trade (like rice and textile items), quarrying and manufacturing (e.g. soap-making, flour-making, squash and jam making and garment-making). Some of the groups which have taken up economic activities perform them well (e.g. some of the bakery units and catering units). However, some groups are content with their savings and credit functions only (Table 6.36).

Table 6.36: The major activities taken up by NHGs during the last years

Type of activities	*Frequency*	*Per cent*
Agriculture	4	3.7
Anniversary	2	1.9
Chitty	5	4.7
Goat Unit	4	3.7
Goat Unit and Agriculture	1	0.9
Microenterprise	1	0.9
Monthly *Chitti*	2	1.9
Nil	82	76.6
NSS Samathi *Chitti*	1	0.9
Onam *Chitti*	4	3.7
Sports	1	0.9
Total	107	100

In short, the neighbourhood groups which are good performers fare well both in organisational functions and proper participation in the activities of NHGs. But the medium and poor performers do not give much importance to the functions of the NHGs, which in turn affect the sustainability and existence of the groups.

Participation in Community Development Activity

Women self-help groups in various parts of the world have taken up serious community issues (e.g. anti-liquor campaign in Orissa) and have fought for their resolution. Participation of members in *grama sabhas* had increased considerably after their becoming the members of NHGs. The panchayat also provided revolving fund assistance to these groups to start enterprise as a part of the Women Component Plan (WCP) of People's Plan Campaign. Revolving fund assistance and the assistance for starting up the income generating activities are also received by NHGs from block panchayat and zilla panchayat.

Table 6.37: Participation in community development activity

Name of the District	*Does the Group participate in community development activity*		*Total*
	Yes	*No*	
Alappuzha	19 (100)	0	19 (100)
Idukki	12 (85.7)	2.(14.3)	14 (100)
Kozhikode	18 (100)	0	18 (100)
Malappuram	21 (100)	0	21 (100)
Thiruvananthapuram	9 (52.9)	8 (47.1)	17 (100)
Wayanad	16 (88.9)	2 (11.1)	18 (100)
Total	95 (88.8)	12 (11.2)	107 (100)

Source: Figures in brackets show percentages.

In the study area, it is found that 89 per cent of the NHGs are engaged in some kind of community development activities, while the rest of the groups are not at all engaged in any of the activities (Table 6.37).

Kind of Community Development Activity

In the case of community activities, 81 per cent of the groups are participating in the *grama sabhas*. Only a very small percentage of NHGs are engaged in other activities (Table 6.38).

Cultural Activities

For building up the cohesion among the group members, cultural activities play a major role. Many groups celebrate their anniversaries with clan. Most of the groups have already arranged some programmes in their respective groups. They range from cultural programmes of members and their children, sweet distribution on special days like Independence Day, conducting anniversary of the NHGs, sports and so on (Table 6.39).

Emergency Fund

The idea of micro-insurance and welfare measures are included in the ambit of micro-finance in recent times. As the majority of the members

Table 6.38: Kind of community development activity

Name of the District	*Kind of activity*						*Total*
	No activity	*Collective action for community problems*	*Participation in grama Sabhas*	*Corporation Meeting*	*Others*	*Collective action for community problems and Participation in grama Sabhas*	
Alappuzha	0	1 (5.3)	17 (89.5)	0 (0)	0 (0)	1 (5.3)	19
Idukki	2 (14.3)	0	12 (85.7)	0 (0)	0 (0)	0 (0)	14 (100)
Kozhikode	0	1 (5.6)	16 (88.9)	0 (0)	0 (0)	1 (5.6)	18 (100)
Malappuram	0	0	21 (100)	0	0 (0)	0 (0)	21 (100)
Thiruvananthapuram	8 (47.1)	2 (11.8)	5 (29.4)	1 (5.9)	1 (5.9)	0 (0)	17 (100)
Waynad	2 (11.1)	0	16 (88.9)	0	0(0)	0 (0)	18 (100)
Total	12 (11.2)	4 (3.7)	87 (81.3)	1 (.9)	1 (.9)	2 (1.9)	107 (100)

Source: Figures in brackets show percentages.

Table 6.39: Cultural activities among members

Name of the District	If yes please specify							Total
	Cultural Programme	Sweet Distribution	Small Programme	Anniversary	Group Account Clearance	Others	Sports	
Alappuzha	12 (63.2)	0	1 (5.3)	6 (31.6)	0	0	0	19 (100)
Idukki	9 (64.3)	2 (14.3)	0	0	0	3 (21.4)	0	14 (100)
Kozhikode	16 (88.9)	0	0	1 (5.6)	1(5.6)	0	0	18 (100)
Malappuram	19 (90.5)	0	0	1 (4.8)	1(4.8)	0	0	21 (100)
TVM	4 (23.5)	0	0	7 (41.2)	3(17.6)	0	3 (17.6)	17 (100)
Wayanad	11 (61.1)	0	2 (11.1)	0(0)	3(16.7)	2 (11.1)	0	18 (100)
Total	71 (66.4)	2 (1.9)	3 (2.8)	15 (14.0)	8 (7.5)	5 (4.7)	3 (2.8)	107 (100)

Source: Figures in brackets show percentages.

are poor, they often face financial stringencies. SEWA in Gujarat, the forerunner of micro-finance in India, put forth the idea of micro-insurance by collecting small amount from members. This fund is usualiy kept in a separate account. It is found that all the NHGs under Kudumbashree maintain a separate emergency fund for meeting the contingencies of the members in the groups.

The method of creating the fund varies from group to group, but the usual method is to make periodic collections on a monthly basis. Sometimes, fines recovered from members are also deposited in the emergency fund. As these groups are already burdened with savings and loan repayment obligations, they have found it difficult to contribute to such a fund.

In 97 per cent of the groups, they are maintaining a common fund of all the members of the NHGs. In most cases, the group secretary or president take care of the operation of emergency fund. Whenever a need arises to any of the group members, the group would be ready to extend a helping arm to her. Rest of the groups keep their amount with post office and other institutions.

Uses of Emergency Fund

The purposes for which the emergency fund is used vary from gifts for marriage, release for festival seasons, expenses related to death and birth, medical expenses, children's education, etc. On enquiry about the major uses of emergency fund to the members, it is found that they used it for a wide range of purposes where exigency is the major concern of the usage.

Rules, Regulations and Enforcements

For the effective conduct of micro-finance activities, adequate regulations, rules and enforcements are needed.

Written Bye-laws

The written bye-laws help the groups to work in unison. It gives the laws and regulations on which the groups are to be managed and the members are to act in the groups. Of the total 107 NHGs surveyed, 85 per cent have written bye-laws while a 15 per cent do not have written bye-laws for the functioning of the groups (Table 6.40).

Table 6.40: Written bye-laws in NHGs

Name of the District	Are there Written bye-laws		Total
	Yes	No	
Alappuzha	19 (100)	0	19 (100)
Idukki	8 (57.1)	6 (42.9)	14 (100)
Kozhikode	18 (100)	0	18 (100)
Malappuram	20 (95.2)	1 (4.8)	21 (100)
Thiruvananthapuram	17 (100)	0	17 (100)
Wayanad	9 (50.0)	9 (50.0)	18 (100)
Total	91 (85.0)	16 (15.0)	107 (100)

Source: Figures in brackets show percentages.

Members' Awareness about the Bye-laws

The awareness about bye-laws of the NHGs is an important factor for the cohesion among the members. From the study, it is found that only 63.6 per cent of the groups have oral, but strong bye-laws while 24.3 per cent have an oral bye-law, but the members are not aware of the bye-laws. Only 8.4 per cent of the groups have written bye-laws and members are well aware of the bye-laws (Table 6.41).

Table 6.41: Members' Awareness about the bye-laws

Name of the District	Members, Awareness about the bye-laws			Total
	Written and Strong awareness	Oral Out Strong	Oral and not aware	
Alappuzha	3 (15.8)	15 (78.9)	1 (5.3)	19 (100)
Idukki	1(7.1)	4 (28.6)	9 (64.3)	14 (100)
Kozhikode	0 (0)	18 (100)	0(0)	18 (100)
Malappuram	0 (0)	15 (71.4)	6 (28.6)	21 (100)
Thiruvananthapuram	4 (23.5)	13 (76.5)	0 (0)	17 (100)
Wayanad	1 (5.6)	7 (38.9)	10 (55.6)	18 (100)
Total	9 (8.4)	72 (67.3)	26 (24.3)	107 (100)

Source: Figures in brackets show percentages.

Sanction and Control Mechanisms

Kudumbashree had instructed the groups to exercise some control over the members to maintain discipline among them. A fine is imposed for late coming to (Rupees two) and absence (Rupees five) from group meetings. For default in repayment of loans, some groups charge double interest. These rules are evolved for the effective functioning of the groups. Unless care is taken to convince the members of the advantages of observing the rules, they may hesitate to cooperate. All the SHGs strictly follow the rules during the initial stages of their formation; after some time, the religion of implementing the rules is progressively lost. The success story of Grameen Bank and MYRADA reveals that they keep on maintaining rules strictly and impose penalties for any deviation from rules.

Table 6.42: Sanction and control mechanisms for repayment of loan

Name of the District	*Sanctions for repayment of loan*		*Total*
	Yes	No	
Alappuzha	19 (100.0)	0	19 (100.0)
Idukki	13 (100.0)	0	13 (100.0)
Kozhikode	18 (100.0)	0	18 (100.0)
Malappuram	19 (90.5)	2 (9.5)	21 (100.0)
Thiruvananthapuram	15 (88.2)	2 (11.8)	17 (100)
Wayanad	18 (100.0)	0	18 (100.0)
Total	102 (96.2)	4 (3.8)	106 (100.0)

Source: Figures in brackets show percentages.

A large majority of the NHGs (96%) agreed that there exists strict compliance of rules and regulations including sanction and control mechanism for repayment of loans. But four per cent of the NHGs denied that there are such controls in their groups (Table 6.42).

Imposition of Fine

The attendance in the group meetings is an important part of the group functioning in micro-finance. In most of the places, penalty is imposed for not attending the meetings/late coming in order to insist the members to be regular in the meetings.

In the study area, only 18.7 per cent of the NHGs strictly enforce the imposition of fine very strictly. 65.4 per cent of the groups impose it sometimes. A small percentage (15.9%) of the groups is not at all enforcing the fine for late coming (Table 6.43).

Table 6.43: Imposition of fine for late coming

Name of the District	*Impose a fine For Late Coming*			*Total*
	Strictly enforced	*Sometimes*	*Not at all*	
Alappuzha	12 (63.2)	7 (36.8)	0	19 (100)
Idukki	4 (28.6)	10 (71.4)	0	14 (100)
Kozhikode	0	17 (94.4)	1 (5.6)	18 (100)
Malappuram	0	6 (28.6)	15 (71.4)	21 (100)
Thiruvananthapuram	3 (17.6)	14 (82.4)	0	17 (100)
Wayanad	1(5.6)	16(88.9)	1(5.6)	18(100)
Total	20 (18.7)	70 (65.4)	17 (15.9)	107 (100)

Source: Figures in brackets show percentages.

The social capital formation of the micro-finance industry is evidently seen in the present chapter. Those who are from vulnerable and backward regions of the local economy of Kerala has definitely benefited out of various activities of the micro-finance institution, Kudumbashree.

7

Inclusive Growth at the Grassroot Level

The challenges of achieving more inclusive growth can only be met by policies that encourage easier and affordable access to financial services. Both theoretical and empirical researches highlight the role of finance in facilitating economic development. It is in this context, the innovative credit delivery system—micro-finance—was a breakthrough in the world of finance. It changes the life of the poor, especially women, not only by providing financial services such as micro-savings and micro-insurance, but also by imparting training in entrepreneurial development. Over the past few decades, micro-finance institutions and programmes all-over the world have adopted numerous innovative ways of providing credit and savings services to the entrepreneurial poor. These include provision of small loans to poor people, especially in rural areas, at full-cost interest rates, without collateral, repayable in easy/frequent instalments. Borrowers are organised into groups, which reduce the risk of default. There are also effective mechanisms to disseminate valuable information on ways to improve the health, legal rights, sanitation and other relevant concerns of the poor.

The present study looked into how the recent progress in the field of micro-finance helped in the capacity-building of women in particular and development of the State in general, in the context of inclusive growth. In the grassroot level, the growth should be inclusive and at the same time distributive.

Sample Population

As per the methodology proposed, it was aimed to cover six districts in Kerala. Almost equal representation could be made from the six different districts of the State, *viz*., Alappuzha, Idukki, Kozhikode, Malappuram,

Thiruvananthapuram, and Wayanad. With slight variation in the representation almost in all the districts, a representation of 16 per cent could be made on an average (Table 7.1).

Table 7.1: Name of the district and the sample size

Name of District	*Frequency*	*%*
Alappuzha	96	16.3
Idukki	100	16.9
Kozhikode	100	16.9
Malappuram	99	16.8
Thiruvananthapuram	95	16.1
Wayanad	100	16.9
Total	590	100.0

The Panchayats/wards selected for the study are given in Table 7.2. The selection of the beneficiaries from the respective wards has been finalized on the basis of availability.

Table 7.2: Name of the panchayats/wards selected with the sample population

Name of Panchayat/Ward	*Frequency*	*%*
Baypore	45	7.6
Chitravilasam Colony	30	5.1
Chokkad	50	8.5
Edakkara	49	8.3
Kavalam	50	8.5
Maradu	55	9.3
Mattupetty	50	8.5
Munnar	50	8.5
Panamaram	44	7.5
PulimKunnu	46	7.8
Rajeev Nagar Colony	65	11.0
Thirunelli	56	9.5
Total	590	100.0

In the present chapter, an attempt is made on the impact of the Kudumbashree programme on the people who are in the grassroot level. The chapter is divided into seven sections, *viz.* socio-religious profile, basic amenities, family profile, savings and liabilities savings and liabilities with Kudumbashree, information and opinion about Kudumbashree participation in NHG and enhancement of economic capacity through micro-finance institution.

Socio-religious Profile

Religious Profile

Religion is an important institution in every society. Religion performs certain important functions in the society. Religions act as an agency of social control and maintain social order. The religious influence on society has been varied in many walks of life. Kerala is a State which has a significant presence of all the major religions *viz.* Hinduism, Islam and Christianity. Of the total of 590 samples surveyed (Figure 7.1), 68 per cent belonged to Hindu religion, another 25 per cent belonged to Muslim religion and seven per cent belonged to the Christian religion. The representation of Muslims in the district of Malappuram is evidently seen in the sample, while in other districts the presence of all the other religions could be seen.

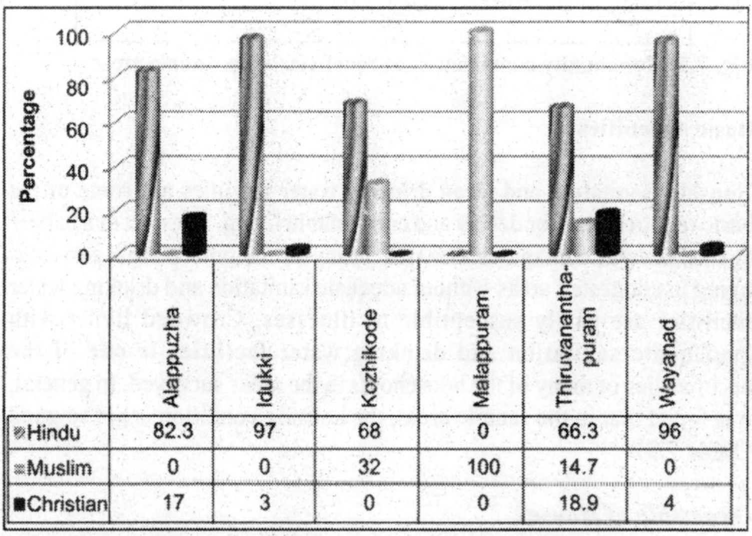

	Alappuzha	Idukki	Kozhikode	Malappuram	Thiruvanantha-puram	Wayanad
Hindu	82.3	97	68	0	66.3	96
Muslim	0	0	32	100	14.7	0
Christian	17	3	0	0	18.9	4

Fig. 7.1: Distribution of religion of beneficiaries in sample areas

Community Composition

Caste is a peculiar feature of Indian society. Caste system divides the people in different strata. Caste is an endogenous system in which mobility is restricted. Caste is, in fact, a closed group. Of the total sample, 22 per cent belonged to SC community while another 17 per cent belonged to ST community, 49 per cent belonged to the OBC and six per cent belonged to the general category. It is evident from the sample selected that the majority of the respondents belonged to the marginalized and vulnerable sections of the Kerala society.

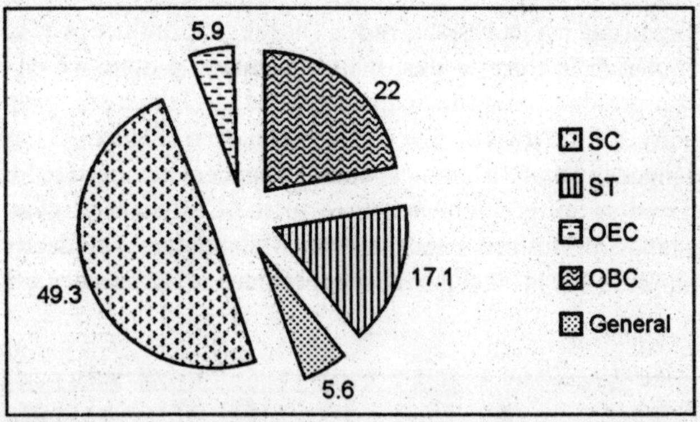

Fig. 7.2: Community composition of beneficiaries in sample areas

Basic Amenities

Housing, sanitation and clean drinking water facilities are some of the basic requirements for decent and comfortable living. They act as a barrier against several contagious diseases. Many of the poor people surveyed living in congested areas without adequate sanitation and drinking water facilities are easily susceptible to illnesses. Crowded living with inadequate sanitation and drinking water facilities is one of the peculiarities of many of the households in the areas surveyed. In general, it is found that in the sample areas, the housing condition is not so good (Table 7.3).

Ownership of House

The type of house in which people stay reveals their economic conditions to a certain extent. Nearly 75 per cent of the sample households have a house of their own. The proportion of rented house is about 18 per cent while another seven per cent lived in a joint family (Figure 7.3). Another important thing to note is that most of the sampled areas are highly congested. For example the highest density of houses is observed in Thiruvananthapuram as the study area is located in slums.

Table 7.3: Housing details of sample population

Housing Details	*Housing facilities*	*Alappuzha*	*Idukki*	*Kozhi-kode*	*Malap-puram*	*Thiru-vanantha-puram*	*Wayanad*	*Total*
Ownership of house	Own	94 (97.9)	0 (0)	84 (84.0)	87 (87.9)	86 (90.5)	89 (89.0)	440 (74.6)
	Rented	0 (0)	99 (99)	0 (0)	3 (3.0)	5 (5.3)	1 (1.0)	108 (18.3)
	Joint family	2 (2.1)	1 (1.0)	16 (16.0)	9 (9.1)	4 (4.2)	8 (8.0)	40 (6.8)
	Others	0 (0)	0 (0)	0 (0)	0 (0)	0 (0)	2 (2.0)	2 (.3)
Type of house	Pucca	1 (1.0)	1 (1.0)	26 (26.0)	11 (11.1)	16 (16.8)	16 (16.0)	71 (12.0)
	Kutcha	92 (95.8)	99 (99)	71 (71.0)	84 (84.8)	72 (75.8)	68 (68.0)	486 (82.4)
	Hut	2 (2.1)	0 (0)	3 (3.0)	4 (4.0)	7 (7.4)	16 (16.0)	32 (5.4)
Type of roof	Thatched	72 (75.0)	56 (56)	43 (43.0)	71 (71.7)	22 (23.2)	65 (65.0)	329 (55.8)
	Sheet	18 (18.8)	44 (44)	15 (15.0)	21 (2.0)	22 (23.2)	17 (17.0)	118 (20.0)
	Tiled/Asbestos	3 (3.1)	0 (0)	3 (3.0)	1 (1.0)	9 (9.5)	2 (2.0)	18 (3.1)
	Concrete	3 (3.1)	0 (0)	39 (39.0)	25 (25.3)	42 (44.2)	16 (16.0)	125 (21.2)
Type of walls	Thatched	3 (3.1)	0 (0)	7 (7.0)	3 (3.0)	0 (0)	7 (7.0)	20 (3.4)
	Mud	13 (13.5)	0 (0)	37 (37.0)	28 (28.3)	31 (32.6)	64 (64.0)	173 (29.3)
	Brick	80 (83.3)	100 (100)	56 (56.0)	65 (65.7)	64 (67.4)	25 (25.0)	390 (66.1)
	Wood	0 (0)	0 (0)	0 (0)	3 (3.0)	0 (0)	4 (4.0)	7 (1.2)
Source of energy for lighting	Electricity	94 (97.9)	100 (100)	98 (98.0)	90 (90.9)	95 (100)	48 (48.0)	525 (89.0)
	Solar	0 (0)	0 (0)	1 (1.0)	0 (0)	0 (0)	1 (1.0)	2 (.3)
	Kerosene	2 (2.1)	0 (0)	1 (1.0)	9 (9.1)	0 (0)	51 (51.0)	63 (10.7)
Sanitary facility	Flush	89 (92.7)	100 (100)	97 (97.0)	98 (99.0)	66 (69.5)	41 (41.0)	491 (83.2)
	Covered Pit	0 (0)	0 (0)	0 (0)	0 (0)	2 (2.1)	4 (4.0)	6 (1.0)
	Open-air	0 (0)	0 (0)	0 (0)	0 (0)	0 (0)	22 (22.0)	22 (3.7)
	Others	7 (7.3)	0 (0)	3 (3.0)	1 (1.0)	27 (28.4)	33 (33.0)	71 (12.0)
Furnishing	Spare	0 (0)	44 (44.0)	0 (0)	0 (0)	0 (0)	0 (0)	44 (7.5)
	Moderate	96 (100)	56 (56.0)	100 (100)	98 (99.0)	95 (100)	100 (100)	545 (92.4)
	Lavish	0 (0)	0 (0)	0 (0)	1 (1.0)	0 (0)	0 (0)	1 (.2)
Fuel used for cooking	Cooking Gas	0 (0)	0 (0)	0 (0)	0 (0)	3 (3.2)	0 (0)	3 (.5)
	Kerosene	0 (0)	0 (0)	0 (0)	1 (1.0)	0 (0)	0 (0)	1 (.2)
	Firewood	45 (46.9)	5 (5.0)	18 (18)	43 (43.4)	15 (15.8)	95 (95.0)	221 (37.5)
	Gas & firewood	51 (53.1)	95 (95.0)	77 (77)	55 (55.6)	75 (78.9)	0 (0)	353 (59.8)
	Kerosene & wood	0 (0)	0 (0)	5 (5.0)	0 (0)	2 (2.1)	5 (5.0)	12 (2.0)
Source of water	Own well	3 (3.1)	0 (0)	42 (42.0)	51 (51.5)	40 (42.1)	25 (25.0)	161 (27.3)
	Neighbours' well	2 (2.1)	0 (0)	5 (5.0)	14 (14.1)	0 (.0)	15 (15.0)	36 (6.1)
	Public well	1 (1.0)	99 (99.0)	53 (53.0)	21 (21.2)	55 (57.9)	47 (47.0)	276 (46.8)
	Public Well and Public Pond	0 (0)	0	0 (.0)	12 (12.1)	0 (0)	4 (4.0)	16 (2.7)
	Others	90 (93.8)	1 (1)	0 (.0)	1 (1.0)	0 (0)	9 (9.0)	101 (17.1)

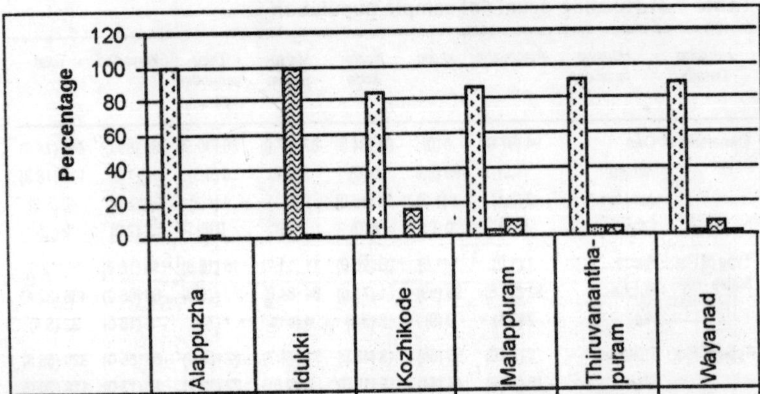

	Alappuzha	Idukki	Kozhikode	Malappuram	Thiruvananthapuram	Wayanad
Own	97.9	0	84	87	90.5	89
Rented	0	99	0	3	5.3	1
Jointed family	2.1	1	10	9.1	4.2	8
Others	0	0	0	0	0	2

Fig. 7.3: Ownership of house

A detailed analysis of districts shows almost the same picture of the rest of the State. However, in Idukki, the prevalence of own house is so low. Most of the respondents surveyed in Idukki are living in the houses provided by the company.

Type of House

Twelve per cent of the houses of the sample households belong to the *kutcha* category and 82 per cent to the *pucca* category. The number of huts is the highest in Wayanad, while Malappuram has the largest number of *kutcha* houses forming 85 per cent. The majority of houses in the sample areas are *pucca*, many had only limited number of rooms and space (Figure 7.4).

Type of Roof

Fifty six per cent of the sample houses had thatched roofs. Twenty per cent of the houses have sheet roof. Taking the disaggregated data together, the picture is different. The housing condition is poor in backward regions like Wayanad and Malappuram (Figure 7.5).

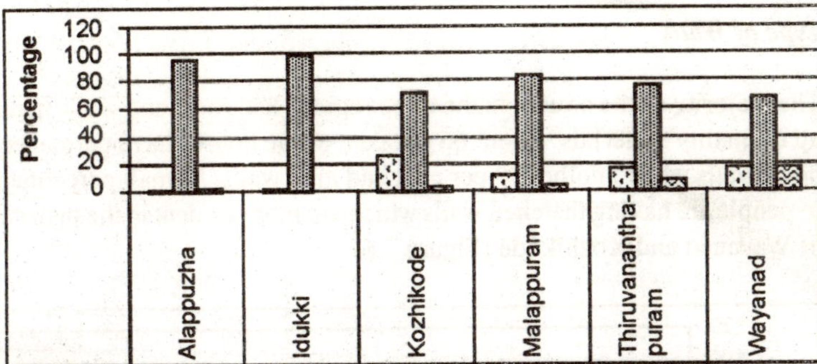

	Alappuzha	Idukki	Kozhikode	Malappuram	Thiruvanantha-puram	Wayanad
Pacca	1	1	26	11.1	16.8	16
Kutcha	95.8	99	71	84.8	75.8	68
Hut	2.1	0	3	4	7.4	16

Fig. 7.4: Type of house

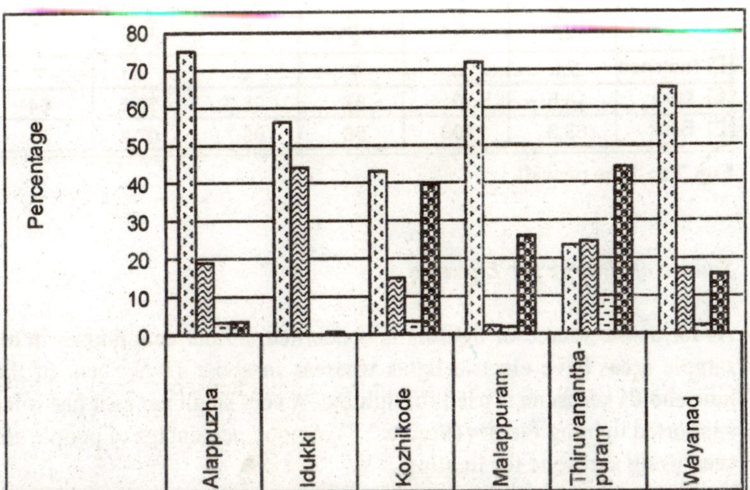

	Alappuzha	Idukki	Kozhikode	Malappuram	Thiruvanantha-puram	Wayanad
Thatched	75	56	43	71.7	23.2	65
Sheet	18.8	44	15	2	23.2	17
Tiled/Asbestos	3.1	0	3	1	9.5	2
Concrete	3.1	0	39	25.3	44.2	16

Fig. 7.5: Type of roof

Type of Walls

The majority of the houses in the three regions had roofs and walls made up of quality materials. About 66 per cent of the houses have permanent brick walls while another 30 per cent had mud walls. A small percentage of people are having thatched walls which are more evident in the districts of Wayanad and Kozhikode (Figure 7.6).

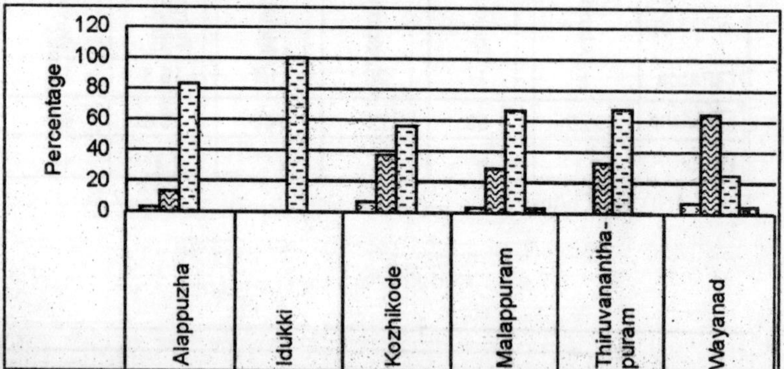

	Alappuzha	Idukki	Kozhikode	Malappuram	Thiruvananthapuram	Wayanad
Thatched	3.1	0	7	3	0	7
Mud	13.5	0	37	28.3	32.6	64
Brick	83.3	100	56	65.7	67.4	25

Fig. 7.6: Type of wall

Source of Energy for Lighting

As far as the source of lighting is concerned, 89 per cent houses in all sample areas have electric lights whereas in about 11 per cent of the households kerosene is used for lighting. A very small per cent has solar supported lighting facility (Figure 7.7). A good percentage of people are seen using kerosene for lighting.

Sanitary Facility

Sanitation facilities are an important requirement for comfortable living. It is an aspect in which the poor people face many difficulties. The type of facility widely spread in the sample areas is the Indian type commode. One of the major issues that must be given priority is the provision of adequate sanitation facilities in this region (Figure 7.8).

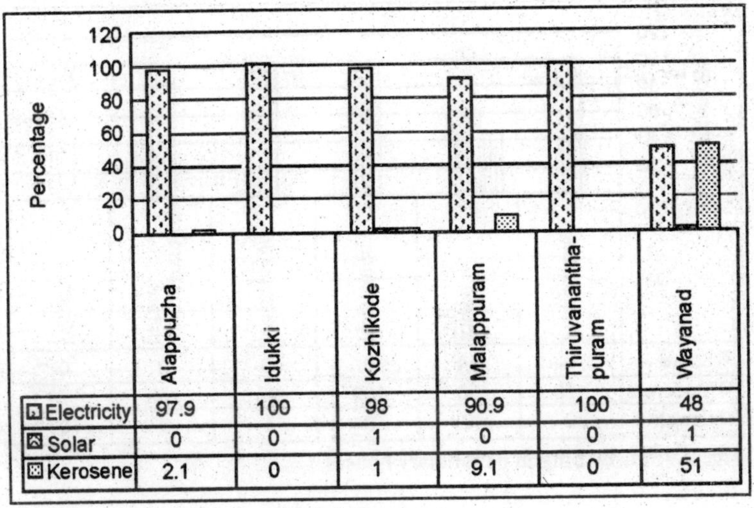

Fig. 7.7: Source of energy for lighting

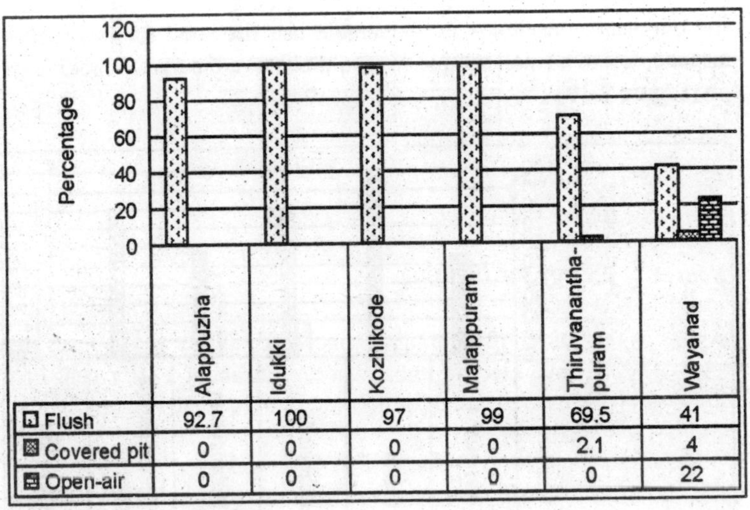

Fig. 7.8: Sanitary facility

Furnishing

As far as furnishing is concerned, nearly fifty per cent of the households in the sample have spare furnishing. In fact, they do not have sufficient space and money and they are not interested in spending their money on furniture (Figure 7.9).

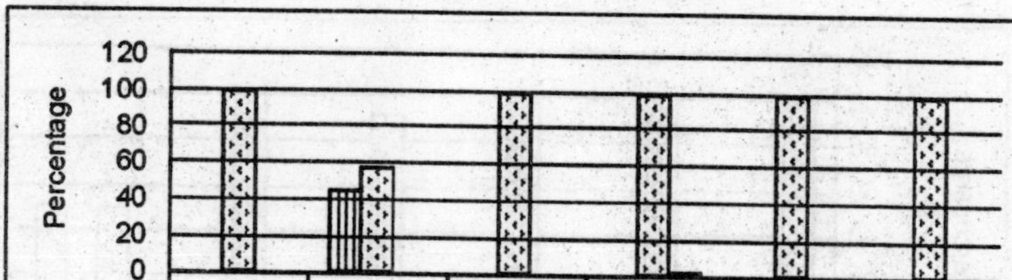

	Alappuzha	Idukki	Kozhikode	Malappuram	Thiruvanantha-puram	Wayanad
Spare	0	44	0	0	0	0
Moderate	100	56	100	99	100	100
Lavish	0	0	0	1	0	0

Fig. 7.9: Furnishing in beneficiary houses

Fuel used for Cooking

The majority households in the sample use firewood for the cooking purpose. Yet in a small sample we could observe the use of cooking gas too (Figure 7.10).

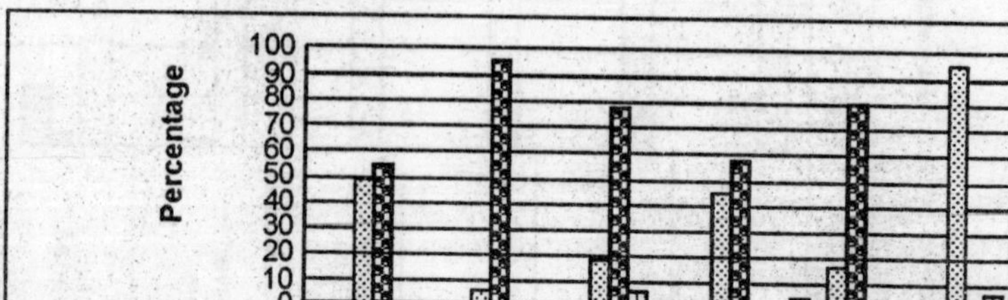

	Alappuzha	Idukki	Kozhikode	Malappuram	Thiruvanantha-puram	Wayanad
Cooking Gas	0	0	0	0	3	0
Kerosene	0	0	0	1	0	0
Fire wood	46.9	5	18	43.4	15.8	95
Gas & firewood	53.1	95	77	55.6	78.9	0
Kerosene & wood	0	0	5	0	2.1	5

Fig. 7.10: Fuel used for cooking

Source of Water

Another important requirement for the people is the drinking water. Though they reside near water sources, drinking water facility is one of the major problems faced by them.

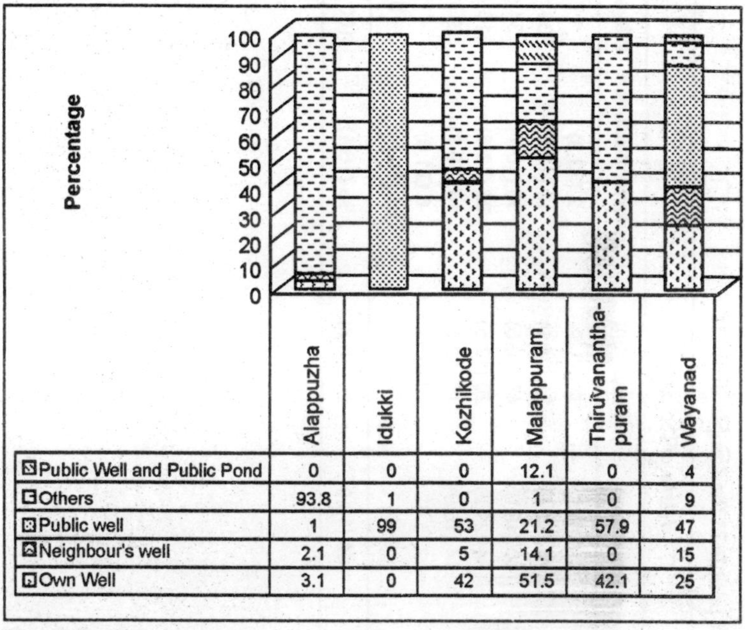

	Alappuzha	Idukki	Kozhikode	Malappuram	Thiruvanantha-puram	Wayanad
Public Well and Public Pond	0	0	0	12.1	0	4
Others	93.8	1	0	1	0	9
Public well	1	99	53	21.2	57.9	47
Neighbour's well	2.1	0	5	14.1	0	15
Own Well	3.1	0	42	51.5	42.1	25

Fig. 7.11: Source of water

Family Profile

The family characteristics of the samples in six areas under study may now be examined. Family background is an important variable determining the income-earning capacity and the consumption pattern of households. They have also an important place in determining the standard of living and educational level of their members.

Age Composition

Age is an important factor which influences or regulates individual activity within or outside the family. Experience and knowledge grow with age, thereby causing change in one's attitude and opinions. Hence, it would

Table 7.4: Age-wise distribution of number of people in the sample districts

Age of beneficiaries	Name of the district						Total
	Alappuzha	Idukki	Kozhikode	Malappuram	Thiruvananthapuram	Wayanad	
<20	0 (0)	1 (16.7)	0 (0)	2 (33.3)	2 (33.3)	1 (16.7)	6 (.6)
20-30	2 (2.3)	8 (9.2)	10 (11.5)	21 (24.1)	10 (11.5)	36 (41.4)	87 (8.7)
30-40	19 (8.8)	43 (20.0)	40 (18.6)	43 (20.0)	36 (16.7)	34 (15.8)	215 (21.5)
40-50	33 (20.6)	35 (21.9)	34 (21.2)	20 (12.5)	22 (13.8)	16 (10.0)	160 (16.0)
50-60	21 (25.3)	13 (15.7)	14 (16.9)	10 (12.0)	16 (19.3)	9 (10.8)	83 (8.3)
60-70	20 (54.1)	0 (0)	2 (5.4)	3 (8.1)	8 (21.6)	4 (10.8)	37 (3.70)
70-80	1 (50.0)	0 (0)	0 (0)	0 (0)	1 (50.0)	0 (0)	2 (.2)
Total	96 (16.3)	100 (16.9)	100 (16.9)	99 (16.8)	95 (16.1)	100 (16.9)	590 (100)

Source: Figures in brackets show percentages.

produce meaningful information by analyzing the respondent age. The women surveyed in the present study fall in seven categories on the basis of age.

The majority of the women in the organization belonged to the middle age group. More than four-fifths of the members were in the age group of 21 to 50 years (Table 7.4). Since, the majority of women in the middle age group are unemployed, it is they who have the urgency and the time to engage themselves in some kind of productive activity. The representation of the elderly is low in the MFI (about 12% above 50 years). In the cases of elderly women members, they take loans in their names, only for the benefit of their children. As the old women may not need money for own use, they help their kith and kin. Some old women help their children in time of needs. They feel that savings with the NHGs may help them in future. In some groups, it was observed that old women were purposely excluded. This was because younger women felt the presence of elderly women unnecessary and a handicap. Obviously, there was a wide generation gap between them and the old people.

Education

From the sample, it is observed that more than three-fifths women in the organisation had education of high school level or more. Graduates formed only about less than two per cent and persons with higher secondary come to eighteen per cent. The percentage of women having lower primary education (5.3%) and upper primary education (4%) was comparatively low. Illiterates accounted for about seven per cent (Table 7.5).

A closer look at the educational status of women in the backward regions of the State showed some dismal situation in many places. For example, in the case of Wayanad, the proportion of illiterate to the total sample comes around 60 per cent.

Women with technical qualification or training were less in number. Some of the untrained had skills in conventional vocations such as tailoring, typewriting, nursery teaching, *anganwadi* teaching and ITI trades. This fact points to the potential need for imparting training to women for enabling them to take up income generating activities.

This trend generally shows that in the sample areas where the different outlier communities are taken for study, they are still remaining far behind in educational level. Adequate investment is needed in the field of education among the marginalised outlier communities in order to get them emancipated.

Table 7.5: Education status of beneficiaries by districts

Education	Name of the District						Total
	Alappuzha	Idukki	Kozhikode	Malappuram	Thiruvananthapuram	Wayanad	
Illiterate	0 (0)	13 (12.1)	4 (5.2)	11 (17.2)	6 (5.2)	35 (60.3)	68 (6.8)
Literate	0 (0)	7 (30.4)	2 (8.7)	11 (47.8)	2 (8.7)	1 (4.3)	23 (2.3)
LP	12 (22.6)	9 (17.0)	8 (15.1)	7 (13.2)	8 (15.1)	9 (17.0)	53 (5.3)
UP	8 (20.0)	5 (12.5)	5 (12.5)	5 (12.5)	9 (22.5)	8 (20.0)	40 (4.0)
HS	42 (23.2)	38 (21.0)	26 (14.4)	26 (14.4)	23 (12.7)	26 (14.4)	181 (18.1)
SSLC	28 (16.8)	23 (13.8)	45 (26.9)	32 (19.2)	23 (13.8)	1 (9.6)	167 (16.7)
PDC/ Higher Secondary	5 (14.3)	2 (5.7)	7 (20.0)	4 (11.4)	14 (40.0)	3 (8.6)	35 (3.5)
Degree	1 (7.1)	2 (14.3)	2 (14.3)	3 (21.4)	6 (42.9)	0 (0)	14 (1.4)
PG	0 (0)	1 (25.0)	0 (0)	0 (0)	3 (75.0)	0 (0)	4 (.4)
Professional	0 (0)	0 (0)	1 (25.0)	0 (0)	1 (25.0)	2 (50.0)	4 (.4)
Others	0 (0)	1 (100)	0 (0)	0 (0)	0 (0)	0 (0)	1 (.1)
Total	96 (16.3)	100 (16.9)	100 (16.9)	99 (16.8)	95 (16.1)	100 (16.9)	590 (100)

Source: Figures in brackets show percentages.

Income

Researchers usually face the problem of underreporting of income by their respondents. From the income data which may contain a certain degree of underreporting, it was found that about 17.5 per cent of the women members had a monthly income of less than Rs. 100. The general observation is that majority of the women's monthly family income is less than Rs. 3000 (Table 7.6). A miniscule population reported that the monthly income can be more than Rs. 5000. Across the State in different districts, the trend is more or less same.

Marital Status

Majority of the beneficiaries (97.1%) are married (Table 7.7). Unmarried women form only 2.9 per cent. Women from female-headed households also take part in the organization's activities. Widows, separated and divorced women who bear the entire burden of looking after their families have found the self-help group a source of sure support. They felt that the women in their group were able to understand their difficulties and they expected that the group would be a great support to them in future. Many of them who had initiated some income generating activities found that the group became a great support for each of them during the time of financial difficulty.

Table 7.7: Marital status of people in the six sample districts

Name of the District	*Marital Status*		*Total*
	Married	*Unmarried*	
Alappuzha	96 (100)	0 (.0)	96 (100)
Idukki	98 (98.0)	2 (2.0)	100 (100)
Kozhikode	100 (100)	0 (.0)	100 (100)
Malappuram	94 (94.9)	5 (5.1)	99 (100)
Thiruvananthapuram	94 (98.9)	1 (1.1)	95 (100)
Wayanad	91 (91.0)	9 (9.0)	100 (100)
Total	573 (97.1)	17 (2.9)	590 (100)

Source: Figures in brackets show percentages.

Landholding

Land is a valuable asset in Kerala. Allotment of plots of ten cents each in rural areas and five cents each in municipal area to poor landless

Table 7.6: Monthly income of the beneficiaries by districts

Monthly Income	*Name of the District*						*Total*
	Alappuzha	*Idukki*	*Kozhikode*	*Malappuram*	*Thiruvananthapuram*	*Wayanad*	
0-100	10 (5.7)	7(4.0)	56 (32.0)	61 (34.9)	27 (15.4)	14 (8.0)	175 (17.5)
100-1000	3 (4.4)	11 (16.2)	26 (38.2)	2 (2.9)	22 (32.4)	4 (5.9)	68 (6.8)
1000-2000	57 (23.3)	81 (33.1)	16 (6.5)	23 (9.4)	26 (10.6)	42 (17.1)	245 (24.5)
2000-3000	23 (25.3)	1 (1.1)	1 (1.1)	11 (12.1)	16 (17.6)	39 (42.9)	91 (9.1)
3000-4000	2 (28.6)	0 (0)	1 (14.3)	1 (14.3)	2 (28.6)	1 (14.3)	7 (.7)
4000-5000	0 (0)	0 (0)	0 (0)	1 (50.0)	1 (50.0)	0 (0)	2 (.2)
5000-6000	0 (0)	0 (0)	0 (0)	0 (0)	1 (100)	0 (0)	1 (.1)
6000 Above	1 (100)	0 (0)	0 (0)	0 (0)	0 (0)	0 (0)	1 (.1)
Total	96 (16.3)	100 (16.9)	100 (16.9)	99 (16.8)	95 (16.1)	100 (16.9)	590 (.1)

Source: Figures in brackets show percentages.

households as part of the Agrarian Reforms implemented in Kerala during the end of the 1960s has improved the standards of living of thousands of families in the State. Yet in the sample, we found nearly 22.9 per cent of the households were absolutely landless. About 64 per cent of the beneficiary households hold land less than ten cents (Table 7.8). Only in districts such as Alappuzha (agricultural land), Malappuram (with a rural setting having importance of agriculture) and in Wayanad (agricultural setting) we could find landholdings of more than twenty cents. In the districts of Idukki, Thiruvananthapuram and Kozhikode the landholding of more than ten or twenty cents is rare.

Livestock Owned

Livestock is a major income generating asset for people in many parts of the developing countries. However, the striking feature of the sample population surveyed is that the ownership of cows and other livestock is very minimal. Of the total sample population only less than one per cent hold cow as an asset. Their mean monthly income has been reported as Rs. 1,327. Regarding the other livestock, the presence is absolutely nil. However, majority of the households do not own any type of livestock for want of land for rearing cattle and poultry. Another reason observed is that most of the women are so poor and they are unable to raise the cattle even if they like to do so. In places like Idukki and Wayanad, the climatic conditions and proximity to forest are cited as reasons for this phenomenon. In Thiruvananthapuram and Kozhikode districts, high density of population is the main reason for the said situation.

Consumer Durables

Of the total sample population, 83 per cent have a television set at their houses, while 57 per cent of houses have gas stove with LPG connection. Another 59 per cent have electric fans at their homes. The tribal settlements in Wayanad do not have electricity connection as most of them are dwelling inside the wildlife sanctuaries. Naturally, electrical and electronic gadgets are not much evident in these areas.

Family Planning

Of the total respondents, 84 per cent are found adopting the family planning measures. The high prevalence of adoption of family planning

Table 7.8: Area of landholding

Area of landholding	*Districts*						*Total*
	Alappuzha	*Idukki*	*Kozhikode*	*Malappuram*	*Thiruvananthapuram*	*Wayanad*	
No Land	2 (1.5)	95 (70.4)	5 (3.7)	5 (3.7)	13 (9.6)	15 (11.1)	135 (22.9)
1-10	85 (22.4)	5 (1.3)	87 (23.0)	60 (15.8)	80 (21.1)	62 (16.4)	379 (64.2)
10-20	7 (18.4)	0 (.0)	6 (15.8)	18 (47.4)	2 (5.3)	5 (13.2)	38 (6.4)
20-30	1 (7.1)	0 (.0)	2 (14.3)	8 (57.1)	0 (.0)	3 (21.4)	14 (2.4)
30-40	0 (.0)	0 (.0)	0 (.0)	4 (80.0)	0 (.0)	1 (20.0)	5 (.8)
40-50	1 (33.3)	0 (.0)	0 (.0)	2 (66.7)	0 (.0)	0 (.0)	3 (.5)
50-100	0 (0)	0 (0)	0 (0)	2 (20.0)	0 (.0)	8 (80.0)	10 (1.7)
above one Acre	0 (0)	0 (0)	0 (0)	0 (0)	0 (0)	6 (100.0)	6 (1.0)
Total	96 (16.3)	100 (16.9)	100 (16.9)	99 (16.8)	95 (16.1)	100 (16.9)	590 (100)

Source: Figures in brackets show percentages.

Table 7.9: Consumer durables

Consumer durables	*Number*	*%age*
Bicycle	6	1.0
Radio	5	.8
Television	490	83.1
Scooter/Motorcycle	53	9.0
Telephone	43	7.3
Electric fan	348	59.0
Electric iron	304	51.5
Gas stove/Electric stove	339	57.5
Mixie/Grinder	294	49.8

in Kerala with respect to other States of the country shows the high level of social development in this regard. But there is a notable variation among the districts.

The districts in which the number of women who are not resorting to family planning measures is higher in Malappuram (24%) and in Wayanad (40%). But in other districts, it is less than 12 per cent which is not up to the mark. The adoption is found to be very less in Malappuram district and Wayanad because of Muslim population and tribal population respectively.

Table 7.10: Members adopted family planning systems

Name of the District	*Adoption of family planning systems*		*Total*
	Yes	*No*	
Alappuzha	91 (94.8)	5 (5.2)	96 (100)
Idukki	93 (93.0)	7 (7.0)	100 (100)
Kozhikode	88 (88.0)	12 (12.0)	100 (100)
Malappuram	75 (75.8)	24 (24.2)	99 (100)
Thiruvananthapuram	89 (93.7)	6 (6.3)	95 (100)
Wayanad	60 (60.0)	40 (40.0)	100 (100)
Total	496 (84.1)	94 (15.9)	590 (100)

Source: Figures in brackets show percentages.

Alcoholics

Kerala is notorious for the presence of alcoholics. The presence of alcoholics seems to be a major problem in many of the sample households too. The menace causes problems like indebtedness, economic and social insecurity, deprivation of other material and social facilities.

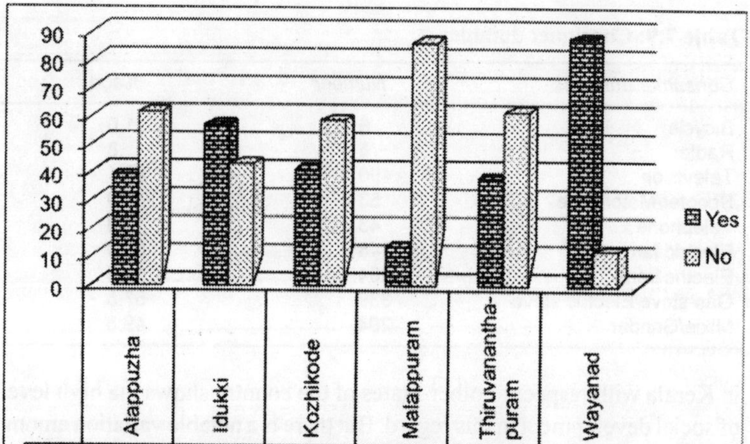

	Alappuzha	Idukki	Kozhikode	Malappuram	Thiruvanantha-puram	Wayanad
Yes	38.5	57	41	13.1	37.9	88
No	61.5	43	59	86.9	62.1	12

Fig. 7.12: Presence of alcoholics in sample households

About 46 per cent of the households in the sample, alcoholism among male is a major problem. Data show that in Malappuram (13%), the proportion of alcoholics is very less; while in Wayanad (88%) it is very high.

Savings and Liabilities

Savings by the poor is an important asset for them as it helps them in times of economic contingencies like diseases, education, needs of children, marriage and other social commitments.

Savings with Formal Financial Institutions

From the field, it is observed that the proportion of beneficiaries having family savings in financial institutions is low and it is less than three per cent.

Problem of Indebtedness

Indebtedness was the major problem observed among the members in the study area. A good percentage of people (47.8%) have outside loan liabilities. Most of the loans were taken from moneylenders. Apart from borrowing from moneylenders, they pledge their gold ornaments in times of difficulties with local moneylenders and informal moneylending institutions (usually not with the institutions such as private banks or nationalised banks).

Table 7.11: Previous loan (loans from other source) outstanding

Name of the District	*Previous Loan outstanding*		*Total*
	Yes	*No*	
Alappuzha	90 (93.8)	6 (6.3)	96 (100)
Idukki	38 (38.0)	62 (62.0)	100 (100)
Kozhikode	42 (42.0)	58 (58.0)	100 (100)
Malappuram	23 (23.2)	76 (76.8)	99 (100)
Thiruvananthapuram	18 (18.9)	77 (81.1)	95 (100)
Wayanad	71 (71.0)	29 (29.0)	100 (100)
Total	282 (47.8)	308 (52.2)	590 (100)

Source: Figures in brackets show percentages.

While looking at the aggregate data on indebtedness among districts, Alappuzha stands first with about 94 per cent of the respondents are indebted. One of the reasons for this trend is that in Alappuzha, the presence of private micro-finance institutions (like ESAF) is more and people are highly depending on them for loans. Next comes the district of Wayanad with 71 per cent of respondents being found to be indebted. High level of poverty and uncertainty in their lives might be the reasons for the same. The districts which show low level of indebtedness are Thiruvananthapuram (18%) and Idukki (38%).

Purpose of Loan

While enquiring about the purpose for which the loans were taken from other sources, the reply was very much varied. It ranges from productive enterprises to household expenditure. A majority (34.6%) of the people who are indebted had taken the loans for meeting their household expenditure. Only 7.8 per cent of the total respondents had taken loans from outside sources for investing in the productive enterprises (Table 7.12).

Table 7.12: Purpose of loan

Name of the District	*Purpose*				*Total*
	Productive Enterprises	*Repayment of Debt*	*Others*	*Nil*	
Alappuzha	71 (34.8)	12 (26.1)	7 (13.5)	6 (2.1)	96 (16.3)
Idukki	14 (6.9)	17 (37.0)	7 (13.5)	62 (21.5)	100 (16.9)
Kozhikode	27 (13.2)	5 (10.9)	10 (19.2)	58 (20.1)	100 (16.9)
Malappuram	21 (10.3)	0	2 (3.8)	76 (26.4)	99 (16.8)
Thiruvananthapuram	11 (5.4)	3 (6.5)	24 (46.2)	57 (19.8)	95 (16.1)
Wayanad	60 (29.4)	9 (19.6)	2 (3.8)	29 (10.1)	100 (16.9)
Total	204 (34.6)	46 (7.8)	52 (8.8)	288 (48.8)	590 (100)

Source: Figures in brackets show percentages.

Experience with Banking

Most of the respondents did not have previous experience in transactions with the formal financial institutions especially the banks. It is to be noted that the prevalence of exclusion from the formal financial system is highly evident among the women in the plantation sector in Idukki. Yet a small number of members responded that they couldn't obtain any loans from the lending institutions (Table 7.13).

Savings and Liabilities with Kudumbashree

Micro-financing with a government sponsored programme is a new experience for the members. The credit and savings facilities rendered by the organization are the key features of the organization which keep the people in the organization. It has its own strengths and weaknesses. Compared to the other private and self-help promoting institutions (SHPIs) promoted by various organizations, the Kudumbashree as a micro-finance institution has a lot of difference in its operations.

Table 7.13: Experience with banking

Name of the District	*Has bank ever refused you a loan application*		*Total*
	Yes	*No*	
Alappuzha	2 (2.1)	94 (97.9)	96 (100)
Idukki	0 (0)	100 (100)	100 (100)
Kozhikode	6 (6.0)	94 (94.0)	100 (100)
Malappuram	2 (2.0)	97 (98.0)	99 (100)
Thiruvananthapuram	6 (6.3)	89 (93.7)	95 (100)
Wayanad	3 (3.0)	97 (97.0)	100 (100)
Total	19 (3.2)	571 (96.8)	590 (100)

Source: Figures in brackets show percentages.

Period of Borrowing

Of the total number of loans disbursed, about 45 per cent was disbursed during 2010. It is also observed that a group of members about 3.5 per cent has not availed any credit from the institution. Obviously, the maximum number of loans were disbursed during the last years especially after 2008. The same trend has been observed irrespective of the entire districts surveyed (Table 7.14).

Amount of Borrowing

Majority of the members (58.6%) have availed amounts ranging from Rs. 1000 to 5000. Yet a small number of members (10.6%) could avail an amount of Rs. 5000-10000. Another five per cent of the members got loan of Rs. 10000 and more. On the other hand, about 23 per cent got loan amount between Rs. 200 and 1000, which is too meagre (Table 7.15).

Number of Loans Availed by Members

It is observed that the maximum number of loans availed by an individual member from the Kudumbashree NHGs comes to around five. Only about 3.5 per cent have not availed loans from NHGs, the rest (97%) have availed loans (Table 7.16). Of the total members, about 36 per cent have availed two loans. But a small percentage of the members have availed more than three loans from the NHGs.

Table 7.14: Date of borrowing from Kudumbashree

Date of Borrowing	*Name of the District*						*Total*
	Alappuzha	*Idukki*	*Kozhikode*	*Malappuram*	*Thiruvananthapuram*	*Wayanad*	
0	1 (2.9)	0	2 (5.7)	6 (17.1)	20 (57.1)	6 (17.1)	35 (3.5)
2004	0	0	0	0	0	1 (100)	1 (1)
2005	1 (2.9)	32 (91.4)	0	0	0	2 (5.7)	35 (3.5)
2006	0	0	0	0	4 (66.7)	2 (33.3)	6 (.6)
2007	7 (31.8)	0	6 (27.3)	0	2 (9.1)	7 (31.8)	22 (2.2)
2008	30 (20.0)	68 (45.3)	30 (20.0)	2 (1.3)	7 (4.7)	13 (8.7)	150 (15.0)
2009	71 (23.7)	2 (.7)	85 (28.4)	50 (16.7)	29 (9.7)	62 (20.7)	299 (29.8)
2010	91 (20.1)	54 (11.9)	97 (21.5)	71 (15.7)	60 (13.3)	79 (17.5)	452 (45.1)
2011	0	1 (50.0)	1 (50.0)	0	0	0	2 (.2)
Total	201 (20.1)	157 (15.7)	221 (22.1)	129 (12.9)	122 (12.2)	172 (17.2)	1002 (100)

Source: Figures in brackets show percentages.

Table 7.15: Amount of Borrowing

Amount of Borrowing	*Name of the District*						*Total*
	Alappuzha	*Idukki*	*Kozhikode*	*Malappuram*	*Thiruvananthapuram*	*Wayanad*	
0	1 (2.9)	0 (0)	2 (5.7)	6 (17.1)	20 (57.1)	6 (17.1)	35 (3.5)
200-1000	17 (7.5)	43 (18.9)	52 (22.9)	40 (17.6)	28 (12.3)	47 (20.7)	227 (22.7)
1000-5000	123 (21.0)	72 (12.3)	145 (24.7)	73 (12.4)	69 (11.8)	105 (17.9)	587 (58.6)
5000-10000	41 (38.7)	22 (20.8)	19 (17.9)	7 (6.6)	5 (4.7)	12 (11.3)	106 (10.6)
10000-15000	16 (38.1)	20 (47.6)	1 (2.4)	3 (7.1)	0 (0)	2 (4.8)	42 (4.2)
15000-20000	2 (66.7)	0 (0)	1 (33.3)	0 (0)	0 (0)	0 (0)	3 (.3)
20000-25000	1 (100)	0 (0)	0 (0)	0 (0)	0 (0)	0 (0)	1 (.1)
25000-30000	0 (0)	0 (0)	1 (100)	0 (0)	0 (0)	0 (0)	1 (.1)
Total	201 (20.1)	157 (15.7)	221 (22.1)	129 (12.9)	122 (12.2)	172 (17.2)	1002 (100)

Source: Figures in brackets show percentages.

Table 7.16: Number of loans availed by members in NHGs

Name of the district	*Number of Loans availed*						*Total*
	0	*1*	*2*	*3*	*4*	*5*	
Alappuzha	1 (.5)	21 (10.4)	92 (45.8)	75 (37.3)	12 (6.0)	0 (0)	201 (20.1)
Idukki	0 (0)	89 (56.7)	33 (21.0)	35 (22.3)	0 (0)	0 (0)	157 (15.7)
Kozhikode	2 (.9)	19 (8.6)	88 (39.8)	80 (36.2)	32 (14.5)	0 (0)	221 (22.1)
Malappuram	6 (4.7)	68 (52.7)	48 (37.2)	3 (2.3)	4 (3.1)	0 (0)	129 (12.9)
Thiruvanantha-puram	20 (16.4)	55 (45.1)	31 (25.4)	6 (4.9)	4 (3.3)	6 (4.9)	122 (12.2)
Wayanad	6 (3.5)	40 (23.3)	73 (42.4)	45 (26.2)	8 (4.7)	0 (0)	172 (17.2)
Total	35 (3.5)	292 (29.1)	365 (36.4)	244 (24.4)	60 (6.0)	6 (.6)	1002 (100)

Source: Figures in brackets show percentages.

Information and Opinion about Kudumbashree

Information

Most of the people come to know about the existence of the organization from those who are very near to them. The members trust their family members, friends, neighbours and ward councillors. But in majority of the cases (67.5%), they depend on others who are in the locality and on those who are influential (Table 7.17).

Arrears

Even though the micro-finance system is known for cent per cent repayment, nowadays, mounting NPA has become a major concern for many of the micro-finance institutions around the world. Contrary to the global trend, in Kudumbashree, majority of the members (99.7%) have said that they are not having any arrears with the Kudumbashree. The proper enforcement mechanism available in most of the NHGs helps to get the repayment in time. As majority of the people are poor, they need credit at the right time and that is the reason why there are no arrears there in most of the groups visited by us (Table 7.18). Only a minority

Table 7.17: Source of knowledge about Kudumbashree providing a loan

Name of the District	*Source of knowledge on Kudumbashree providing loan*				*Total*
	Family/ Friends	*Neighbours*	*Ward Councillor*	*Others*	
Alappuzha	6 (6.3)	5 (5.2)	0 (0)	85 (88.5)	96 (100)
Idukki	60 (60.0)	0 (0)	1 (1.0)	39 (39.0)	100 (100)
Kozhikode	0 (0)	0 (0)	95 (95.0)	5 (5.0)	100 (100)
Malappuram	0 (0)	0 (0)	0 (0)	99 (100)	99 (100)
Thiruvananthapuram	11 (11.6)	14 (14.7)	0 (0)	70 (73.7)	95 (100)
Wayanad	0 (0)	0 (0)	0 (0)	100 (100)	100 (100)
Total	77 (13.1)	19 (3.2)	96 (16.3)	398 (67.5)	590 (100)

Source: Figures in brackets show percentages.

(0.30%) felt that they lag behind in repayment of loans. Major reasons cited here were business failures, economic shocks due to diseases, other contingencies, etc.

Table 7.18: Arrears of the respondents

Name of the District	*Arrears*		*Total*
	Yes	*No*	
Alappuzha	0 (0)	96 (100)	96 (100)
Idukki	0 (0)	100 (100)	100 (100)
Kozhikode	1 (1.0)	99 (99.0)	100 (100)
Malappuram	0 (0)	99 (100)	99 (100)
Thiruvananthapuram	1 (1.1)	94 (98.9)	95 (100)
Wayanad	0 (0)	100 (100)	100 (100)
Total	2 (.3)	588 (99.7)	590 (100)

Source: Figures in brackets show percentages.

Effectiveness of the Programmes

As explained in chapter four, a large number of programmes and activities have been implemented as part of Kudumbashree movement in Kerala. But in the field, the other support systems for the poor people are not much evident. They think that the compulsory saving (with 92% of the responses) is the only evident arrangement they are getting out of the programme (Table 7.19). The respondents are strictly adhering to the mandatory requirement stipulated in the programme.

Table 7.19: Arrangements addition to loans

Name of the District	*Arrangements addition to loans*				*Total*
	Training	*Compulsory Saving*	*Others*	*Nil*	
Alappuzha	0 (0)	96 (100)	0 (0)	0 (0)	96 (100)
Idukki	0 (0)	57 (57.0)	0 (0)	43 (43.0)	100 (100)
Kozhikode	0 (0)	99 (99.0)	1 (1.0)	0 (0)	100 (100)
Malappuram	0 (0)	99 (100)	0 (0)	0 (0)	99 (100)
Thiruvananthapuram	1 (1.1)	93 (97.9)	1 (1.1)	0 (0)	95 (100)
Wayanad	0 (0)	100 (100)	0 (0)	0 (0)	100 (100)
Total	1 (.2)	544 (92.2)	2 (.3)	43 (7.3)	590 (100)

Source: Figures in brackets show percentages.

The members are totally unaware of the other components like training and other purposes. In most of the cases, the members are not exposed even to a single type of training. One of the reasons is the geographical distance between the district centre and the locality. They are to pay for their commutation from their home to the training centre which in most of the cases is unviable. This shows some more about vulnerability. The vulnerability accentuates their inability to take part in many of the opportunities provided by the organization. The members in Idukki, Malappuram and Wayanad have genuine problems in taking part in these activities.

Need of More Credit

Credit is a necessary component which keeps the people to hold around the micro-finance system. Apart from the micro-savings, the most important component which attracts people into the system is the credit. All the members feel that they need credit for the future. But a small per cent of the members feel that debt is a burden and they may not need it for the future period (Table 7.20).

Table 7.20: Need of more credit from Kudumbashree

Name of the District	*Need of more credit*		*Total*
	Yes	*No*	
Alappuzha	95 (99.0)	1 (1.0)	96 (100)
Idukki	100 (100)	0 (0)	100 (100)
Kozhikode	100 (100)	0 (0)	100 (100)
Malappuram	94 (94.9)	5 (5.1)	99 (100)
Thiruvananthapuram	95 (100)	0 (0)	95 (100)
Wayanad	101 (100)	0 (.0)	100 (100)
Total	584 (99.0)	6 (1.0)	590 (100)

Source: Figures in brackets show percentages.

While asking about the problems regarding obtaining credit from Kudumbashree, a majority has the opinion that they never faced any problem in obtaining credit from Kudumbashree. While a quarter of the beneficiaries feel that they have some problems in getting credit from the micro-finance institution (Table 7.21).

Table 7.21: Do you have problem regarding obtaining credit from Kudumbashree

Name of the District	*Do you have problem regarding obtaining credit from Kudumbashree*		*Total*
	Yes	*No*	
Alappuzha	31 (32.3)	65 (67.7)	96 (100)
Idukki	9 (9.0)	91 (91.0)	100 (100)
Kozhikode	24 (24.0)	76 (76.0)	100 (100)
Malappuram	40 (40.4)	59 (59.6)	99 (100)
Thiruvananthapuram	36 (37.9)	59 (62.1)	95 (100)
Wayanad	15 (15.0)	85 (85.0)	100 (100)
Total	155 (26.3)	435 (73.7)	590 (100)

Source: Figures in brackets show percentages.

Participation in NHG

Attendance in Meetings

While asking the members' opinion on whether all the members attend group meetings, almost all feel that they are doing so. On the other hand, a small percentage of people think that the members are not regular in attending meetings of Kudumbashree (Table 7.22).

Table 7.22: Attendance in Group Meeting

Name of the District	*Attendance in group meeting*		*Total*
	Yes	*No*	
Alappuzha	96 (100)	0 (0)	96 (100)
Idukki	99 (99.0)	1 (1.0)	100 (100)
Kozhikode	100 (100)	0 (0)	100 (100)
Malappuram	97 (98.0)	2 (2.0)	99 (100)
Thiruvananthapuram	95 (100)	0 (0)	95 (100)
Wayanad	98 (98.0)	2 (2.0)	100 (100)
Total	585 (99.2)	5 (8)	590 (100)

Source: Figures in brackets show percentages.

Official Role in the NHG

About 53 per cent of the people do not hold any position in the NHGs while rest of the people holds any one of the posts in the unit (Table 7.23). About 11.5 per cent of the respondents are presidents of their respective units, while another 12 per cent hold the position of secretary. Another 16 per cent of the people are the committee members of the units. By assuming the responsibilities thrown open by such avenues, leadership quality could be imbibed at the grassroot level. The women were actually home managers. But now they are found to be competent in decision making process including financial and organizational matters.

Training

Of the total sample population surveyed, about 53 per cent of them have received some kind of training from the organization. 47 per cent of the sample population has not received any kind of training till date (Table 7.24). Wayanad topped in the list of districts where the maximum number

Table 7.23: Official role in the group

Name of the District	*Official role in the group*						*Total*
	No	*Chairman*	*Secretary*	*Treasurer*	*Committee Members*	*Others*	
Alappuzha	62 (64.6)	6 (6.3)	7 (7.3)	0 (0)	17 (17.7)	4 (4.2)	96 (100)
Idukki	36 (36.0)	12 (12.0)	11 (11.0)	2 (2.0)	39 (39.0)	0 (0)	100 (100)
Kozhikode	38 (38.0)	14	16 (16.0)	2 (2.0)	4 (4.0)	26 (26.0)	100 (100)
Malappuram	58 (58.6)	11 (11.1)	10 (10.1)	4 (4.0)	15 (15.2)	1 (1.0)	99 (100)
Thiruvananthapuram	64 (67.4)	10 (10.5)	13 (13.7)	0 (0)	5 (5.3)	3 (3.2)	95 (100)
Wayanad	57 (57.0)	15 (15.0)	14 (14.0)	0 (0)	14 (14.0)	0 (0)	100 (100)
Total	315 (53.4)	68 (11.5)	71 (12.0)	8 (1.4)	94 (15.9)	34 (5.8)	590 (100)

Source: Figures in brackets show percentages.

of members received training (77%) followed by Malappuram (74.7%) and Kozhikode (70%).

Table 7.24: Any training received

Name of the District	*Training*		*Total*
	Yes	*No*	
Alappuzha	50 (52.1)	46 (47.9)	96 (100)
Idukki	19 (19.0)	81 (81.0)	100 (100)
Kozhikode	70 (70.0)	30 (30.0)	100 (100)
Malappuram	74 (74.7)	25 (25.3)	99 (100)
Thiruvananthapuram	22 (23.2)	73 (76.8)	95 (100)
Wayanad	77 (77.0)	23 (23.0)	100 (100)
Total	312 (52.9)	278·(47.1)	590 (100)

Source: Figures in brackets show percentages.

The effectiveness of training offered by the Kudumbashree programmes is more evident in the northern districts than in the southern districts. The Urban Basic Services for the Poor (UBSP) programme which was successful among the districts like Malappuram was more evident here. The districts like Idukki (19%), Thiruvananthapuram (23%) and

Alappuzha (52%) collectively accounted for less than that recorded by Malappuram. The district of Idukki is peculiar in nature as all the beneficiaries are plantation workers whose time is taken away by the plantation work and so, they are not in a position to spare any time for other activities like going for training or conducting micro-enterprises.

Micro-savings

All the sampled population unanimously said that all of them were enjoying the facility of compulsory saving. The Kudumbashree programme has given them a chance to save in a safer place. As the savings of the members are kept in the banks, they are assured of the money. The interest on savings is usually given to the members as an incentive to their savings. In many of the groups, they keep the interest amount in a common fund and it would be considered as the capital to give loans to the members themselves. Some of the groups keep the amount in emergency fund. In the sampled areas, about half of the groups distribute their interest amount to the members, whereas in the rest of the groups, the members have not received any amount as interest on their deposits.

Table 7.25: Receipt of any Interest from the savings

Name of the District	*Received Interest from the savings*		*Total*
	Yes	*No*	
Alappuzha	96 (100)	0 (0)	96 (100)
Idukki	0 (0)	100 (100)	100 (100)
Kozhikode	95 (95.0)	5 (5.0)	100 (100)
Malappuram	35 (35.4)	64 (64.6)	99 (100)
Thiruvananthapuram	36 (37.9)	59 (62.1)	95 (100)
Wayanad	29 (29.0)	71 (71.0)	100 (100)
Total	291 (49.3)	299 (50.7)	590 (100)

Source: Figures in brackets show percentages.

In Alappuzha district, all the groups have given out the interest money to their members (Table 7.25). On the other hand, in the district of Idukki, not even a single member has received any money as interest. In the other districts, the picture is mixed.

A small per cent (11%) of members have a feeling that their savings have been used to cover bad debts of other group members (Table 7.26). Vast majority of members do not feel so. This shows that the repayment of the loans is more prompt in the groups under Kudumbashree. Hence, there is no need of covering bad debts of some members by the savings of rest of the group members.

Table 7.26: Whether the savings been used to cover bad debts of group member

Name of the District	*Savings been used to cover bad debts of group members*		*Total*
	Yes	*No*	
Alappuzha	21 (21.9)	75 (78.1)	96 (100)
Idukki	0 (0)	100 (100)	100 (100)
Kozhikode	1 (1.0)	99 (99.0)	100 (100)
Malappuram	25 (25.3)	74 (74.7)	99 (100)
Thiruvananthapuram	17 (17.9)	78 (82.1)	95 (100)
Wayanad	5 (5.0)	95 (95.0)	100 (100)
Total	69 (11.7)	521 (88.3)	590 (100)

Source: Figures in brackets show percentages.

Further analysis shows that the presence of bad debts never stopped the members from saving or reducing the size of the member's deposits (Table 7.27). Regular savings increase the credit fund and it has an added advantage for the members.

Table 7.27: Debts stopped from saving or reduced the size of deposits

Name of the District	*Debts stopped from saving or reduced the size of your deposits*		*Total*
	Reduced savings	*No effect on saving*	
Alappuzha	0 (0)	96 (100)	96 (100)
Idukki	0 (0)	100 (100)	100 (100)
Kozhikode	1 (1.0)	99 (99.0)	100 (100)
Malappuram	4 (4.0)	95 (96.0)	99 (100)
Thiruvananthapuram	0 (0)	95 (100)	95 (100)
Wayanad	0 (0)	100 (100)	100 (100)
Total	5 (.8)	585 (99.2)	590 (100)

Source: Figures in brackets show percentages.

Even though the data show a very rosy picture on the micro-savings of the NHGs, there are instances which the researcher came across that some of the groups would like to get back their savings. The contractural non-withdrawal feature of the savings in the micro-finance makes them a bit frustrated.

Participation in Organizations other than Kudumbashree

Participation in Grama Sabhas

As a result of the People's Plan Campaign, *grama sabhas* have become the fora for discussing people's problems and development needs. However, it was only after joining SHGs that most of the women in the study area came to know about *grama sabhas*. In fact, the SHGs motivated many of the beneficiaries to take part in *grama sabhas*. In the group meetings of the SHGs, the members used to discuss their needs and problems which included drinking water, toilet, public hygiene and housing. Identification of problems and formulation of ideas for their solution have helped them to take part in the planning process effectively and meaningfully. Thus, women from financially and educationally backward classes were empowered to take part in development process and discourse on gender-sensitive planning.

Table 7.28: Attendance in the meeting of *grama sabha*

Name of the District	*Attending the meeting of grama sabha*		*Total*
	Yes	*No*	
Alappuzha	79 (82.3)	17 (17.7)	96 (100)
Idukki	90 (90.0)	10 (10.0)	100 (100)
Kozhikode	93 (93.0)	7 (7.0)	100 (100)
Malappuram	58 (58.6)	41 (41.4)	99 (100)
Thiruvananthapuram	22 (23.2)	73 (76.8)	95 (100)
Wayanad	98 (98.0)	2 (2.0)	100 (100)
Total	440 (74.6)	150 (25.4)	590 (100)

Source: Figures in brackets show percentages.

Reported 75 per cent participation of the Kudumbashree members in their respective *grama sabhas* is a tribute to the democratic values being propagated by the NHGs. As the benefits of the poor are discussed and decided through the *grama sabha* meetings, the beneficiaries are keen to attend the meetings. Among the members surveyed, about three-fourths of them are attending the *grama sabha* meetings regularly. Among the districts of the State, Thiruvananthapuram has very low participation with only 23 per cent and the highest is in Wayanad where 98 per cent of the women are participating in the *grama sabha* meetings. In districts like Kozhikode (93%) and Idukki (90%) participation level is high. Apart from Thiruvananthapuram, the participation in Malappuram is low with about 58 per cent participation.

Many of them have received benefits such as cow, poultry, sewing machine, construction, renovation or maintenance of houses, toilets and wells through *grama sabhas*. This must be the reason why participation of the poor in *grama sabhas* was higher, especially in places like Wayanad than in the rest of the State. This is due to the reason that the districts like Wayanad the *grama sabhas* and other social groupings are only place where the poor are expecting monetary and physical support for their survival. Whereas in places like Thiruvananthapuram, people have other avenues and engagements towards this cause. It was also observed that the NHGs of Kudumbashree all-over the State could effectively enhance the democratic capacities of poor women by making them participate in *grama sabhas.*

Participation of Members in Social and Business Organizations

It was observed that participation of the beneficiaries of Kudumbashree in social and business organizations is very low (less than three per cent). The vast majority of members (97.3%) are not participating in any of these organizations. It is further observed that participation of the poorest is lower than that of the non-poor areas (Table 7.29). This is evident in the groups working in Wayanad and Idukki, that none of them are participating in any of the groups or organizations in the locality or around.

Women participate, in general, in various political, cultural and social organisations. Some take part in activities of political parties and trade unions. Some among them are also members of Parent Teacher Association (PTA) and Residents' Association and various welfare groups. Many of them are participating in NSS karayogams and SNDP *yogams*. It instils confidence in women and attracts them to MFO. The majority of women did not have any previous exposure to such organisations.

Knowledge of other MFIs

There exist multiple MFIs operating in all the areas surveyed. Of the total sample size, 88 per cent of the people are aware of other institutions providing similar credit facilities in their localities. On the other hand,

Table 7.29: Participation in other social organizations

Name of the District	*Participation in other social organizations*					*Total*
	None	*School Committee*	*Political group*	*Welfare group*	*Other*	
Alappuzha	96 (100)	0 (0)	0 (0)	0 (0)	0 (0)	96 (100)
Idukki	100 (100)	0 (0)	0 (0)	0 (0)	0 (0)	100 (100)
Kozhikode	95 (95.0)	5 (5.0)	0 (.0)	0 (.0)	0 (.0)	100 (100)
Malappuram	90 (90.9)	0 (0)	0 (0)	5 (5.1)	4 (4.0)	99 (100)
Thiruvananthapuram	93 (97.9)	0 (0)	2 (2.1)	0 (0)	0 (0)	95 (100)
Wayanad	100 (100)	0 (0)	0 (0)	0 (0)	0 (0)	100 (100)
Total	574 (97.3)	5 (.8)	2 (.3)	5 (.8)	4 (.7)	590 (100)

Source: Figures in brackets show percentages.

about 12 per cent of the sample population has not heard of any other of the micro-financial institutions functioning in the locality (Table 7.30).

Table 7.30: Knowledge of other institutions in locality

Name of the District	*Knowledge of other institutions in locality*			*Total*
	Yes	*No*	*Unknown*	
Alappuzha	96 (100)	0 (0)	0 (0)	96 (100)
Idukki	57 (57.0)	43 (43.0)	0 (0)	100 (100)
Kozhikode	100 (100)	0 (0)	0 (0)	100 (100)
Malappuram	99 (100)	0 (0)	0 (0)	99 (100)
Thiruvananthapuram	85 (89.5)	10 (10.5)	0 (0)	95 (100)
Wayanad	83 (83.0)	16 (16.0)	1 (1.0)	100 (100)
Total	520 (88.1)	69 (11.7)	1 (.2)	590 (100)

Source: Figures in brackets show percentages.

Enhancement of Economic Capacity through Micro-finance Organization

For analysing women's empowerment, Mayoux (1998) has developed a framework. In the framework, the power or the capacity to accommodate change for individual woman includes the following:

(a) Access to income
(b) Access to productive assets and household property
(c) Control over loan use
(d) Control over income from loan and other household productive activities
(e) Control over productive assets and household property
(f) Freedom from the burden of domestic work including childcare.

This section deals with the role played by the micro-finance organisation, Kudumbashree, in initiating, organising, managing and enhancing micro-enterprises and other income generating activities for the NHGs under them is discussed.

Micro-enterprises

Micro-savings and micro-credit are the major components of micro-finance. Micro-finance helps the poor to mobilise and pool their meagre savings and to use them as a major source to cushion the economic shocks. Likewise, micro-credit enhances economic choices and opportunities of the poor. Micro-finance institutions also provide credit to the poor for meeting their various needs. Micro-credit is given to the poor for production and also for consumption.

The major objective of micro-finance is to ensure sustainable livelihood for poor women. Micro-credit is given for starting a new business or for improving the existing business. In other words, micro-finance is the first step for launching micro-enterprise. The enterprise may be either individual or group-based. The basic approach of the micro-finance organization is to address the economic problems first, and then to pursue their social problems. The self-help groups addressed the economic problems of the poor women by providing access to credit, technical advice and training. To some extent, the organization was able to expand the resource base through improvement of socio-economic status of women in the family and community. It also helped to increase the level of awareness and confidence among women by giving them training in micro-savings, banking habits and starting micro-enterprises. Thus, self-help groups are striving for a change in the status of women.

At the same time, micro-finance is viewed as a panacea for many ills of women. It is true that the NHGs could become agents for change, but the expected change would be possible over a long period of time only. Change on a sustainable basis would come about by enhancement of the level of public awareness, active participation in group discussions, broadening of the sphere of activities, and appropriate training.

Initiation of micro-enterprise is the major focus of all the micro-finance programmes in the world. In Kudumbashree also the major focus is on micro-enterprises. Of the total 590 members surveyed, only 22 per cent of the members (i.e. 128) are conducting any kind of micro-enterprise. About 78 per cent of the members do not have any enterprise of their own. The major reason for this trend is that many of them are not having confidence to start entrepreneurial activity of any kind. Lack of education and previous experience in conducting business, fear of failure and marketing problems are some of the reasons cited by the respondents.

Year of Establishment

More than ninety per cent of the women started any of the economic activities only after joining the groups. This shows that the micro-finance organization helped them to gain confidence to initiate an economic activity. Less than ten per cent of the enterprises had been started even before the MFI started functioning in the respective areas (Table 7.31). However, those who are engaged in economic activities for a long period show more confidence and consistency in business than others. This indicates that experience in doing economic activity is very important.

Table 7.31: Year of establishing

Name of the District	*Year of establishing*						*Total*
	1-5	*5-10*	*10-15*	*15-20*	*20-25*	*25-30*	
Alappuzha	13 (72.2)	1 (5.6)	2 (11.1)	2 (11.1)	0	0	18 (14.1)
Kozhikode	23 (92.0)	2 (8.0)	0	0	0	0	25 (19.5)
Malappuram	3 (100)	0	0	0	0	0	3 (2.3)
Thiruvananthapuram	32 (59.3)	15 (27.8)	4 (7.4)	1 (1.9)	1 (1.9)	1 (1.9)	54 (42.2)
Wayanad	28 (100)	0	0	0	0	0	28 (21.9)
Total	99 (77.3)	18 (14.1)	6 (4.7)	3 (2.3)	1 (.8)	1 (.8)	128 (100)

Source: Figures in brackets show percentages.

The number of enterprises started during the recent periods is found to be more in Wayanad and Malappuram. On the other hand, Thiruvananthapuram as the sample area is near a famous tourist spot (Shangumugham beach) in the city, some of them have started the enterprises beforehand. For the people living in the slums of the city, Kudumbashree has offered an opportunity to make a living out of the situation opened up by the tourism industry. The women in the locality have set-up trading businesses, especially small eateries (both moveable and non-moveable) in and around the tourist spot.

Home-based Business

In India, most of the enterprises run by women are home-based and form an extended home activity. In our sample also, the majority (93.8%) of the enterprises are located in homes (Table 7.32). It helped them to look after the household chores and to manage their enterprises simultaneously.

Table 7.32: Home-based business

Name of the District	*Home Based Business*		*Total*
	Yes	*No*	
Alappuzha	18 (100)	0	18 (14.1)
Kozhikode	24 (96.0)	1 (4.0)	25 (19.5)
Malappuram	3 (100)	0	3 (2.3)
Thiruvananthapuram	47 (87.0)	7 (13.0)	54 (42.2)
Wayanad	28 (100)	0	28 (21.9)
Total	120 (93.8)	8 (6.3)	120 (100)

Source: Figures in brackets show percentages.

Looking into the district-wise data, in Alappuzha, Malappuram and Wayanad, all the units and the members' residents were located in the same place. In the primarily backward regions of the State, this trend is very evident. But in places like Thiruvananthapuram, as indicated earlier, some of the units are working outside the homestead.

Ownership Structure

About fifty per cent of the entrepreneurs organized, ran and managed their enterprises, all on their own. Another 47 per cent of the enterprises are run by the group enterprises. It is evident in the case of Kudumbashree that they have initiated a large number of group enterprises under various State and centrally sponsored schemes such as SGSY, SJSRY, RMK, etc. Many group enterprises are found to be established in Wayanad and Kozhikode with about 90 per cent of the micro-enterprises (Table 7.33). But the number of group enterprises formed in places like Thiruvananthapuram and Alappuzha is comparatively low.

Table 7.33: Ownership structure of the enterprise

Name of the District	*What is the Ownership Structure of the Enterprise*				*Total*
	Proprietor-ship	*Family Partnership*	*Non-Family Partnership*	*Group*	
Alappuzha	11 (61.1)	0	0	7 (38.9)	18 (14.1)
Kozhikode	3 (12.0)	0	0	22 (88.0)	25 (19.5)
Malappuram	0	1 (33.3)	0	2 (66.7)	3 (2.3)
Thiruvananthapuram	50 (92.6)	0	0	4 (7.4)	54 (42.2)
Wayanad	0	0	3 (10.7)	25 (89.3)	28 (21.9)
Total	64 (50.0)	1 (.8)	3 (2.3)	60 (46.9)	128 (100)

Source: Figures in brackets show percentages.

Location of Operation

The majority of the enterprises have a permanent place of operation (41.1%). About 36 per cent of the women enterprises have no assured localities for their business. Those women, who are not having an outlet infrastructure, walked all the way carrying their wares on their heads or in hand-bags searching for customers to buy their products.

Other Income Generating Activities

The survey showed that 69 per cent of the entrepreneurs have no income generating activity other than activity of the micro-enterprise (Table 7.34). They were forced to take some kind of income generating activity for sustaining their families. On the other hand, for 46 per cent of the entrepreneurs, the enterprise is not the sole source of income. The overall data show that the entrepreneurs in Wayanad are depending on the enterprise more than the other entrepreneurs in the State.

Table 7.34: Loan assisted enterprise is main source of income

Name of the District	*Loan assisted enterprise is main source of Income*		*Total*
	Yes	*No*	
Alappuzha	15 (83.3)	3 (16.7)	18 (14.1)
Kozhikode	22 (88.0)	3 (12.0)	25 (19.5)
Malappuram	0	3 (100)	3 (2.3)
Thiruvananthapuram	5 (9.3)	49 (90.7)	54 (42.2)
Wayanad	27 (96.4)	1 (3.6)	28 (21.9)
Total	69 (53.9)	59 (46.1)	128 (100)

Source: Figures in brackets show percentages.

Source of Start-up Fund

The enterprises started by women used various sources of funds as seed money for setting-up their units. The amount of investment varies from one another depending on the nature and scale of activity. Nearly 41 per cent of them availed loans from the neighbourhood groups while about one-fifth managed to get loans from financial institutions and other sources (Table 7.35). Household or personal savings provided the initial funds in the case of more than one-tenth.

Employment Structure

As most of the enterprises are maintained by the groups, the number of people being employed by majority of the enterprises is about ten. Yet in a small number of enterprises, the people engaged in the activity are more than ten (Table 7.36).

Working Hours

About 57 per cent of the enterprises spent about five to ten hours of time for running and maintaining their respective enterprises, while another 43 per cent have less than five hours of time in enterprises.

Table 7.35: Main source of start-up funds

Name of the District	*Main source of start-up funds*					*Total*
	Kudumbashree Loan	*Other Loan*	*Household Savings*	*Borrowing from Other Sources*	*Others Specify*	
Alappuzha	12 (66.7)	3 (16.7)	0	0	3 (16.7)	18 (14.1)
Kozhikode	10 (40.0)	10 (40.0)	1 (4.0)	0	4 (16.0)	25 (19.5)
Malappuram	2 (66.7)	0	1 (33.3)	0	0	3 (2.3)
Thiruvananthapuram	2 (3.7)	14 (25.9)	14 (25.9)	17 (31.5)	7 (13.0)	54 (42.2)
Wayanad	27 (96.4)	0	1 (3.6)	0	0	28 (21.9)
Total	53 (41.4)	27 (21.1)	17 (13.3)	17 (13.3)	14 (10.9)	128 (100)

Source: Figures in brackets show percentages.

Table 7.36: Number of employees in enterprise

Name of the District	*Number of employees*				*Total*
	1-5	*5-10*	*10-15*	*15-22*	
Alappuzha	15 (83.3)	1 (5.6)	2 (11.1)	0	18 (14.1)
Kozhikode	15 (60.0)	10 (40.0)	0	0	25 (19.5)
Malappuram	3 (100)	0	0	0	3 (2.3)
Thiruvananthapuram	51 (94.4)	0	1 (1.9)	2 (3.7)	54 (42.2)
Wayanad	14 (50.0)	9 (32.1)	5 (17.9)	0	28 (21.9)
Total	98 (76.6)	20 (15.6)	8 (6.3)	2 (1.6)	128 (100)

Source: Figures in brackets show percentages.

Table 7.37: Average hours of working

Name of the District	*Average hours of working*		*Total*
	1-5	*5-10*	
Alappuzha	9 (50.0)	9 (50.0)	18 (14.1)
Kozhikode	6 (24.0)	19 (76.0)	25 (19.5)
Malappuram	0	3 (100)	3 (2.3)
Thiruvananthapuram	24 (44.4)	30 (55.6)	54 (42.2)
Wayanad	16 (57.1)	12 (42.9)	28 (21.9)
Total	55 (43.0)	73 (57.0)	128 (100)

Source: Figures in brackets show percentages.

Changes Occurred

The major performance highlight of the units can be attributed to the expansion of their respective businesses with 61.7 per cent doing it with positive intent. While enquiring about the achievements of the present loan and the enterprises of the entrepreneurs, the only substantial change

Table 7.38: Changes occurred during business

Name of the District	*Over the period of the present loan have you succeeded in doing any of the following*						*Total*
	Increase the volume of goods/service	*Improve the quality of goods/service*	*Purchase new tools or equipment*	*Move to better premises*	*Expand the business*	*Others*	
Alappuzha	0	0	1 (5.6)	0	16 (88.9)	1 (5.6)	18 (14.1)
Kozhikode	0	0	0	3 (12.0)	15 (60.0)	7 (28.0)	25 (19.5)
Malappuram	0	0	0	3 (100)	0	0	3 (2.3)
Thiruvananthapuram	2 (3.7)	5 (9.3)	4 (7.4)	9 (16.7)	29 (53.7)	5 (9.3)	54 (42.2)
Wayanad	0	0	0	7 (25.0)	19 (67.9)	2 (7.1)	28 (21.9)
Total	2 (1.6)	5 (3.9)	5 (3.9)	22 (17.2)	79 (61.7)	15 (11.7)	128 (100)

Source: Figures in brackets show percentages.

has taken in the case of the expansion of the business (61.7%). The other options like diversification, improvement in the quantity and quality of goods and services, modification premises, etc. were seen given lesser attention (Table 7.38).

Financial Records

To a query as to whether any change has taken place in the entrepreneur's style of functioning, especially in the maintenance of financial records of the business after receiving micro-enterprise loan, it was reported that a vast majority of them (98%) have continued to maintain the records in their old formats (Table 7.39).

Table 7.39: Status of financial records

Name of the District	*After receiving Micro-enterprise loan have you changed the way in which you keep financial records for your business*		*Total*
	None	*Regular*	
Alappuzha	18 (100)	0	18 (14.1)
Kozhikode	25 (100)	0	25 (19.5)
Malappuram	3 (100)	0	3 (2.3)
Thiruvananthapuram	52 (96.3)	2 (3.7)	54 (42.2)
Wayanad	28 (100)	0	28 (21.9)
Total	126 (98.4)	2 (1.6)	128 (100)

Source: Figures in brackets show percentages.

Profits

Only 50 per cent of the entrepreneurs feel that they are able to sell their products or there exists a market for their products and their respective enterprises are making profits. But the rest of the people feel that they are incurring huge operating expenses and they are yet to reach the point of break even (Table 7.40).

Cash Banked

As the enterprises are not being operated on a large-scale, most of them (89%) are not using the banking facility for keeping their surplus cash reserves. Only a small number of enterprises are keeping their money in the banks for meeting future eventualities (Table 7.41).

Table 7.40: Sales or operating expenses

Name of the District	*Sales or operating expenses*		*Total*
	Sales	*Operating expenses*	
Alappuzha	3 (16.7)	15 (83.3)	18 (14.1)
Kozhikode	17 (68.0)	8 (32.0)	25 (19.5)
Malappuram	0	3 (100)	3 (2.3)
Thiruvananthapuram	37 (68.5)	17 (31.5)	54 (42.2)
Wayanad	8 (28.6)	20 (71.4)	28 (21.9)
Total	65 (50.8)	63 (49.2)	128 (100)

Source: Figures in brackets show percentages.

Table 7.41: Cash banked

Name of the District	*Is the cash Banked*		*Total*
	Yes	*No*	
Alappuzha	10 (55.6)	8 (44.4)	18 (14.1)
Kozhikode	4 (16.0)	21 (84.0)	25 (19.5)
Malappuram	0	3 (100)	3 (2.3)
Thiruvananthapuram	0	54 (100)	54 (42.2)
Wayanad	0	28 (100)	28 (21.9)
Total	14 (10.9)	114 (89.1)	128 (100)

Source: Figures in brackets show percentages.

About 69 per cent do not have separate bank accounts for their enterprises. But group enterprises to which the unit belonged (about 31%) have separate bank accounts for their respective enterprises (Table 7.42).

Table 7.42: Separate bank account for enterprise

Name of the District	*Separate bank account for enterprise*		*Total*
	Yes	*No*	
Alappuzha	11 (61.1)	7 (38.9)	18 (14.1)
Kozhikode	18 (72.0)	7 (28.0)	25 (19.5)
Malappuram	2 (66.7)	1 (33.3)	3 (2.3)
Thiruvananthapuram	9 (16.7)	45 (83.3)	54 (42.2)
Wayanad	0	28 (100)	28 (21.9)
Total	40 (31.3)	88 (68.8)	128 (100)

Major activity Undertaken by Enterprises

The micro-enterprises run by the entrepreneurs are varied in nature. They range from agriculture and allied activities, production, services and trade (Table 7.43). Of all the activities, agriculture and allied activities accounted for 67 per cent, while production activity constituted 16 per cent, services occupied 13 per cent and trade activities consist of only three per cent.

Table 7.43: Business processes adopted by enterprises

Name of the District	*Category*				*Total*
	Agriculture	*Production*	*Services*	*Trade*	
Alappuzha	20 (76.9)	5 (19.2)	1 (3.8)	0	26 (20.3)
Idukki	9 (50.0)	0	5 (27.8)	4 (22.2)	18 (14.1)
Kozhikode	0	8 (66.7)	4 (33.3)	0	12 (9.4)
Malappuram	3 (50.0)	3 (50.0)	0	0	6 (4.7)
Thiruvananthapuram	0	5 (50.0)	5 (50.0)	0	10 (7.8)
Wayanad	54 (96.4)	0	2 (3.6)	0	56 (43.8)
Total	86 (67.2)	21 (16.4)	17 (13.3)	4 (3.1)	128 (100)

Nature of Enterprise

Under the aegis of Kudumbashree various NHGs initiated group enterprises. They include group farming and enterprise run by a group members. Of the total entrepreneurs, 87 per cent are running group enterprises while only 12 per cent run individual enterprises (Table 7.44).

Table 7.44: Type of enterprise

Type of enterprise	*Frequency*	*%*
Group	112	87.5
Individual	16	12.5
Total	128	100.0

It is observed that many units like bakery, soap-making and flour-making face the problems of marketing the products. There is no support system for this kind of enterprises either at the organisation level or at the Panchayat level. The major drawback faced by these group enterprises is that most of them are not economically viable. Hence, the profits earned by them are very low or even negative.

Another failure of this kind of group enterprises (e.g. provision store) is that all the members in the range of ten to twenty do not actively participate in the activity. Two or three members take care of all the activities. But the profits are to be shared equally among the members. Such a situation creates ill-will among members. Hence, most of the groups had been reluctant to take up any remunerative activity, while some others have expressed their readiness to take up additional responsibilities.

The specific case of Sparsham (the soft touch) which is initiated by the Collector of Kozhikode is a noted experience. In this case, the micro-enterprises had been initiated by the district administration and have been successfully conducted by the NHG members in Marad.

From the ongoing discussion, it is made clear that the poor sections of the society are depending on the micro-finance industry for their survival. The inclusive growth component of the policy proposition is to some extent made apparent using micro-finance tool.

8

Summary, Conclusion and Suggestions

The 'inclusive growth' as a strategy of economic development received attention owing to a rising concern that the benefits of economic growth have not been equitably shared. Growth is inclusive when it creates economic opportunities along with ensuring equal access to them. Apart from addressing the issue of inequality, the inclusive growth may also make the poverty reduction efforts more effective by explicitly creating productive economic opportunities for the poor and vulnerable sections of the society. After the mid-1990s, economic growth in India has failed to be sufficiently inclusive. A key element of the strategy for inclusive growth must be an all out effort to provide the teeming mass of people the access to basic facilities such as health, education, clean drinking water, etc. that they need. In the longer run they will be instrumental in creating economic opportunities for the future. It is important to recognise that access to these basic services is not necessarily assured simply by a rise in per capita income.

The concept of social capital has taken a central role in the modern development discussions, especially in the case of local level development. The concept was developed by Robert Putnam in his study of Italy (1993) which was then employed in the US situation (1995). He had stressed the association between group bonding and political development. In general, the term of social capital can be explained as the quality and quantity relationships, networks and norms among people and organizations that facilitate collective action. Putnam (1993) has defined social capital as "features of social organisation such as networks, norms and trust that facilitate coordination and cooperation for mutual benefit". According to Putnam (1996), social capital "refers to the collective value of all 'social networks' and the inclinations that arise from these networks to do things for each other". Further, he explained that it "refers to connections among individuals—social networks and the norms of reciprocity and trustworthiness that arise from them." Without 'bridging' social capital, 'bonding' groups may become isolated and disenfranchised from the rest of the society. Bonding social capital is a necessary antecedent for development of a more powerful form of bridging social capital. Bonding and bridging social capital can work together productively if in balance, or they may work against each other. Bonding social capital can also perpetuate sentiments of certain groups, allowing the bonding of individuals together upon common radical ideals. In mild cases, it just isolates certain communities such as suburbs of cities because of the bonding social capital.

The challenges of achieving more inclusive growth can only be met by policies that encourage easier and affordable access to financial services. Both theoretical and empirical researches highlight the role of financial development in facilitating economic development. At the cross-country level, evidence indicates that various measures of financial development are positively related to economic growth. The approach of forming social capital for inclusive growth is used widely nowadays. Micro-finance, by providing small loans and savings facilities to those who have been excluded from commercial financial services, has been promoted as a key strategy for reducing poverty in all its forms by agencies all-over the world. The innovative credit delivery system—micro-finance—was a breakthrough in the world of finance. It changes the life of the poor, especially women, not only by providing financial services such as micro-savings and micro-insurance, also by imparting training in entrepreneurial development. Over the past few decades, micro-finance institutions and programmes all-over the world have adopted numerous innovative ways of providing credit and savings services to the entrepreneurial poor. These include the provision of small loans to poor people, especially in rural areas, at full-cost interest rates, without collateral, repayable in frequent instalments. Borrowers are organized into groups, which reduce the risk of default. There are also effective mechanisms which disseminate valuable information on ways to improve the health, legal rights, sanitation and other relevant concerns of the poor.

Kerala has gained international acclaim due to its development experience during the second half of the twentieth century. The basic characteristic of Kerala's experience is that it has gained high levels of social development despite low levels of per capita income. Kerala's development achievements have been considered by many as a model of viable development achieved through equitable distribution against the background of a relatively low economic growth. It has been attributed to the combination of public action and responsive governance. The achievement has been mainly due to the twin engines of education and health. In spite of these achievements in the social sector, women in Kerala face a variety of problems such as educational discrimination, gender discrimination in the labour market, wage discrimination, deprivation, lack of health care, violence and sexual atrocities and lack of public space. Many of the problems of women have gone unattended and neglected by social reform movements and organisations in Kerala.

There now exist a rich crop of literature on micro-finance—both theoretical and empirical studies. The theoretical issues relating to micro-finance may be broadly classified under categories: sustainability of MFIs, outreach to the poor, outreach to the extreme poor, impact on the poor, mistargeting and non-participation, drop-outs, delinquent clients, overlapping memberships, informal finance, commercialization of micro-finance, etc. The various debates existing in the field of micro-finance are to be given proper attention.

In India, financial inclusion has been viewed as one of the major aspects of inclusive growth. The process of financial inclusion is an attempt to bring the weaker and vulnerable sections of society within the ambit of the organized financial system. Economic theory supports the view that access to affordable financial services enlarges livelihood opportunities and empowers the poor to change their lives. Such empowerment aids social growth as well as sustainable development of the economy. It is in this sense that the inclusive growth cannot be complete without financial inclusion. The mainstream financial institutions have nowadays recognized that the poor too are bankable. They feel that the modern technology help them to make this possible. India has also introduced technology into different financial products and financial services. The country has allowed using its citizens the debit/credit cards and mobile banking. She also has allowed regional rural banks and cooperative banks to sell insurance and financial products. Different commercial banks have opened no-frills accounts with overdraft facility for their customers. The approach to financial inclusion in developing countries such as India is different from that of the developed countries. In the developed countries, the focus is on the relatively small share of population not having access to banks or the formal payments system. But in countries like India, majority who are excluded are focused and aimed to be financially included.

Since, formal credit institutions rarely lend to the poor, special institutional arrangements become necessary to extend credit to those who have no collateral to offer. Micro-finance, the provision of a wide range of financial services to the poor on a sustainable basis, has proved to be immensely valuable in this regard. Access to financial services has allowed many families to make significant progress in their own efforts to escape poverty. The need for informality in credit delivery and easy access is demonstrated by the fact that Self-Help Groups (SHGs) and Micro-finance Institutions (MFIs) constitute the fastest growing segment in recent years in reaching out to small borrowers. One can easily spell out five factors distinguishing micro-finance bodies from traditional banking institutions and they are: (a) client base (poor/low income); (b) lending methodology (no collateral, peer or character lending); (c) labour-intensive nature of work (with a cost structure reflecting it); (d) portfolio (small, short-term loans); and (e) institutional structure and governance.

Four important models have been tried out by the poor to help themselves in rural India such as the SHG Model, Grameen replicators, Co-operative societies and NBFCs. Micro-finance is a recent development in which Indian institutions have acquired considerable expertise and where up-scaling holds great promise both to expand the nature of financial services offered to micro-enterprises and to make these the springboard for entrepreneurial development. The SHG movement is bringing about a profound transformation in rural areas of India. MFIs play a significant role in facilitating inclusion, as they are uniquely positioned in reaching out to the rural poor. Many of them operate in a limited geographical area, with a greater understanding of the issues specific to the rural poor, enjoy greater acceptability amongst the rural poor and have flexibility in operations providing a level of comfort to their clientele.

Kudumbashree is a multi-faceted women based participatory poverty eradication programme of the Government of Kerala. It was launched on 1 April, 1998. It is a partnership between four major actors (Central Government, State Government, Local Bodies and National Bank for Agriculture and Rural Development—NABARD). The objective of the project is to eliminate absolute poverty from the State of Kerala within a decade. It is exclusively focussed on women, women in family and women in community. It is an organization of women from below poverty line. The core activity is women empowerment through micro-finance, micro-enterprise and convergent community action. Kudumbashree stands for organising the poor under a community based organization called Community Development Society (CDS).

Kudumbashree is a Government programme for poverty alleviation of women experimented first in an urban setting in Alappuzha, which was later scaled up to selected panchayats. In this scheme woman representatives of all the neighbourhoods in a ward are grouped into an Area Development Society (ADS) chaired by the Panchayat Member. The ADS of all the wards in a panchayat are federated into a panchayat level development committee chaired by the Panchayat President. In other words, this is a programme for poverty alleviation that seeks to bring all poor women organised for micro-credit under the governmental umbrella. The programme looks upon the NHGs as similar to SHGs oblivious of the different contexts in which they arose.

As the economy grows, certain sections of the society get naturally marginalized. They are left out of the mainstream economic development and social reform agenda. In the case of Kerala, even though the State is much forward in the area of social development, some of the social and economic groups are still found as outliers in the society. From the available evidences, it is found that the Kerala society has its outliers all over the State. Some of them are marginalized historically (for example, the SC/ST population), some others are marginalized culturally or religiously (for example, the Muslim population), some others locationally (for example, the urban poor in the slums), and yet others are occupationally (plantation workers). The overriding peculiarity of these people would be underlying poor economic and social status. The backwardness in social arena makes them economically stagnant or vulnerable too. The type of work assigned to these people by the society, wages given to them and public utility services rendered to them are accentuating their status.

Kerala, a State renowned for social sector development witnessed the emergence of several marginalized sections. They live in remote places (the mountainous tracts, protected forest areas), make a livelihood from nature (fisher folk) and so they are open to the vagaries of the nature for their livelihood. Resourcelessness is their major problem. The ownership of land would be a problem for many of them. The land ownership issues prevailing among tribal, plantation workers, marine fisher folk and alienation from their present dwellings are the major problems faced by them. Lack of assets such as physical, social, human, financial and economic make them more vulnerable. The advent of globalization, liberalization and privatization has a major impact on the economy. Indian economy is showing a robust growth, but the faceless teeming population has been forgotten due to various reasons. Withdrawal of State machinery from various social sectors like education, health and infrastructural development has an adverse impact on these people.

It is in the present context that the broad objective of the study is to look into how the recent progress in the field of micro-finance helped in the capacity-building of women in particular and development of the State in large, especially in the context of inclusive growth. The major findings on the work are presented below:

Major Findings

Since, the inception of Kudumbashree in 1998, the NHGs were initiated all-over the State during different periods. At that time, the membership was allowed at 40 per group. For the purpose of bank linkage and other administrative purposes, the group membership had been fixed at 20. So, many of the groups have been reorganised and made into groups of 20 members each. But many groups have a membership even less than 15.

Of the total members, sixty per cent of them belong to the age group of 30 to 50 years. They are mainly the homemakers and always they are keener in what is happening around them. The majority of the members belong to the age group of 30 to 40 (32.1%), another 27.6 per cent belong to the age group 40 to 50. Younger women less than age of 30 years have less representation, forming about 19 per cent.

About 97 per cent of the women in the NHGs are married and the rest of the women are unmarried. The majority of the unmarried women belong to younger age group. In the field, it is found that the married women are found to be more active in these types of financial institutions as they have to shoulder a lot of responsibilities in the society. They have children to get educated, they have husbands to be self-employed, and they too have a dream about livelihood in the form of micro-enterprises. In many of the cases, the women are said to be currently married. But, many of them are female headed households. They have to take care of survival of themselves and of their families, especially their children. The benefits they reap from the Kudumbashree help them meet some of their needs.

Kerala is a State which gives utmost importance to education. But the results show that the status of education among women belonging to socially and economically backward regions is still lagging behind. One of the indicators of poverty among women is the lack of human capital. The theoretical suggestion can be clearly visible in the field also. The present study concentrated its focus on the backward regions of Kerala State and this result has been obtained. Most of the members in the NHGs belong to backward and marginalized sections of the society. Yet in another way one can view the result in such a manner that the organization reached out to the various sections of the society in Kerala and the extent of its spread is not small.

A striking feature which one can observe in the field is that, whatever be the educational status, the women are so keen to send their wards to school and for higher education. They are ready to spend any amount of money for the purpose. Exception to this trend was seen only in Wayanad, where the mothers in most cases are head of the family and the facilities available to them for sending their children to school are very limited.

Even though many of the NHGs were constituted more than a decade ago, the level of savings is very low. As the area of study is confined only to the women in the poorer sections of the society, it is evident that the inability of the poor to save is the major problem. The other point they have raised is that, they are not allowed to withdraw a portion of their savings when they are in urgent need. The micro-finance industry usually keeps the savings to extend loans to the members. They are not aware of those principles, many are defaulting the savings although the amount saved is very low.

It is found that out of the total 1880 respondents, about 30 per cent of the people have not availed any loans at all. About 40 per cent of the members availed loans less than Rs. 5000 while a small percentage of people (15%) have availed a loan more than Rs. 7500. It is observed that four per cent of the members have availed a loan more than Rs. 10000. When looking into the mean it is Rs. 3288.89 and the median is Rs. 2000. The standard deviation of the data is Rs. 4332.46.

It is observed that the Kudumbashree mission has rendered the micro-finance services in the right spirit among the women, especially to those who are underprivileged in the society. About 58 per cent of the women have admitted that they have received some kind of training from the micro-finance organization while about 42 per cent have not received any such kind of training. On enquiry, it is observed that many of the members have been offered different types of training. But due to the traditional settings (as in Malappuram), very poor background (as in Wayanad) and other engagements (as in Idukki), the women could not participate in these kinds of training.

The survey results show that only 3.8 per cent of the total groups were started due to self-motivation or the initiative of the other NHGs in the locality. The friends helped in the formation of 6.7 per cent of the total groups. 89 per cent of the groups were started under the initiative of others in the locality. They include the office bearers like ADS president, ADS secretary, Panchayat Member, Ward Councillor and CDS chairperson. In addition to their normal services, Block Panchayat Members, Scheduled Tribe promoters in the case of Wayanad, Welfare officer of plantation in the case of Idukki district, etc. too played a crucial role. An important thing one can observe is that the representatives of local self-government, local level politicians, and Kudumbashree leaders play a very important role in initiating new groups.

The direction from the authorities of Kudumbashree insisted the members to have a group meeting every week. 90.7 per cent of the groups strictly follow the instruction. But a percentage less than ten does not follow the instruction. While 5.6 per cent of the total groups meet only once in a month, another 3.7 per cent meet twice a month.

About 99 per cent of the NHGs witnessed that they meet without fail. Only less than one per cent of NHGs admit that they do not meet regularly. While 62.6 per cent of the groups conduct their group meeting on rotational basis, the rest of the 37.4 per cent groups have a permanent place to conduct their group meetings. The question that naturally arises is why permanent place is selected though it is being instructed otherwise. The simple answer is that there is no space for them to get together in the members' dwellings. Most of the poor people live in very small spaces and it may be difficult for them to share their own spaces to convene meetings. For example, slum dwellers in Thiruvananthapuram stay in rental buildings; plantation workers in Idukki live in company allotted lines and tribal people dwell in settlements. As they have very limited space for them and their families, it would be difficult for them to open their own houses for convening the meetings. So, there is a little chance for having the group meetings on a rotational basis.

Many members in the groups felt that the time they spend for group meetings gives them exposure to the world of friends and fellows for sharing experiences and gaining insights. Housewives from lower middle class families have a lot of time to spare and invariably attend the meeting. But the poor people give more importance for their living and survival. They can hardly spare time for this purpose. In the districts of Malappuram and Wayanad, all the groups meet for less than one hour duration, while in districts like Alappuzha and Idukki one can see that more groups are engaged in meeting for a duration of more than one hour.

It is also observed that in some of the groups even now, the number is as high as 38. One of the reasons for the high number is that some of the groups were formed as early as in 1990s under the UBSP project. After those groups were linked to Kudumbashree programme, many of them have broken up and have formed new groups. Still some of the groups do not want to break up and so, the number of members is so high in those groups. The number of members of a group plays a very important role in disbursement of loan, waiting period between different loan cycles, distribution of capital, and distribution of bank loans among members. So, even if a member drops out, the groups are reluctant to include a new person. The major reason is that the new person has to raise the savings because in many of the groups, savings play a major role in sanctioning and distribution of loans. Loans are sanctioned on the basis of the savings of the respective members. Many groups feel that when they take new members, it takes time for them to adjust with the tradition and rules of the groups. So, they often opt for a smaller group. In many cases, the groups prefer to be exclusive. Hence they are hesitant to entertain new members. The reason is that it would create problems within the group's cohesion.

In 79 per cent of NHGs, there are no new members after the formation of the groups. In some of the groups, the number of new members is two to six, but in some groups, 15 to 16 new members are added. It is stipulated that the members of the neighbourhood groups should be residents of the same area and must have an affinity towards other members in the NHGs. The theory of group lending always emphasizes the point that the groups must be homogeneous. The homogeneity of relationship could be in terms of caste/occupation/gender or economic status, whichever is critical in the specific local settings. In other words, by homogeneity it means that the members should be from the same social and economic status, so, that the functioning of the groups becomes smooth and effective. Social capital explains a chance of having exclusions by other groups. Some level of reluctance to accept new members or incorporate people from other social groups can be seen in some areas. Formation of tribal groups in Wayanad or SC groups in Thiruvananthapuram has been given emphasis by the authorities. This may be done on the basis of giving benefits to them collectively.

The major reasons cited for drop-out from NHGs were due to marriage, migration or death. Some have said that their inability to repay loan and other financial problems are the major reasons. Lack of time is also mentioned as another reason. Some blame the conditions and reluctance on the part of the members to have an effective participation in the meetings. Some others felt that they do not get any benefit from the group.

The official recognition of being poor is holding of a BPL card. In the field, all the poor people do not hold BPL cards. A striking example is seen in the case of Idukki where the plantation workers are sampled. As the plantation workers are permanent employees of the tea estates, they are not provided with the BPL cards. But the living standards of these people are in no way better than the rest of the poor population (BPL) of the State. They are living in residential quarters provided by the estate, with low living standards. They are presumably poor but in some way they are excluded from the BPL list. On the other hand, the NHGs found that the people living in the tribal areas of Wayanad are predominantly poor and they hold BPL ration cards.

Nowadays in Kerala, many other organizations and government programmes have also emerged to support SHGs of poor women. These 'promoting' agencies try to hijack the existing self-help groups in a particular area. It is now noted that some of the members of Kudumbashree are also joining the groups formed by other 'promoting' agencies. This creates problems for the existing groups as some of the members make willful defaults and migrate to other groups putting the NHGs in jeopardy.

In different localities of Kerala, the presence of other MFIs is also felt. They try to attract the members of Kudumbashree to their organizations for various reasons. One of the reasons cited is that training the members had gained from Kudumbashree is much worthy. If they are taken to other groups, indeed they are going to be assets for the new groups. Many of the members have already learnt the key micro-finance activities such as convening meetings, preparing agenda, writing reports, maintaining records, importance of discipline, calculation of interest and other related functions. The members in Kudumbashree are regular in group meetings, loan repayment and savings. Even the decision-making capacity is high as they have gained good exposure to the outside world.

The field experience revealed that even though the authorities are giving strict instructions, Kudumbashree members are taking part in other micro-finance institutions/organizations. They have membership in Nair Service Society (NSS), Sree Narayana Darma Paripalana Yogam (SNDPY), church organizations and other private micro-finance organizations. They are very much active in those organizations too. Obviously, when the respective communities start the self-help groups, the women who are already in Kudumbashree movement would be the sure members of them. They are happy about their multiple memberships. They hold key positions like secretary or president. Some of them have been identified for acting as facilitators to other MFI/Ps too.

Private MFIs like ESAF, Muthoot, etc. have been found working among the beneficiaries of Kudumbashree. These NBFC-MFIs have spread their tentacles even among the poorest of the people. Their prevalence is seen more in Thiruvananthapuram and Kozhikode where the members are having affinity to cities.

The mode of activity is entirely different from the traditional micro-finance activities. The traditional micro-finance institutions try to raise the savings of the poor as seed capital and rotate the savings among the members as credit, but the new generation micro-finance institutors do the reverse. For example, one of the MFIs (ESAF) which is seen working among the fishing villages of Kozhikode, has another mode of operation. It grants loan of Rs. 10000/- to each member. There is no need of a group meeting or any other informal gatherings. They collect ten members in the locality and disburse the loans to all the members. In many cases, the husbands offer guarantee for wives and *vice versa.* The interest rate is apparently high. It is a re-emergence of moneylenders in a new form in the backward areas.

Poor repayment history of some members may invite sanctions and enforcements. When one member does not repay loans, naturally the other members become alert as the loan may turn bad. The peer pressure works in these cases, and the result would be repayment without default. But at times, some members make willful default. This affects the solidarity of the groups. In most of the areas of study, where very poor people are living, they really feel it difficult to repay it. In such situation, they silently leave the group.

Availability of time is a major factor behind the participation of group meetings and other activities. As people become busier, they do not find time to participate in these kinds of groups. Time is also a commodity for modern people having alternative uses. If participation in these groups is not found to be fruitful; they may quit and give more preference to other things.

Only 4.7 per cent of the groups said that more than 75 per cent of the members are making their savings regularly. 76 per cent of the leaders said that in their respective groups 50 to 75 per cent members are saving regularly, while in another 26 per cent of the groups less than 50 per cent of the members are saving regularly.

In some of the NHGs, an elected member takes care of the responsibilities of going to banks, while in a small number of NHGs everybody share the responsibility on a rotational basis. In 44 per cent of the groups secretary performs the above duty and in another 27 per cent of NHGs, president undertakes the responsibility.

Only 42 per cent of the NHGs say that 50 per cent of the members in their respective NHGs are aware of the loan rules and bank loan details. The leaders of the rest of the groups (58%) hold the opinion that 50 to 75 per cent of the groups have the awareness about the loan rules and bank loan details. It is striking to note that the district of Wayanad has a higher proportion (83%) of persons with lower level of awareness. The literacy level as well as mobility from their local areas is low among the tribal women.

Most of the NHGs are already linked with the banks in the locality. Many of the NHGs have enjoyed the facility and they are in a position to get more money than that they can disburse using their own funds. They are leveraging on it and make prompt repayment to take the advantage of the lower interest incidence supplemented by government subsidy.

It is observed that ten per cent of the groups have not yet received any kind of bank loans. They are meeting their needs with their own funds or by other available sources. On the other hand, the groups which availed the loans said that they are very prompt in repayment of their loans. 83 per cent of the groups are of this opinion. A small number of NHGs confessed that they have either delayed their repayments or defaulted the payment. Some of the members in the NHGs default repayment of loans. In majority of groups (92%) defaults are not reported. But in some groups, up to 10 members defaulted their repayment. Decisions on loan are taken at the group meetings of NHGs. From the field study, it is found that in 95 per cent of the groups the decision is taken by all the members in the NHGs. Only less than five per cent of the NHGs said that it is taken by other people including the elected members or persons from outside.

It is mandatory on the part of the Kudumbashree to audit the accounts of the NHGs on a regular basis. It is found that auditing was done by all the groups under study. It has been done under the aegis of different persons in the locality. They include bank manager, CDS chairperson, Kudumbashree auditors, corporation authorities, Panchayat Members, etc.

Even though the micro-credit given to the members is meant for productive purposes, it is a well-known fact that the micro-credit is largely being used for consumption smoothing purposes. The evidence is seen with the result of 42 per cent of groups who are denying the claim that there is not much misutilisation of the loans. 62 per cent of the groups said that there is a steady increase in the loans for productive purposes.

One of the major reasons for this state of affairs is the poor background of the members in the NHGs in the study area. Lack of education and skill, lack of entrepreneurial capacity, lack of mobility, laxity of marketing avenues, social taboos and livelihood issues are the reasons for this problem.

While enquiring about the reasons for less quantity of amount spent for productive purposes, the members gave varied replies. Some have said that they did not get a loan from the bank. Some others said that they have already applied for a loan but they have not got any loan. In Idukki area, the women surveyed belonged to the plantation estates and so they have no time for conducting a micro-enterprise as they are fully engaged in their jobs.

According to the opinion of the leaders in 77 per cent of NHGs, less than 50 per cent members in their respective NHGs possess resource or skill asset for regular income. 23.4 per cent of the NHGs said that about 50 to 75 per cent of their members have some sort of resource or skill for creating regular income.

Along with the micro-finance activities such as dealing with loans and savings, some NHGs are engaged in other activities. It is found from the results that 77 per cent of the NHGs are not engaged in any other activities. Only 23 per cent of the groups are said to have been engaged in some kind of activities. In short, the NHGs which are good performers fare well both in organisational functions and proper participation in the activities of NHGs. But the medium and poor performers do not give much importance to the functions of the NHGs, which in turn affect the sustainability and existence of the groups.

Besides dealing with loans and savings, NHGs take up other activities—financial, economic and cultural. In the study area, it is found that 89 per cent of the NHGs are engaged in some kind of community development activities, while the rest of the groups are not engaged in any activity. In the case of community activities, 81 per cent of the groups are participating in the *grama sabhas*. Only a very small percentage of NHGs are engaged in some other activities. For building up the cohesion among the group members, cultural activities play a major role. Most of the groups have already arranged some programmes in their respective groups. They range from cultural programmes of members and their children, sweet distribution on special days like Independence Day, conducting anniversary of the NHGs, sports meets and so on.

Ninety seven per cent of the groups are maintaining a common fund of all the members of the NHGs. In most cases, the group secretary or president take care of the operation of the emergency fund. Whenever any of the group members requires money, the group would be ready to extend a helping arm to her. Rest of the groups keep their amount with post office and other institutions.

The purposes for which the emergency fund is used vary from gifts for marriage, release for festival seasons, expenses related to death and birth, medical expenses, children's education, etc. While asked about the major uses of emergency fund to the members, it is stated that they used it for a wide range of purposes where exigency is the major item of the usage.

Of the total 107 NHGs surveyed, 85 per cent have written bye-laws while 15 per cent do not have written bye-law for the functioning of the groups. From the study, it is found that only 63.6 per cent of the groups have oral but strong bye-laws while 24.3 per cent have an oral byelaw, but the members are not aware of the bye-laws. Only 8.4 per cent of the groups have written bye-laws and members are well aware of the bye-laws A large majority of the NHGs (96%) agreed that they were having rules and regulations including sanction and control mechanism for repayment of loans. But four per cent of the NHGs denied that there are such controls in their groups. In the study area, only 18.7 per cent of the NHGs strictly enforce the imposition of fine. 65.4 per cent of the groups impose it occasionally. A small percentage (15.9%) of the groups is not imposing the fine for late coming.

Nearly 75 per cent of the sample households have own houses. The proportion of rented house is about 18 per cent while another seven per cent live in joint families. It is important to note that most of the sampled areas are highly congested, with the highest density of houses being observed in Thiruvananthapuram as the study area is situated in the slum areas.

Twelve per cent of the sample households belong to the *kutcha* category and 82 per cent to the *pucca* category. The number of huts is the highest in Wayanad, while Malappuram has the largest number of *pucca* houses forming 85 per cent. The majority of houses in the sample areas are *pucca*; many houses have only limited number of rooms and space. Fifty six per cent of the sample houses have thatched roofs. Twenty per cent of the houses have sheet roof. The housing condition is poor in backward regions like Wayanad and Malappuram. About 66 per cent of the houses have permanent brick walls while another 30 per cent have mud walls. A small percentage of houses are having thatched walls which are more relevant in the districts of Wayanad and Kozhikode. 89 per cent houses in all sample areas have electric lights whereas in about 11 per cent of the households kerosene is used for lighting. A very small per cent has solar supported lighting facility. Nearly fifty per cent of the households in the sample have sparse furnishing. In fact, they do not have sufficient space and money and they are not interested in spending their money on furniture.

The majority of the women in the organisation belonged to the middle age group. More than four-fifths of the members were in the age group of 21 to 50 years. Since, the majority of women in the middle age group are unemployed, it is they who have the urgency and the time to engage themselves in some kind of productive activity.

The representation of the elderly is low in the MFI (about 12 per cent above 50 years). In the cases of elderly women members, they take loans in their names, only for the benefit of their children. As the old women do not need money for their own use, they help their kith and kin. Some old women help their children in times of needs. They feel that savings with the NHGs may help them in future. In some groups, it was observed that old women were purposely excluded. Younger women felt the presence of elderly women unnecessary and a handicap. Obviously, there was a wide generation gap between them and the old people.

From the sample, it is observed that more than three-fifths of women in the organisation had education of high school level or more. Graduates formed less than two per cent and persons with higher secondary level education come to eighteen per cent. The percentage of women having lower primary education (5.3%) and upper primary education (4%) was comparatively low. Illiterates accounted for about seven per cent. A closer look into the educational status of women in the backward regions of the State showed some dismal situation in many places. For example, in the case of Wayanad, the proportion of illiterate to the total sample comes around 60 per cent.

Women with technical qualification or training were less in number. Some of the untrained women had some skills in conventional vocations such as tailoring, typewriting, nursery teaching, *anganwadi* teaching and ITI trades. This fact points to the potential need for imparting training to women for enabling them to take up income generating activities. This trend generally shows that in the sample areas where the different outlier communities are taken for study, they are still remaining far backward in educational level.

Nearly 22.9 per cent of the households were absolutely landless. About 64 per cent of the beneficiary households hold land less than ten cents. Only in districts such as Alappuzha (agricultural land), Malappuram (with a rural setting having importance of agriculture) and in Wayanad (agricultural setting) we could find landholding of more than twenty cents. In the districts of Idukki, Thiruvananthapuram and Kozhikode, the land holding more than ten or twenty cents is rare. The striking feature of the sample population surveyed is that the ownership of cows and other livestock is very minimal. Of the total sample population, less than one per cent hold cow as an asset. Their mean monthly income has been reported as Rs. 1,327. Regarding the other livestock, the presence is absolutely nil. However, majority of the households do not own any type of livestock for want of land for rearing cattle and poultry. Another reason observed is that most of the women are very poor and they are unable to raise the cattle even if they like to do so. In places like Idukki and Wayanad, the climatic conditions and proximity to forest are cited as reasons for the same. The density of population is very high in Thiruvananthapuram and Kozhikode and that has been cited as the major reason.

Of the total sample population, 83 per cent have a television set at their houses, while 57 per cent of houses have gas stove with LPG connection. Another 59 per cent have electric fans at their homes. The tribal settlements in Wayanad do not have electricity connection as most of them are dwelling inside the wildlife sanctuaries. Naturally, the electrical and electronic gadgets are not much in use in these areas.

Eighty four per cent women are found adopting the family planning systems. The high prevalence of adoption of family planning in Kerala in comparison to the other States of the country shows the high level of social development in the State. But there is a notable variation among the districts. The districts in which the number of women who are not adopting family planning is higher in Malappuram (24%) and Wayanad (40%). But in other districts, it is less than 12 per cent which is not substantial. The adoption is found to be very less in Malappuram district and Wayanad because of Muslim and tribal population respectively.

About 46 per cent of the households in the sample had alcoholism as a major problem. Data show that in Malappuram (13%), the proportion of alcoholics is very less; while in Wayanad (88%) it is very high.

From the field, it is observed that the proportion of beneficiaries having family savings in financial institutions is low. A good percentage of people (47.8%) have outside loan liabilities. Most of the loans were taken from moneylenders. Apart from borrowing from moneylenders, they pledge their gold ornaments in times of difficulties with local moneylenders and informal moneylending institutions.

While looking at the aggregate data on indebtedness among districts, Alappuzha stands first with about 94 per cent of the respondents are indebted. One of the reasons for this trend is that in Alappuzha, the presence of private micro-finance institutions (like ESAF) is more and people are highly depending on them for money. Next comes the district of Wayanad with 71 per cent of respondents found to be indebted. High level of poverty and uncertainty in their lives can be the reasons for the same. The districts which show low level of indebtedness are Thiruvananthapuram (18%) and Idukki (38%). A majority (34.6%) of the people who are indebted had taken loans for their household expenditure. Only 7.8 per cent of the total respondents had taken loans from outside sources for investing in the productive enterprises.

Most of the respondents did not have previous experience with the formal financial institutions especially banks. It is to be noted that the prevalence of exclusion in the formal financial system is highly evident among the women in the plantation sector in Idukki. Yet a small number of members responded that they couldn't obtain any loans from the lending institutions.

It is observed that a group of members about 3.5 per cent has not availed any credit from the institution. Majority of the members (58.6%) have availed loans ranging from Rs. 1000 to 5000. But a small number of members (10.6%) could avail an amount of Rs. 5000-10000. Another five per cent of the members got loan of Rs. 10000 and more. 23 per cent of the members got loan amount between Rs. 200 and 1000, which is too meagre. It is observed that the maximum number of loans availed by members in the Kudumbashree NHGs comes to around five. About 3.5 per cent have not availed loans from NHGs, the rest (97%) have availed loans. Of the total members, about 36 per cent have availed two loans. But a small percentage of the members have availed more than three loans from the NHGs.

Most of the people come to know about the existence of the organization from those who are very near to them. The members trust their family members, friends, neighbours and ward councillors. But in majority of the cases (67.5%), they depend on others who are in the locality and on those who are influential.

Although the micro-finance system is known for cent per cent repayment, nowadays, mounting non-performing assets (NPAs) have become a major concern for many of the micro-finance institutions around the world. Contrary to the global trend, in Kudumbashree, majority of the members (99.7%) have said that they are not having any arrears with the Kudumbashree. The proper enforcement mechanism available in most of the NHGs helps to get the repayment in time. As the majority of the people are poor, they need credit at the right time and that is the reason why there are no arrears in most of the groups visited. Only a minority (0.3%) felt that they lag behind in repayment of loans. The major reasons cited here were business failures, economic shocks due to diseases, contingency, etc.

A large number of programmes and activities have been implemented as part of Kudumbashree. But the other support systems for the poor people are not much evident. They think that compulsory saving (with 92 per cent of the responses) is the only tangible benefit they are getting out of the programme. The respondents are strictly adhering to the mandatory requirement stipulated in the programme.

Credit is a necessary component which keeps the people to hold around the micro-finance system. Apart from the micro-savings, the most important component which attracts people into the system is the credit. All the members feel that they need credit for the future. But a small per cent of the members feel that debt is a burden and they may not need it for the future period also.

While enquiring about the problems in obtaining credit from Kudumbashree, a majority of the members have the opinion that they never faced any problem in obtaining credit from Kudumbashree. A quarter of the beneficiaries feel that they have some problems in getting credit from the micro-finance institution.

While asking the members' opinion on whether all the members attend each group meeting, almost all are of the opinion that they are doing so. On the other hand, a small percentage of people think that the members are not regular in their meeting in Kudumbashree.

About 53 per cent of the people do not hold any position in the NHGs while rest of the people hold any one of the posts in the unit. About 11.5 per cent of the respondents are presidents of their respective units, while another 12 per cent hold the position of secretary. A rest of 16 per cent of the people is the committee members of the units.

Of the total sample population surveyed, about 53 per cent of them have received some kind of training from the organization. 47 per cent of the sample population have not received any kind of training till date. Those who have received the highest level of training are in Wayanad (77%) followed by Malappuram (74.7%) and Kozhikode (70%). Many of the members surveyed are totally unaware of the training. In other words, they are not exposed to any type of training. One of the reasons for the same is the geographical distance between the district centre and their locality. They are to pay for their commutation from their home to the training centre which in most of the cases is very high. The vulnerability of the poor people accentuates their inability to take part in many of the opportunities provided by the organization. The members in Idukki, Malappuram, and Wayanad have genuine problems like geographical, cultural and social reasons which forbid them in taking part in these kinds of activities.

The effectiveness of the Kudumbashree programmes is more evident in the northern districts than in the southern districts. The Urban Basic Services for the Poor (UBSP) programme which was successful among the district like Malappuram was more evident here. The districts like Idukki (19%), Thiruvananthapuram (23%) and Alappuzha (52%) accounted for less effectiveness. The district of Idukki is peculiar in nature as all the beneficiaries are plantation workers whose time is taken away by the plantation work and so they are not in a position to spare any time for other activities like going for training or participating in micro-enterprises.

All the sampled population unanimously said that all of them were having the facility of compulsory saving. The Kudumbashree programme has given them a chance to save in a safe place. As the savings of the members are kept in the banks, they are assured of the money. The interest on savings is usually given to the members as an incentive to their savings. In many of the groups, they keep the interest amount in a common fund and it would be considered as the capital for giving loans to the members themselves. Some of the groups keep the amount in emergency fund. In the sampled areas, about half of the groups distribute their interest amount to the members, whereas in the rest of the groups, the members have not received any amount as interest on their savings. In Alappuzha district, all the groups have given out the interest money to their members. In the district of Idukki, no members have received any money as interest. In the other districts, it is a mixed picture.

A small per cent (11%) of members have a feeling that their savings have been used to cover bad debts of other group members. Vast majority of members do not feel so. This shows that repayment of loans is more prompt in the groups under Kudumbashree. Hence, there is no need for covering bad debts of some members by the savings of rest of the group members. Further analysis shows that the presence of bad debts never stopped the members from saving or reducing the size of the member's deposits. Regular savings increase the funds available for credit and that has an added advantage for the members.

Even though the data show a very rosy picture on the micro-savings of the NHGs, there are instances that some of the groups would like to get back their savings. The contractual non-withdrawal feature of the savings in the micro-finance makes them a bit frustrated.

As a result of the People's Plan Campaign, *grama sabhas* have become the fora for discussing people's problems and development needs. However, it was only after joining NHGs that most of the women in the study area came to know about *grama sabhas*. In fact, the NHGs motivated many of the beneficiaries to take part in *grama sabhas*. In the group meetings of the NHGs, the members used to discuss their needs and problems which included drinking water, toilet, public hygiene and housing. Identification of problems and formulation of ideas for their solution have helped them to take part in the planning process effectively and meaningfully. Thus, women from financially and educationally backward classes were empowered to take part in development process and discourse on gender-sensitive planning.

Attending the *grama sabha* is a key improvement one can observe in the case of Kudumbashree members. As the benefits of the poor are discussed and decided through the *grama sabha* meetings, the beneficiaries are keen to attend the meetings. Among the members surveyed, about three-fourths of them are attending the *grama sabha* meetings regularly. Among the districts of the State, Thiruvananthapuram has very low participation with only 23 per cent and the highest is in Wayanad where 98 per cent of the women are participating in the *grama sabha* meetings. In districts like Kozhikode (93%) and Idukki (90%) participation level is high. Apart from Thiruvananthapuram, the participation in Malappuram is low with about 58 per cent participation.

It was observed that participation of the beneficiaries of Kudumbashree in social and business organizations is very low (less than 3%). The vast majority of members (97.3%) are not participating in any of these organizations. It is further observed that participation of the poorest is lower than that of the non-poor areas. This is evident in the groups working in Wayanad and Idukki, that none of them are participating in any of the groups or organizations in the locality or around. Those women who are participating in other organizations participate in various political, cultural and social organizations. Some take part in political parties and trade unions. Among them are also members of Parent Teacher Association (PTA) and Residents' Association and various welfare groups. Many of them are participating in NSS *karayogams* and SNDP *yogams*. It instils confidence in women and attracts them to MFI. The majority of women did not have any previous exposure to such organizations.

There exist multiple MFIs operating in all the areas surveyed. Of the total sample size, 88 per cent of the people are aware of the other institutions providing similar credit facilities in their localities. About 12 per cent of the sample population has not heard of any of the micro-financial institutions in the locality.

In Kudumbashree also the major focus is on micro-enterprises. Of the total 590 members surveyed, only 22 per cent of the members (i.e. 128) are conducting any kind of micro-enterprise. About 78 per cent of the members do not have any enterprise of their own. The major reason for this trend is that many of them are not having confidence to start an enterprise. Lack of education, lack of experience in conducting business, fear of failure, and marketing problems are some of the reasons cited by the respondents.

More than ninety per cent of the women started their activities after joining the groups. This shows that the micro-finance organization helped them to gain confidence to initiate an economic activity. Less than ten per cent of the enterprises had been started even before the MFI started functioning in the respective areas. However, those who are engaged in economic activities for a long period show more confidence and consistency in business than others. It is very evident that experience is very important for doing any economic activity.

In India, most of the enterprises run by women are home-based thereby running an extended home activity. In our sample also, the majority (93.8%) of the enterprises are operated from homes. It helped them to look after the household chores and manage their enterprises simultaneously.

About fifty per cent of the entrepreneurs organized and managed their enterprises. Another 47 per cent of the enterprises are run by the group enterprises. It is evident in the case of Kudumbashree that they have initiated a large number of group enterprises under various State and centrally sponsored schemes such as SGSY, SJSRY, RMK, etc. Many group enterprises are found to be established in Wayanad and Kozhikode with about 90 per cent of the micro-enterprises. But the number of group enterprises formed in places like Thiruvananthapuram and Alappuzha is comparatively low.

The majority of the enterprises have a permanent place of business (41.1%). About 36 per cent of the women enterprises have no assured localities for their business. Those women, who are not having a permanent place of business, walked all the way carrying their wares on their heads or in hand-bags searching for customers.

The survey showed that 69 per cent of the entrepreneurs have no income generating activity other than the micro-enterprise. They were forced to take some kind of income generating activity for sustenance of their families. But for 46 per cent of the entrepreneurs, the enterprise is not the sole source of income. The overall data show that the entrepreneurs in Wayanad are depending on the enterprises started under NHGs more than the other entrepreneurs in the State.

The enterprises started by women used various sources of funds as seed money for setting up their units. The amount of investment varies from one another depending on the nature and scale of activity. Nearly 41 per cent of them availed loans from the neighbourhood groups to which they belonged, while about one-fifth managed to get loans from financial institutions and other sources. Household or personal savings provided the initial funds in the case of more than one-tenth of the enterprises.

As most of the enterprises are maintained by the groups, the number of people being employed in majority of the enterprises is about ten. In a small number of enterprises, the persons engaged in the activity are more than ten. About 57 per cent of the enterprises spent about five to ten hours of time for conducting their enterprises, while another 43 per cent have less than five hours of time in enterprises.

The major performance highlight of the units can be attributed to the expansion of their respective businesses with 61.7 per cent doing it with positive intent. While enquiring about the achievements of the present loan and the enterprises of the entrepreneurs, the only substantial change that has taken place in the case of the expansion of the business (61.7%). The other options like diversification, improvement in the quantity and quality of goods and services, modification premises, etc. were seen given lesser attention.

To a query as to whether any change has taken place in the entrepreneur's style of functioning especially in the maintenance of financial records of the business after receiving micro-enterprise loan, it was reported that a vast majority of them (98%) have not changed their way in keeping the records of their mioro-enterprises.

Only 50 per cent of the entrepreneurs feel that they are able to sell their products or there exists a market for their products. But the rest of the people feel that they are incurring huge operating expenses and they are yet to reach break even point.

As the enterprises are not operating on a large-scale, most of them (89%) are not using the banking facility to keep their surplus cash. Only a small number of enterprises are keeping their money in the bank for their business purposes.

About 68 per cent do not have separate bank accounts for their enterprises. But group enterprises (about 31%) have separate bank accounts.

The micro-enterprises run by the entrepreneurs are varied in nature. They range from agriculture and allied activities, production, services and trade. Of all the activities, agriculture and allied activities accounted for 67 per cent, while production activity constituted 16 per cent, services occupied 13 per cent and trade activities consist of mere three per cent.

Under the aegis of Kudumbashree, various NHGs initiated group enterprises. They include group farming and enterprise run by a group of members. Of the total entrepreneurs, 87 per cent are running group enterprises while only 12 per cent run individual enterprises.

Conclusions

Regarding the objective of analyzing the factors leading to the inequalities of women in rural/backward areas, it is found that they are varied and diverse. The evidences from the field and secondary sources of data show that some of them are marginalized historically (for example, the SC/ST population), some others are marginalized culturally or religiously (for example, the Muslim population), some others locationally (for example, the urban poor in the slums), and yet others are occupationally (plantation workers). While enquiring into the problems of inequality among the women, relative lack of assets—human, natural, physical, social and financial—emerged as the striking problem behind their backwardness. Distribution of human assets such as the capacity for basic labour, skills and good health is heavily biased against women. In the developing countries like India, ownership of natural assets such as land has tended to be heavily biased in favour of the male members of the family. Access to physical assets such as infrastructure is restricted by institutional barriers. Social assets, such as networks of contacts and reciprocal obligations that can be called on in time of need, and political influence over resources are also low for women. Lack of access to financial assets such as savings and to formal credit is another stumbling block to their progress.

While verifying the objective of how micro-finance helps in the formation of social capital, it is found that the micro-finance institutions try to reach the poor population in the society in a broader way. As the idea of micro-finance involves small-scale transactions in credit and savings designed to meet the needs of small- and medium-scale producers and businesses, it could penetrate into the depths of the poor sections in a country like India, specifically in a State like Kerala. While the micro-finance programmes offer skill-based training to augment productivity and organizational support and consciousness-raising training to empower the poor, it enhances the capacities of the poor people in a huge way. The social capital formation angle of the micro-finance industry is to work in such a manner that the women could be able to gather together and act for their welfare as well as the progress of the nation as a whole. The Kudumbashree movement, an unique programme by its own, which was the prime focus of the present study has promoted women empowerment and improved the condition of the poor families. This project has evolved a new strategy in Kerala that enables the successful operationalisation of anti-poverty programmes by the poor themselves. It offered ample opportunities to the poor, who are neglected by the formal banking sector, to avail of financial services in the form of thrift and credit and promoted economic empowerment of the poor women. Through their involvement in the activities of the project, their social and political empowerment is also ensured.

While examining whether micro-finance helps in the enhancement of democratic, economic and social capabilities of poor women, the evidences clearly pointed out the fact that the enhancement of capabilities among the womenfolk in Kerala has taken place under the aegis of Kudumbashree mission. Special attention has been given on the investment in social inputs, initiation of individual as well as group enterprises, implementation of varied kinds of programmes and projects, conduct of training programmes for the skill enhancement, etc. It has created ample opportunity for women to come forward and take part in different activities and improve their participation in different vistas of society. Participation in the decision-making processes in the democratic institutions such as local self-government bodies which is evident with the improved participation of Kudumbashree members in *grama sabhas* and getting the benefits out of them are a positive impact of the MFI in the grassroot level. The political participation of the women has gone up with the activities of the MFI. It could be seen in the context of local self-government elections where a large number of Kudumbashree members are contesting for various posts in Gram, Block and Zila Panchayat. Improved participation in economic activities, namely micro-savings, micro-credit and micro-enterprise, surely improved their economic situation. Increased mobility, enhanced confidence, improved decision-making power and better position in family and society are some of the changes which occurred in the social life of the women in the field. In short, one can conclude that the economic empowerment of women undisputably has enhanced the political and social capabilities of the women in rural and backward regions of Kerala.

In the case of the objective of the study which tried to analyse the factors affecting bonding and bridging of social capital through micro-finance, it is found that the peculiar method of gathering members for the micro-finance meeting plays a crucial role. The development programmes like Kudumbashree mission could create social ties and enhance social capital among members of a highly localised community in a strikingly short time. Close neighbours from similar socio-economic backgrounds ought to know one another to cooperate among themselves. It creates a sense of oneness among the people under the NHGs and it creates in a bonding kind of social capital. The federated system of Kudumbashree mission, which has NHG at the lower level and ADS at the ward level and CDS at the Panchayat level naturally helped to bridge the local people with a larger and higher platform of development activities. Many of the members have learnt the key micro-finance activities such as convening meetings, preparing agenda, writing reports, maintaining records, importance of discipline, calculation of interest and other related functions. The members in Kudumbashree are regular in group meetings, loan repayment and savings. The decision-making capacity is at new heights as they have gained good exposure to the outside world.

While trying to examine how the actions taken by the authorities are effective in helping the women to have access to various financial and other services, the indications from the data point out the fact that a positive impact is made. The entrepreneurial development programmes conducted by the Kudumbashree movement have augmented the existing capacities of the women in the backward regions. Evidences clearly show that various poverty alleviation programmes such as BSUP, SJSRY, EMS housing programme, etc. could reach the poor in an adequate manner. The mission helped the authorities to target the beneficiaries in the right sense and a lot of the poor have benefited out of it.

An enquiry into the reasons for deficiencies in the system of micro-finance in reaching poor women effectively was also conducted as part of the study. The evidences show that micro-finance is a ground-breaking innovation for removing poverty. The developing countries like India have used it intensively and extensively. Yet in the case of outreach there are still some issues to be settled. Even though the system is envisaged to target the poor only, in due course, inclusion of non-poor into the structure has become common. The reason is that those who are in the borderline naturally get attached to the realm of the groups. In the process, the effective targeting on the poor won't take place. The MFI instructed that the members in a neighbourhood should be the members of the NHGs irrespective of their economic background.

While looking into the contribution of micro-finance to the poor women in accessing various financial products, it is observed that the MFI could enhance the financial inclusion of the members in an immense way. It is found that those who were not generally attached to the banks have access to the banking business after becoming the members of the MFI. It is also observed that many of the members could develop better banking habits after getting the membership. In due course, as a result of this, they could avail various financial products such as savings bank account, subsidized loans, bank linkage with their NHGs, etc.

In the present study, it is hypothesized that micro-finance helps to enhance the resource base of women and micro-finance institutions can effectively act as a sub-system of local bodies and commercial banks for conferring inputs and services upon the poor. The study clearly supports the hypotheses. The resource base of the once resourceless women has been enhanced considerably. Though not in adequate measure, the MFI is acting as a major force to enhance the various capabilities of the poor women in backward regions of the States. As Kudumbashree is a government sponsored programme, it could significantly change the lives and outlook of the poor women in the local settings of the State. It is a programme which has become an unprecedented success hitherto in the development history of the State. As it is a governmental programme which acted as a conduit of all the poverty alleviation programmes sponsored by State and Central Governments, it could instruct the NHGs to take part in the development activities and policies of the government at large. As a result, the members as well as NHGs become the beneficiaries of almost all the programmes initiated by the government.

Active and effective participation of the local people in the local bodies and the commercial banking activities are the result of the same.

From the study, in general, it is understood that the provision of micro-finance has enabled the poor women to access financial services. While the facility of savings is being used optimally, credit retrieval is seen to face problems. While some of the deserving borrowers are discriminated against, some others depend on other similar institutions for credit at lower rates of interest. Problems of discrimination against certain members, high rates of interest and overlapping memberships can be seen here. It can also be seen that many old women face the problem of receiving credit. Office bearers usually avoid providing them with credit, even in times of urgency. Also, they are sometimes dropped out of groups on the excuse that they are too old and inefficient. This is against the goal of outreach of micro-financial organizations. Many women, in need of funds, decline to take loans because of the fear of debt burden. This has led them to the same level of poverty pre- and post-admission to the NHGs. This shows the ineffectiveness of the micro-financial tools in administering poverty reduction.

It is understood that a level of mistargeting exists. Many of the members are from non-poor households, and these are the ones who are usually holding the responsibilities as office bearers and leaders. These individuals usually take decisions in finalizing the list of borrowers. It is seen that the poorest ones in the group are usually denied credit and non-poor members are favoured with credit. This has led to further discrimination against the poor. Hence, mistargeting within the group and outside the group is a prominent problem. Many members face difficulties in attending training and workshops due to the distances to the institutes, and due to household responsibilities. Hence their entrepreneurial initiative is suppressed.

From the present study, it is understood that the contribution of micro-finance to the well-being of the poor women in terms of mobilisation of micro-savings, utilisation of micro-credit and organization, management and performance of income generating activities are substantial in the study area. It has also proved that micro-finance helped in building up economic and political capacity of women and thereby enabling empowerment of women. The performance of neighbourhood groups is largely influenced by the attendance and participation of members in meetings. But other factors such as keeping of records and registers, implementation of sanctions and enforcement of discipline also help their performance. On the other hand, drop-out of members, lack of incentives to the leaders who organize everything are weakening the organisational performance of the NHGs.

From the level of participation of women in self-help groups and the group dynamics that influence their participation, it was found that majority of NHGs have taken up some kind of activities. On the other hand, low confidence level, economic unviability and marketing problems have held back many groups from taking up any of the income generating activities. While assessing the extent of participation of the poor in the micro-finance institution, it is found that participation of hardcore poor is declining. The reasons are varying. As many of the neighbourhood groups do not have homogeneity and as they become a mixed group, the poor would fall out of place. Penalties and sanctions also exert pressures on the poor. Hence, they are automatically expelled from the group.

The study has clearly proved that micro-finance has definitely helped the beneficiary women to enhance their resource base by improving their micro-savings, micro-credit and micro-enterprises. It has also helped them to develop banking habits. The economic, political and social empowerment of women has enabled them to improve their overall capacity building. In the study area, networking of NHGs at the Panchayat level has helped to achieve some common goals of the groups. Also linkages with local institutions such as Panchayats and financial institution have improved the overall resource base of the NHGs. Thus, it is proved that micro-finance institutions can effectively act as a sub-system of local bodies and commercial banks for conferring inputs and services on the poor.

It is also observed that for those who are marginalized and who are living in backward regions of the country, mere provision of micro-finance is not adequate. There is no doubt that micro-finance has penetrated into the masses of the population and could make obvious transformations among the poor. The poorest of the society need some more provisions. Adequate healthcare system, protection from economic shocks, agricultural insurance, subsidized food provisions, viable income generating activities, pension benefit mechanism, are some of them.

Suggestions

Adequate investment and support are needed in the field of education among the marginalised outlier communities in order to get them emancipated.

Micro-finance organizations should arrange work-related training courses for the benefit of women entrepreneurs. Entrepreneurship development programmes (EDPs) should be tailored to suit the requirements of women entrepreneurs, to train them in specific areas such as decision making, discipline, communication skills and management without imposing much financial burden on them.

A team of experts for providing counselling to women entrepreneurs at the time of difficulties like demotivation, marketing problems, etc. may also be put in position. Since not all the members are literate, it is essential for them to go through special classroom activities.

At present, there exists no organizational support at the government level to assist micro-enterprises in marketing their wares. The government should think in terms of setting up organized marketing channel. The proposed organization could have its own umbrella brand name for different products that it buys from the units. It could also lay down qualitative standards and could evolve a system of quality control. It could help the small entrepreneurs in their input needs.

However, it will be necessary to equip the micro-finance organization with an expert marketing body concerned with both domestic and export markets, of products exclusively of micro-units. Technical advice for value addition and quality improvement of NHG products should also be made available. At present, the micro-finance organizations in Kerala give training only in a few activities such as soap-making and catering.

Coordination and networking of self-help groups are necessary on both vertical and horizontal basis.

In order to obviate the difficulties experienced by the extremely poor among the members of MFIs, it is necessary to make the terms and conditions of savings and borrowings more pro-poor than they are at present.

Penalties and sanctions need to be made less stringent in order to keep the poorest from drop-out of the groups.

Setting up of a welfare fund at the NHG level is necessary so, that it can be used in times of emergency.

The membership ceiling of a NHG may be kept in the range of 20 to 25. Large groups may lead to problems of cohesion and management.

Development of a mechanism to constantly monitor neighbourhood groups to check whether members are unduly discriminated and for the strict compliance of provisions in the bye-laws. The State and district mission offices should be constantly engaged in checking on the needs, priorities and complaints of the poor people.

Reasonable restrictions on the entry of non-poor are to be imposed by putting in place some kind of targeting tools.

Development of flexible financial products at low cost which suit the needs of the poorest in the society is the need of the hour. This should take special care in the context of emergence of private MFIs and moneylenders.

Charging high interest rate is not suitable for micro-finance industry as most of the beneficiaries are from the vulnerable sections of the society. It is suggestive to follow subsidized rate of interest from the banks. The governmental support in this context is preferred.

As the marginalized and vulnerable sections are living far away from the district headquarters and other training centres, adequate attention should be taken to conduct training programmes at locations convenient to majority of the members. Since, the literacy levels of most of the members are low, they should be offered with such training modules through class room activities.

Model groups and best practices identified with groups across the State shall be located and portrayed at appropriate meetings, so that others will be motivated to join the band wagon in the immediate future. Hope that one day will come, when Kudumbashree model of Kerala will become the flagship bearer of all poverty alleviation and empowerment programmes of India.

Bibliography

Adams, Dale W., and J.D. von Pischke. 1992. "Micro-enterprise Credit Programmes: deja vu." *World Development* 20(10):1463-1470.

Adams, Dale W., and Robert C. Vogel. 1986. "Rural Financial Markets in Low-Income Countries: Recent Controversies and Lessons." *World Development* 14(4): 477-487.

Adler, Paul S. and Seok-Woo Kwon. 2002. "Social Capital: Prospects for a New Concept". *The Academy of Management Review,* 27(1): 17.

Agarwal, K.P., V. Puhazhendhi, and K.J.S. Satyasai. 1997. "Gearing Rural Credit for the Twenty-First Century." *Economic and Political Weekly,* 32(42): 2717-2728.

Aghion, P., and P. Howitt. 1998. *Endogenous Growth Theory*. Boston: MIT Press.

Aghion, P., and P. Howitt. 2006. "Appropriate Growth Policy: A Unifying Framework.", *Journal of the European Economic Association*, 4(2-3): 269-314.

Alamgir, A.H.D. 1998. "Current Interventions for Hard-core Poor in Bangladesh and How to Reach Them with Financial Services", in Micro-finance News Vol. 1. Dhaka.

Ali, I., and J. Zhuang. 2007. Inclusive Growth toward a Prosperous Asia: Policy Implications. ERD Working Paper Series No. 97, Economics and Research Department, Asian Development Bank, Manila.

Baker, W. 1990. "Market Networks and Corporate Behaviour". *American Journal of Sociology,* 96:589-625.

Bateman, Milford. 2010. *Why doesn't Microfinance Work?* London: Zed Books.

Beck, Thorsten, Asli Demirguc,-Kunt, and Maria Soledad Martinez Peria. 2008. "Banking Services For Everyone? Barriers to Bank Access and use around the World." *The World Bank Economic Review,* 22(3): 397-430.

Belliveau, M.A., O'Reilly, C.A., and Wade, J.B. 1996. "Social capital at the top: Effects of social similarity and status on CEO compensation". *Academy of Management Journal,* 39: 1568-1593.

Bourdieu, P. 1986. "The forms of capital". Richardson, J.G. (ed.), *Handbook of Theory and Research for the Sociology of Education*. New York: Greenwood Press.

Boxman, E.A.W., P.M. De Grant, and H.D. Flap. 1991. "The Impact of Social and Human Capital on the Income Attainment of Dutch Managers". *Social Networks,* 13:51-73.

Brehm, J., and Rahn, W. 1997. "Individual-level evidence for the causes and consequences of social capital." *American Journal of Political Science,* 41(3): 999-1023.

Burt, R.S. 1992. *Structural Holes: The social structure of competition.* Cambridge, MA: Harvard University Press.

Chakrabarty, K.C. 2010. "Financial Deepening by putting Financial Inclusion Campaign into Mission Mode1." Address at the 23rd Skoch Summit on 17 June in Mumbai.

Chakrabarty, K.C. 2009. "Banking: Key Driver for Inclusive Growth." The Address delivered at the Mint's "Clarity through Debate" series on August 10th at Chennai.

Chathukulam, Jos. 2002a. "Survival through Social Capital Formation: The Case of Women's Self-Help Groups." *Proceedings of International Workshop on Research for Poverty Alleviation, Kerala Research Programme on Local Level Development,* Centre for Development Studies, Thiruvananthapuram.

Chathukulam, Jos. 2002b. "Building Social Capital through State Initiative: The case of Participatory Planning in Kerala." *Economic and Political Weekly,* 37(20) 1939-48.

Chaudhury, Iftekhar A., and Imran Matin. 2002. "Dimensions and Dynamics of Microfinance Membership Overlap: A Micro Study." *Small Enterprise Development,* 13(2): 46-55.

Chen, Greg, Stephen Rasmussen, and Xavier Reille. 2010. "Growth and Vulnerabilities in Microfinance", CGAP Focus Note 61, CGAP, Washington.

Christabell, P.J. 2009. *Women Empowerment through Capacity Building: The Role of Micro-Finance.* New Delhi: Concept Publishing Company Pvt. Ltd., Delhi.

Christabell, P.J. 2011. "Inclusive Growth through Social Capital Formation: How Micro-finance helps in Targeting Poor Women?" in M.K. Saralamma and Manju. S. Nair (eds) *Development* vs. *Deprivation in the Era of Globalization,* Vol. II, Sonali Publications, New Delhi.

Christabell, P.J. 2013a. "Microfinance and Empowerment Politics—Missing the Balancing Act", in Maciek Michalek and Krzysztof Antosik (eds.) *Development, Security, Democracy.* Faculty of Journalism and Political Science, University of Warsaw, Poland.

Christabell, P.J. 2013b. "Social Capital Formation—Endurance Assured with Neighbourhood Groups." *ISDA Journal,* 23(3): 349-370.

Christabell, P.J. 2013c. "Social Innovation for Women Empowerment: Kudumbashree in Kerala." *Innovation and Development,* 3(1):139-140.

Christen, Robert Peck. 2000. Commercialization and Mission Drift, The Transformation of Microfinance in Latin America. Occasional Paper No. 5, Consultative Group to Assist the Poorest (CGAP), Washington DC.

Coleman, James S. 1988. Social capital in the creation of human capital. *American Journal of Sociology*, 94: S95-S120.

Coleman, James S. 1990. *Foundations of Social Theory.* Cambridge: Harvard University Press.

Conlin, Michael. 1999. "Peer Group Micro-lending Programmes in Canada and the United States." *Journal of Development Economics,* 60(1): 249-269.

Consultative Group to Assist the Poor (CGAP) 2009. *Financial Access 2009* CGAP/World Bank, Washington.

Dasgupta, Partha, and Serageldin, Ismail. (eds.). 2000. *Social Capital: A Multifaceted Perspective*. Washington, DC.: World Bank.

Dekker, Paul and Uslaner, Eric. (eds). 2001. *Social Capital and Participation in Everyday Life.* New York: Routledge.

Duflos, Eric and Barbara Gahwiler. 2008. "Impact and Implications of the Food Crisis on Microfinance", CGAP, November.

Evans, Timothy G. 1999. Demystifying non-participation in micro-credit: A population-based analysis. *World Development*, 27: 419-430.

Fernando, Nimal. 2007. *Low-Income Households' Access to Financial Services', International Experience, Measures for Improvement and the Future*. Manila: Asian Development Bank.

Fukuyama, Francis. 1995. *Trust: The Social Virtues and the Creation of Prosperity*. Free Press: New York.

Ghate, Prabhu. 2007. "Learning from the Andhra Pradesh Crisis", in Dichter, Thomas and Malcolm Harper (eds.) *What's Wrong with Microfinance?*, Practical Action Publishing, UK.

Glisovic, Jasmina, and Xavier Reille. 2010. "Microfinance Investors Adjust Strategy in Tougher Market Conditions", CGAP Brief, October.

Gonzalez, Adrian. 2008. "Microfinance, Incentives to Repay, and Over-indebtedness: Evidence from a Household Survey in Bolivia", Ph.D. Dissertation, The Ohio State University.

Gonzalez, Adrian. 2010. "Is Microfinance Growing Too Fast?", MIX Data Brief No. 5, Microfinance Information Exchange, June.

Gonzalez, Adrian. 2011. "Lessons for Strengthening Microfinance Institutions through Financial Crises, Fluctuations in Food and Fuel Prices, and Other Major Risks". Global Microcredit Summit Commissioned Workshop Paper, Valladolid, Spain.

Government of Andhra Pradesh (GoAP). 2010. Andhra Pradesh Micro Finance Institutions (regulation of money lending) Ordinance, 2010.

Government of India (GoI). 2006. *Towards Faster and More Inclusive Growth: An Approach to the Eleventh Five Year Plan*. New Delhi: The Planning Commission.

Government of India (GoI). 2007. *Towards Inclusive Growth: The Gender Dimension.* New Delhi: The Planning Commission.

Government of India (GoI). 2010. *Economic Survey 2009*. New Delhi: The Planning Commission.

Government of Kerala (GoK). 2012. *Economic Review 2011.* Thiruvananthapuram: Kerala State Planning Board.

Gupta, K.R., Gunnar Lind Haase Svendsen and Prasenjit Maiti (eds). 2008. *Social Capital* (Vol 1). New Delhi: Atlantic Publishers and Distributors.

Inglehart, R. 1977. *The Silent Revolution: Changing Values and Political Styles among Western Publics*, Princeton, NJ: Princeton University Press.

John, Jacob. 2009. A Study on Kudumbashree Project, A Poverty Eradication Programme in Kerala: Performance, Impact and Lessons for other States. Kerala Development Society (KDS-Delhi).

John, M.S., and Jos Chathukulam. 2002. "Building Social Capital through State Initiative: Participatory Planning in Kerala." *Economic and Political Weekly,* 37(8): 1939-1948.

Johnson, Susan and Ben Rogaly. 1997. *Microfinance and Poverty Reduction.* London: Oxfam Publication.

Jose, A.V. 1977. "Origin of Trade Unionism among Agricultural Labourers in Kerala", *Social Scientist.* 5 (12): 24-44.

Kadiyala, Suneetha. 2004. Scaling up Kudumbashree collective action for poverty alleviation and Women's Empowerment. FCND Discussion Paper No. 180, Food Consumption and Nutrition Division, International Food Policy Research Institute, Washington, DC.

King, R.G and R. Levine. 1993. "Finance, Entrepreneurship, and Growth: Theory and Evidence." *Journal of Monetary Economics,* 32: 513-542.

Knoke, David. 1999. "Organizational Networks as Social Capital" in *Corporate Social Capital and Liability*, by Roger Leenders and Shaul Gabbay (eds.). Dordrecht, Netherlands: Kluwer Press.

Kochhar, Sameer. 2009. *Speeding Financial Inclusion.* New Delhi: Academic Foundation.

Levine, R. and S. Zervous. 1998. "Stock Markets, Banks and Economic Growth." *American Economic Review,* 88: 537-58.

Littlefield, Elizabeth and Christoph Kneiding. 2009. "The Global Financial Crisis and Its Impact on Microfinance", Focus Note No. 52, CGAP.

Littlefield, Elizabeth. 2008. "CGAP Virtual Conference: Microfinance and the Financial Crisis", CGAP, November.

Llanto, Gilberto M. and Jocelyn Alma R. Badiola. 2009. "The Impact of the Global Financial Crisis on Rural and Microfinance in Asia". Discussion Paper Series No. 2009-24 Philippines Institute for Development Studies.

Loury, G. 1992. "The economics of discrimination. Getting to the core of the problem." *Harvard Journal for African American Public Policy*, 1: 91-110.

Marguerite, Robinson. 2001. *The Micro-finance Revolution Sustainable Finance for the Poor.* Washington, DC: The World Bank.

Meehan, Jennifer. 2004. "Tapping the Financial Markets for Microfinance", Grameen Foundation USA's Promotion of this Emerging Trend. Grameen Foundation USA Working Paper Series.

Nahapiet, J. and Ghoshal, S. 1998 "Social capital, intellectual capital and the organizational advantage", *Academy of Management Review*, 23(2): 242-266.

Navajas, Sergio and Mark Schreiner. 1998. Apex Organisations and the growth of microfinance in Bolivia, Economics and Sociology Occasional Paper No. 2500, Rural Finance Programme, Dept of Agriculture and Environment and Development Economics, Ohio State University.

Nidheesh, K.B. 2009. "Study on the changing process of Kerala Women through Kudumbashree." *Kerala International NGO Journal,* 4(8): 352-361.

Oh, H., M. Kilduff, and D.J. Brass. 1999. "Communal social capital, linking social capital, and economic outcomes." in *Paper presented at the annual meeting of the Academy of Management.* Chicago.

Oommen, M.A. 2008. Micro Finance and Poverty Alleviation: The Case of Kerala's Kudumbashree. Working Paper No. 17. Centre for Socio-economic and Environmental Studies (CSES) Kochi-Kerala.

Peachey, Stephen and Alan Roe. 2004. *Access to Finance: A Study for the World Savings Banks Institute.* Brussels: Oxford Policy Management.

Portes, A., and Sensenbrenner, J. 1993. "Embeddedness and Immigration: Notes on the social determinants of economic action." *American Journal of Sociology,* 98: 1320-1350.

Portes, A., 1998. "Social Capital: Its origins and applications in modern sociology." *Annual Review of Sociology,* 24: 1-24.

Poyo, Jeff, and Robin Young. 1999. "Commercialization of Micro Finance: A Framework for Latin America." United State Agency for International Development Micro Enterprise Best practices project, Development Alternatives, INC. Washington, DC.

Putnam, Robert D. 1993. *Making democracy work: Civic traditions in modern Italy.* Princeton: Princeton University Press.

Putnam, Robert D. 1993. "The prosperous community: Social capital and public life." *American Prospect,* 13: 35-42.

Putnam, Robert D. 1995. "Bowling Alone: America's Declining Social Capital", *Journal of Democracy,* 6(1): 65-78.

Putnam, Robert D. 2000. *Bowling Alone: The Collapse and Revival of American Community.* New York: Simon and Schuster.

Raghavan, V.P. 2009. "Micro-Credit and Empowerment: A Study of Kudumbashree Projects in Kerala". *India Journal of Rural Development,* 28 (4): 469-484.

Rahman, Sayma. 2000. "Consumption Difference between Microcredit Borrowers and Non-borrowers: A Bangladesh Experience", *The Journal of Developing Areas,* 43(2): 313-326.

Rajan, R.G. and L. Zingales. 2003. *Saving Capitalism from Capitalists.* New York: Crown Business.

Reinhard H. and C P. Schmidt/Zeitinger. 1994. Critical Issues in Small and Micro Business Finance, IPC Working Paper No. 1.

Reserve Bank of India (RBI). 2009. Report of the Working Group to Review the Business Correspondent Model, Mumbai.

Rosenberg, Richard, Adrian Gonzalez, and Sushma Narain. 2009. "Are Microcredit Interest Rates Excessive?", CGAP Brief, Washington.

Rozas, Daniel. 2011. "Weathering the Storm: Hazards, Beacons, and Life Rafts Lessons in Microfinance Crisis Survival from Those Who Have Been There", Centre for Financial Inclusion, ACCION.

Rutherford, S. 2000. The Poor and Their Money: An Essay about financial services for poor people, Institute for Development Policy and Management, University of Manchester.

Sander, Thomas H. 2002. "Social capital and new urbanism: Leading a civic horse to water." *National Civic Review,* 91: 213-221.

Sanjeev, Prakash and Per Selle. 2003. *Investigating Social Capital: Comparative Perspectives on Civil Society, Participation and Governance.* New Delhi: Sage Publications.

Sapundzhieva, Ralitsa. 2011. "Geographical Concentration of Lending in Bosnia and Herzegovina", *MIX Microfinance World,* March 2011.

Schiff, M. 1992. "Social capital, labour mobility, and welfare: The impact of uniting states." *Rationailty and Society,* 4.

Schmidt, Reinhard H. and C.P. Zeitinger. 1994. Critical Issues in Small and Micro Business Finance, IPC Working Paper No. 1.

Seibel, Hans Dieter. 2005. Does History Matter? The Old and the New World of Microfinance in Europe and Asia. Working paper/University of Cologne, Development Research Centre, No. 2005, 10, http://hdl.handle.net/10419/23654

Serra, Renata, 2001. "Social Capital: Meaningful and Measurable at the State Level?" *Economic and Political Weekly,* 36 (8): 693-704.

Srinivasan, N. (2010) *Microfinance India: State of the Sector Report 2010.* Sage: New Delhi.

Thorat, Usha. 2007. "Banking in the Hinterland." Keynote address delivered at the Conference organised by the Indian Banks Association and Rural Marketing Agencies Association of India at Mumbai on February 14, 2007.

Thorat, Usha. 2008. "Financial Inclusion and Information Technology", Keynote address at 'Vision 2020—Indian Financial Services Sector' hosted by NDTV at The Ballroom, Taj Lands End, Mumbai.

Wright, Graham A.N., Christen, Robert Beck, Matin, Imran. 2000. "Introducing Saving Services in to ASA, A Micro Credit Institution." *Small Enterprise Development* 12(3): 20-32.

Index

CONCEPT

75C/ 28/9/16